Mister Psykonaut

By Kris Ayrton

Copyright 2016 Kris Ayrton

Smashwords Edition

Mister Psykonaut

Life's a beach

Sky blue, bright and beautiful is all that I can see, as if it has been freshly sprayed painted on to the domed ceiling of the earth. A gloopy swathe of deep navy blue has been daubed across the horizon by the broad, sure stroke of some colossal brush; by an artist who has just moved out of view. She's probably stepped back to admire her handiwork, gripping the dripping brush in her clenched teeth and making that picture frame gesture with her hands; smiling on the inside. The deep navy blue gradually lightens as it flows toward me, like gradients down a paint colour chart until it becomes a rich translucent aqua green all around my body. I am floating in a sea that is sparkling with the afternoon sunlight; a magical shimmering that seems to dance above the surface of the water. Looking at just the strip of sky and sea stretching out in front of me it fizzles with a vibrancy that seems to be truly alive. The sky sighs a breath of satisfied delight. The fresh ocean waves gurgle, rhythmically splashing my naked body, whispering longingly into my ear "Hush, hush, *hush*"

Above the surface of the water my skin is golden brown but in the ocean it glows brighter, dappled by the sunlight. I squish my feet into the sand and watch the smoky cloud lazily rise and disperse. I feel as if I could just dissolve and merge into the flow of the waves, quietly joining their tide. I could just unceremoniously drift away into oblivion. I let myself float up flat in the water again; it lifts me up and cradles me. Slowly I relax and find my balance so that only my face is exposed to the air like a discarded mask. I imagine a whole flock of masks gently floating on the surface, a sea of faces staring up into the sky. Up and down, with the waves gliding gracefully past me, up and down as I breathe. I cannot tell where I end and where the ocean begins. I can't feel my edges, no boundary - just surface. I am but a lump of meat floating here in this water. This water doesn't know it's called the Mediterranean Sea, it is just water; and I am just flesh and bones. All the seas are really just one massive connected body of water that humans have carved up and allocated names to. They don't actually have any boundaries separating them one from another. Floating here in the Mediterranean I am in the same piece of water that is the Pacific or Atlantic and so forth, I'm just in The Ocean. Here where I am, to me, the ocean is tranquil but somewhere else in this water, to somebody else, it might be rough. Somebody might be surfing its powerful waves- somebody else may be drowning. Follow its surface to the other side of this globe and it is twinkling with moonlight rather than the sun. People may be paddling along its shore sharing a kiss. Just think of all the animals that are living in this water, the amazing variety of species. There are penguins diving about, massive whales majestically rising above the surface, jellyfish, and sharks. This piece of water is shark infested! They are just a long way away - hopefully.

Aargh! Something just touched my leg! I splutter and jolt around, there's a little leaf-shaped silver and black fish darting around me. "Oh hello Fish" I stand really, really still and it comes back to investigate me, gingerly circling closer, probably wondering what this big lump of meat in the water is. It doesn't know that I am what we humans call a human, it doesn't know that it's a fish either; we call it a fish for our own benefit. I suppose it's like I got named by my parents so that they could identify me. Then they gradually taught me my identity, they *identified* me. This is who you are and where you fit in to the scheme of things. If I had been born somewhere else to different people I would have had a different name and fit into a different part of the scheme of things. Where you get born is a bit of a lottery really, which country and culture you end up in. Like being a drop of water and someone labelling you as Mediterranean or Indian or Atlantic, you're still just a drop of water. Each of us is born without an identity and we're gradually taught who we are; born wild but domesticated into society. Fish has swum off - I don't blame him. He could probably smell the crazy, actually can fish smell?

I idly glance across the glistening surface of the sea, the sunlight is dancing, and in its shimmering I can see little patterns; a swirling number 8, shooting stars, all kinds of letters and symbols twinkling all around me. Golden sparkly circles start to shoot up out of the water in front of me and slowly a familiar face rises up with the last circle crowning her head like a halo. This glorious blond vision of beauty - I'm sure that I can hear a fanfare blasting inside my head. I smile at her and simply say "Hello lover" and punctuate it with a wink. She throws her head back and laughs, then her eyes lock onto mine and I can feel her looking inside of me. She raises her hand to her mouth and blows me a kiss; with her breath golden twinkling letters float into the air between us - they spell out a word. Lover. As the letters rise up like slo-mo fireworks into the sky she too bursts into a cloud of twinkling sunlight that dances along the surface of the sea. Whenever I see her it is so intense that I can almost feel the memory being made as the moments pass by. The connection is so great that each time we are face to face it knits us tighter together, we become ever more entwined in this beautiful dance.

I slowly spin around in the water and look directly at the coast. As with the sea, so with the land - it also has no idea of its identity. It doesn't know that it is Cala Cielo, next to Punta Prima in the Valencian Community of Spain, in Europe, Northern Hemisphere, Planet Earth, etc, etc. It's just land. I know this stretch of coast like the back of my hand; I'd shudder to calculate how many hours I've whiled away here - so many. I've got this little cove to myself today; you have to climb down the rocks and through a tree to get on to the tiny little beach. The boulders have fallen away from the cliffs over years of erosion.

Out from behind one of them I see a scraggly little black beach cat skulking along, probably tracking a beach rat. People have always said that I look like a cat, angular face and big eyes. But I suppose I'm quite feline in my character as well, I wander about by myself, a satellite orbiting a world of my own. Along the top of the cliffs there are groups of people strolling along together, walking their dogs, going for a jog; there's a dude riding a BMX pulling wheelies and hopping about. It seems a bit of a dodgy place to be doing stunts because it's so rocky and he keeps puffing up clouds of dust. He has really cool long blonde dreadlocks, I love dread locks; I've had them three times in my life so far. If I look like a cat then he definitely looks like a lion. Oh shit… he has stopped and is staring right down at me! He gets off of his bike and is pushing it along looking for the pathway down to the cove. What do I do? I'm stark bollock naked and it's a bit weird if I get out of the sea, plus I don't want him to think I'm getting out to guard my bag and towel that are laid out on the shore; I'll wait and see what he does. He puts his bike up on his shoulder and slowly struggles down the rocky pathway and through the tree and emerges on the tiny little beach. He rests his bike against a boulder and pops his rucksack down at his feet, beckoning me with his hand. Oh well, I'll just have to grin and bear it, so to speak, I walk up out of the water and he thankfully doesn't even bat an eyelid at my nudity. I grab my towel and half dry myself whilst covering up my junk.

"Hey man" He says with a foreign accent "Do you wanna buy any weed?" I say 'foreign' accent but again that's just a matter of perspective when you're an Englishman living in Spain, it's only foreign to me.

"Oh, um, no I'm okay thanks man. I don't really smoke thanks though."

"Ah okay, I just saw the tattoos and punk hair and I was thinking that you might do. I just have some and need to sell it because I need the money." He shrugged, kicking a pebble.

"Sorry I don't bring any money with me to the beach." I shrugged. I can't help but notice how unique his looks are, real long surfer blond dreadlocks and a strikingly fierce bone structure. He does actually look like a morph of lion with a man; like a funky BMXer caveman in a faded orange vest and camouflage shorts.

"Do you have any tobacco?" He asks. Cigarettes in Spain are virtually communal as it is quite normal for a random stranger to stop you in the street and ask for one.

"Yeah of course, I smoke menthol though." It always makes me laugh when you say that to those random cig-scroungers and they turn their noses up at menthol ones. But Caveboy says that's fine and I try to negotiate nakedly crouching down and searching for my packet of cigs in my bag without dropping my towel - awkward. I grab my packet (of cigarettes!) and drop my towel down onto the sand and sit on it, shielding myself as much as possible. Caveboy retrieved a Jamaican flag beach towel from his rucksack and laid it out next to mine, peeling his vest off as he sits down. There's not an ounce of fat on him, the bastard, I fight the urge to suck my little belly in. We both light up.

"So you're English no? Are you on holidays?" He turns and sits square on to me, crossing his legs.

"Yeah I'm from the UK, but I live here."

"What, all year long?"

"Yep, I've been here 11 years now."

"You must really like it no?"

"Yeah I always wanted to live in Spain since I was a little kid, I love it. Where are you from?"

"My family live in Madrid, but I go to University in London. I'm back here for holiday and like all Madrileños we come down to the coast for the summer. My family has an apartment in Torrevieja. That's why I have too much weed, I got a lot in Madrid because I knew I'd be down here with my family but now I want to sell it for spending money instead." He let out a guttural laugh. "Everyone needs money in this country no? Even the banks ran out of it!"

"Amen to that. So what do you do at University?"

"Mostly I smoke, drink and sleep. But I am studying journalism."

"Oh cool."

"Are you studying here in Spain?"

"No I did go to University a long time ago in England but now I just teach a bit of Spanish and do translations, this and that you know - surviving."

"Oh I thought you were the same age as me! What age are you? If I guessed I would say 24 at the oldest."

"Nope, I'm 37. People always think I look younger, I don't know why."

"Oh my god. You will have to tell me your secret! Ha-ha but that's a good thing you now have an extra ten years before people think you need to grow up."

"I don't plan on growing up any time soon so that suits me fine. What's your name by the way? I'm Kristoff." I reach out and shake his hand

"Adonai. Encantado or should I say pleased to meet you, charmed." He attempted a posh English accent. "Kristoff like Cristobal , yeah Colon the explorer. How do you call him in English? Don't tell me … Christopher Columbus."

"Yep that's right. In 1492 Columbus sailed the ocean blue"

"Ha-ha I've never heard that before. Talking of the ocean blue, it is calling to me saying 'Adonai, you are hot and I am cool, come on in and have a swim for a while' Are you coming too Mister Columbus? The explorer."

"Sure, the water's really nice today."

"Come on then" He flicked his dreadlocked head towards the water. He was already kicking his trainers off, he stood up and slowly took off his shorts, momentarily looking like a poster boy in red Calvins, he crossed himself and said "When in Rome." Then he whipped off his trunks and went running into the water, letting out some sort of primal scream and splashing about wildly. The naked caveman. I followed him into the water, he stopped still when it had reached his chest and turned around and waved to me to come closer.

"I do this kind of ritual when I first get in to the sea. My family are religious and one thing I learned from their bible stories was about the baptism." He sort of flushed shyly, as if he'd caught himself talking too candidly, but he soldiered on. "It always sticks in my head about how you can cleanse your spirit by going in the water as well as cleaning your body. So I baptise myself, I think about the negative things that I want to have washed away from me and then go under the water and imagine that when I come up again I am clean and new. It may sound a little loco but it is good for your soul. I think it would be good for you to try as well with me no? That is if you don't think I am too crazy now?" I was really surprised at how openly he was speaking to me, but a lot of Spanish people speak like this, they love to talk and random strangers greet each other in public places. It's not the talking that surprises me it is the fact that he sounds like he's on the same wavelength as me.

"That sounds like a good thing to do and I don't think you're crazy. My parents raised me as a Baptist actually. I think like that sometimes too. Well, a lot of the time."

"Ha? No way, well I thought you might do. Okay then, well you just think for as long as it takes about the things you want to be washed away and then lower yourself under the water and maybe swim about a little to shake them off really good. Vamos." He closed his eyes and scrunched his face up in mock concentration, opening one eye to check whether I'd joined in. I laughed and closed my eyes too. It took me a few moments to stop thinking about the actual randomness of the situation, nakedly standing in the sea with an absolute stranger, our eyes closed for some pseudo baptism. There is something vulnerable about closing your eyes in the presence of someone else; I suppose it's an unspoken declaration of trust that you feel safe. So blindly we stand together, the stoner and the punk performing some new version of an ancient ritual. I did genuinely then start to concentrate on stuff that I would like to have washed away, more in an energy kind of way rather than events. I thought of it like a defragmentation or reboot of a computer. I had been baptised when I was a toddler and again when I was 13 or so and that memory came to the surface. I heard Adonai sploosh down into the water and could feel the ripples of him moving about; then I just let myself fall back. It did feel like I was letting energy flow out of me, like when you piss in a pool, a cloud of negative waste was dispersing away from me. Maybe not the best analogy but for whatever reason it felt like that kind of release. It was weird being underwater with my eyes closed knowing that someone else was doing the same thing close by. The waves were rolling past and it seemed like I held my breath for a really long time before coming back up for air. When I did Adonai was stood there smiling broadly.

"You must have had some serious bad vibes to shift man!" He giggled and then raised his hand up and we high-fived. "Hey can you just put your head under again I want to see your crazy coloured hair under the water it looks like the fins from a tropical fish, very trippy!" I laughed and dunked my head under and swooshed my hair about. "Yeah man, you have angel fish fins... you're the rainbow man! Yeah and all your colour tattoos, how they say? The rainbow warrior!" He giggled whilst flexing his best warrior pose. He was confident and carefree, I couldn't help but glance up to the cliffs to see if there was an audience peering down on this unusual scene; the people were just meandering by, oblivious.

"Now you have to do yours, I want to see your dreads underwater that must look cool. I've had dreadlocks a few times too." He immediately crouched down and slowly swung his head about with his long dreadlocks splaying out like a jellyfish or crazy blond fronds of seaweed. He waved his arms and hands about in some psychedelic 1960s dance. Hilarious. He jumped back up with a splash and we high-fived again.

"It's really cool to meet a new person. In my family we come down here to the coast and all that my cousins want to do is just lie on the same beach and just get tanned. I like to ride my bike and see what all the other people are doing. It is always good to bump into new people and try to talk to them. I'm glad that I came down and spoke to you."

"Thanks yeah me too, I don't really speak to a lot of people I just walk about with my headphones on listening to music. The seaside is right on my doorstep so it seems silly not to enjoy it. I like to swim then lie down and soak up the sun and then swim again, there's no better way to spend an afternoon."

"Okay come on then let's soak up some rays - it will take an age for my dreads to dry!" We waded back up into the little cove and sat on our towels. I handed him a cigarette and we smoked. He cocked his head to one side as he shook his dreads and looked at me.

"I am guessing that you are okay with me sitting here, um, *au naturel*... you like the men no?" He winked.

"Er, yeah I like the men yep."

"Hey it's cool with me. I like the ladies, I've messed about with guys don't get me wrong, hasn't everyone? But I like women. No-one cares now though, boys, girls so long as you're happy that's the main thing. Just so long as you can resist my beautiful self, I wouldn't want you to feel so distracted that you are uncomfortable. Ha ha ha!" He flung his head back laughing.

"I think I can control myself, don't worry." I really like that people his age, or of his generation are so comfortable with their sexuality and can talk so naturally about it, it's such a relief compared to what it was like when I was his age. Things are a lot more fluid now, gender and sexuality – it's a healthy way to be. Adonai lies back on his towel still giggling and arranges his dreadlocks out around his head to dry in the sun.

"So Kristoff, these bad boys are going to take a long time to cook. I'm guessing that behind those tattoos there are a fair few stories to be told no? You are now required to humour me as a journalist and give me your stories." He rolls his head to the side to catch my eye and waves his hand above him inviting me to 'take the floor'. "Come on, you've already seen me naked and been baptised with me, now tell me your stories."

"Er, yeah I suppose there are stories, I've just never really explained them all in one go before. You know people stare at my ink in the street and give their opinion about whether they like tattoos or what ones they want. Or they think that because you have tats that you no longer have personal space and that it is completely fine to grab your arms and start mauling you to inspect them."

"Well now's your chance. I tell you what I will supply

the herb in exchange for you telling me. I'm genuinely interested and I have to lie here and dry me hair so what better opportunity; think of it as providence. You have a story and a captive audience - what's that great word in English? Serendipity, that's it."

"You saw that written on me didn't you?"

"What do you mean?

"I have that tattooed around my wrist the word 'serendipity' - here look." I leant over and showed him the word tattooed around my left wrist.

"Oh my god! Seriously man, I did not see that. I just like that word somebody taught it to me and the meaning - one of my mates at University. That's crazy! See now you have to tell me! I am rolling us joints!" He sat up and hunted around in his rucksack gathering up his paraphernalia and started rolling two joints still shaking his head in disbelief but making me wait. "I'm going to make you a joint and you smoke until you feel relaxed then I will say 'once upon a time' and you can tell me your fairytale. Ha ha ha - no offence"

I laughed "None taken, okay deal. But I can't smoke more than a couple of puffs as I'm a real lightweight. I have got to admit that this is a freaky coincidence and I don't really believe in coincidences rather than synchronicity."

"Yeah man, me too. Okay we'll be quiet and chill

while I roll and you conjure up your fairy story." He looked at me and we both laughed, then we both did go silent as he concentrated on constructing the joint and I psyched myself up for 'giving him my story'. I felt nervous. Without a word he handed me a lit joint. It felt like a kind of time bomb, with each puff I was getting closer to having to talk. But also I did start to feel that warm glow rising in me and a blurring around my edges as the joint cast its spell. Adonai let out a satisfied humming sound, it was good stuff. Then he spoke.

"Okay Mister Kristoff, I'm going to help you out, I'm going to have a look and pick a tattoo from those two sleeves of yours and that's the first story to start from." He came over and took both of my hands in his and looked up and down both of my arms, turning them so that he could see all around them. "Say 'aah'- only joking I pick this one" He said pointing at the letter B on the inside of my right wrist. "Tell me about this first...once upon a time." He lay back on his towel face down resting on his elbows looking at me expectantly. It is now or never, just go with the moment I thought.

"Well it's weird that you should pick that one because the story behind that is about a person."

"Aha I thought it might be." He said touching his nose and pointing at me. "Carry on."

Today is actually the anniversary of a really important thing that happened with that person and I was just thinking about it earlier when you came along"

"Ooh freaky…go on."

"But you see I'm a bit worried if I tell you that story you'll be freaked out and think I'm a complete weirdo."

"Okay now you have to tell me. I love being freaked out and I'm really open minded so you can say whatever you want, the weirder the better. In fact I challenge you to tell me the weirdest story that I've ever heard! And not the short version either I want to hear all the gory details, so don't be embarrassed. You could say I am a story voyeur…ha ha!" He winked cheekily.

"Alright then." I took a deep breath and somewhere inside of me I made a decision, to tell him the truth. It may have been the weed or the weird coincidences but a voice inside of me was emphatically saying 'Go on - just tell it'- so I did.

"Eight years ago today something happened to me that changed my beliefs about everything that had happened before and opened my eyes to a completely different reality than the one that I thought I had been living in. It was in some ways the middle of my journey, or the start of a new one or the end of my old way of thinking. But as seen as today is the anniversary of that day it seems like the right place to start."

"Definitely, this sounds like it's going to be epic! Keep going." Adonai said with a genuinely excited look on his face and shaking two thumbs up in the air.

"Okay it's eight years ago and I'm sat in a room with a stranger and what do you think is the weirdest question that a stranger could ask you?"

"Do you know who you are?"

That is the question that I have just been asked, by a complete stranger. For a moment I mull the answer over and I can see a brainstorm gathering in my mind's eye, a large grey cloud bursting with the identities I could use to describe myself. The ceiling above me turns into a loaded sky, the cloud rolling and rumbling around laden with my history. Downpours of labels splash out around me – son, brother, twin, human, Englishman and all of the things that I am by birth. Then the roles that I have assumed – listener, wanderer, wonderer, mental patient, lover of women, lover of men, liar, failure, satellite friend, drifter, hustler, hippy, barbarian, bohemian and a myriad of other activities that may serve to define me. Also the occupations that I have had – shop assistant, student, barman, dancer, model, door to door salesman, white van man, translator, teacher, receptionist, prostitute, chef, waiter. I think I must also consider that other people's opinions and views of me as a person also count into that picture of myself. There are so many facets to a life that it is difficult to determine which pieces are the more significant. My Ego may bear no similarity to anyone else's view of me; I may not actually exist as who I think I am to anybody else at all. At this particular juncture of my existence I think 'lost soul' might just be the best way to answer the question. I glance at Adonai to check his reaction so far; he's smiling slightly and waves his hand for me to proceed.

It is August 2008, I'm 29 and life is a bit of a mess. Here I am in this room with this stranger who is about to turn my world upside down. How did I get here? Which events made me who I am? In amongst that cloud of identity I can see my life flashing before me. I don't know if you've ever been in that kind of situation where your life flashes before you, I have been in a few of them over the years. It doesn't matter if you're in a river drowning, got a gun to your head, on a hospital bed with anaesthesia being administered into your vein or any other show stopping episode - for a moment time stops. Something in your brain presses pause on the external world whilst your mind's eye fires up a cacophony of memories. It is as if every single image that you've seen and every sound that you've heard all get played at the same time. If you imagine that each particular memory of your past is a different musical instrument with its own unique sound then in that life flashing moment there's an intake of breath then a wall of noise as each instrument sounds its last blast. So here I am in one of those noisy moments and my brain has pressed pause.

The place that I am in right now is a small white

room. I'm sat in an armchair, in front of me is a coffee table and then another identical armchair in which is sitting the psychic medium woman who has just asked me the question "Do you know who you are?" This room is frozen because my brain has paused it. From behind me emerges a familiar female figure, she places a reassuring hand on my shoulder; I look at her hand and notice her sapphire and diamond bejewelled nails. My gaze moves up her porcelain arm to her shoulder where her snow white hair is framing her beautiful face. Those dark eyes and blood red lips are gently smiling. She stands tall before me, clothed in an ornate white ball gown sprinkled with sparkling diamond. Where her ball gown meets the ground it has a blue ombre effect, as if she's been wading through a pool of blue ink. I have always nicknamed her Blue because whenever I see her she appears to have an electric glow. For most of my life I have been having hallucinations, a kind of day dream so vivid that I often wonder why other people cannot see the things that I see or hear the voices that are talking to me. The hallucinations interact with reality, warp it and manipulate it. To me they seem real, like another version of reality being projected into this one. An augmented reality kind of thing. I had always thought that I just had a vivid imagination. When I was a child I would be in my bedroom alone orchestrating fantastic stories and enacting them with my toys Barbie, Ken, and Action Man. Ken would be having a fight with Action Man and Barbie would fly in and save Ken, carrying him off into the sky, safe in her arms. In my dreams at night I would fly. I would watch films on television, musicals and love stories and incorporate them in to my play. When my twin brother and I were asked to pick our favourite dressing up clothes at nursery for a photo he chose to be a cowboy and I wore a blue ball gown. It was natural to me, the same as asking my teacher at primary school how to spell Barbie when we were writing our letters to Santa. My world was just full of romance, fairytales and make-believe. Another big part of my life was listening to my parents' music The Carpenters, Abba, Elaine Paige, Cliff Richard; I would sing along in the car or dance around the lounge when they played music. My earliest ever memory is of sitting on the floor in our lounge listening to the song Heartbreaker by Dionne Warwick on vinyl whilst my mother did the housework. When I told my mother about this memory and described the dress that she was wearing she says that I must have been only 6 months old at the time. As I grew I would draw the figure of this same woman over and over, so much that I remember when I was about 6 years old my paternal grandfather telling me to stop drawing her as it was inappropriate. I couldn't stop; I didn't understand what I was doing wrong. She lived in my dreams, in the music and in my make-believe, an imaginary Barbie. She always dresses according to the occasion and conducts the hallucinations as if my senses are instruments in her orchestra. Once I became an adult she also had a voice and a personality; she had grown with me. And here she is now in this frozen moment, standing before me; her voice is inside my head.

"At this moment you want to know how you got here

and which events made you who you are. Can I just remind you that you have already answered those questions in the last 24 hours? You read your books, your history; you recorded your journey. Yet the question still remains 'Do you know who you are?' Consider what led you here to this present moment." She speaks to me as if the answer should be obvious, as if just by her saying it I will have some sort of revelation.

"So the 'B' is for Blue then?" Adonai asks.

"Yep."

"Okay, I really need to hear the story of who She is! What happened in that room then when She's there and your brain is on pause?" He seems really excited about the stuff I'm saying, it's weird, perhaps sometimes you just need the right audience in order to feel comfortable enough to open up - actually, a thought rises up in my consciousness; I have the journals with me because I copied them out onto the computer for safe keeping and they're on my phone.

"Well She reminds me about my journals that I kept - if you really want the full story I can read them to you?"

"Hell yeah! Oh this is gonna be good! Where are they? Do you have to go get them or something?"

"Nope they're right here on my phone. I didn't do them all of the years but I can fill in the blanks, if you don't get too bored." I smile.

"Oh sweet. The power of technology! Well carry on Mister Kristoff."

Okay well I started to think over what actually lead me 'here' to this frozen room with the psychic medium woman. I suppose it's the story of the day before. I set the scene for myself and retrace my steps. The day of the week is insignificant because here in Spain during August, as you know, everyday seems the same; all the days feel like the weekend. Yesterday I was at work. My Mother and Step-father own a wholesale company that delivers frozen food to a chain of English cafes all along the south coast. I receive the orders and with the help of the other employee Gary make the deliveries. Me and Gary get on really well, he's a proper blokey bloke and obviously I'm not, so you'd think that ' on paper' we shouldn't but we've become really good friends. I think that must happen with a lot of co-workers, you just get thrown together and find common ground or learn off of each other. He's a big bear of a man and I'm a little punk but we get on. We drive a big white freezer van, so yes we are white van men. We set off at 6am to the warehouse that holds the stock. We spend half an hour in the storeroom that is set to -20°c picking out the boxes that we need for the days deliveries. I have a circulation disease called Raynauds which means I'm really sensitive to the cold. So even with protective clothing on I go numb. When I get back outside in the heat and the blood starts to re-enter my hands and feet it is excruciatingly painful, proper breathtaking. Not my favourite time of the day. Gary drives the two hours southwards to the furthest café and I take over as we work our way back up the coast so that he can have a sleep. It's a boring drive on a deserted toll road and yesterday my head was playing tricks on me. As I was driving along I had a weird flashback to a place in my mind. But instead of it just being like a day dream my senses were filled by the memory. I was standing inside the workshop on my grandparents' farm between the tractor and the big tank of red diesel. I could smell the farm, the diesel, the mud. I could hear all the sounds of the farm. I put my hand out and touched the muddy tyre of the tractor and Nell the sheepdog who was lay next to it stirs and looks at me. I felt as if I had been fully transported to that place. It must have only lasted a matter of seconds and I hadn't closed my eyes or jerked back to consciousness, my driving hadn't been effected but I really felt that for however long that episode lasted I wasn't sat in the van. Somehow part of my consciousness had separated off into the hallucination and the rest had stayed operating in reality. The memory wasn't a significant one either; I had no idea why that place would pop into my head so vividly. I didn't wake Gary as I wanted to just write it off as some sort of cognitive blip and carry on with the day; also I didn't want him to think I was a dangerous lunatic.

We swapped back over on the driving after the next delivery and bantered away in our normal manner. He's a proper man's man but we are able to really talk to each other about stuff, we're never short of conversation. But I kept having the flashbacks.

Climbing a big oak tree in the forest near one of my childhood homes. Sitting in the back of my Mum's Citroen Dianne with the grey furry seat covers when I was about 5 years old stroking fuzzy patterns on the fabric. At Bristol zoo watching the polar bear crazily walk back and forth in its plastic habitat. Sat on the beach overlooking Sydney Harbour watching the beautiful woman (Blue) emerge out of the sea. All the scenes were unrelated and of unimportant events. I wasn't reliving dramatic episodes that made any sense to me. This was a new form of craziness to me. I'd had visions and voices in my head before but what made this different was that I really felt somehow transported into these places. I had felt like my actual location had vanished and my senses were being fed by my memory. Usually reality is added to when I have a crazy mental episode, like a special effect superimposed on a film. An augmented reality rather than flashing in to a similar but alternate reality. But this was like something had cut a few frames out and selotaped a memory in amongst them. There was nothing else significant about the working day, completely average. I wasn't affected enough for anyone to notice, I was still engaging with the mundane reality that I was physically in. Once we had finished doing the deliveries on the van I did the banking and set off on my scooter to my afternoon occupation.

I'm helping out in the tattoo shop that my friends own Bagwa Tattoo. I'm doing reception work, doing some tattoo design, drawing the transfers and making coffee in exchange for tattoos. The shop is a kind of solace and sanctuary for me; it's a little apartment that has been converted into a studio and has a really friendly, bohemian atmosphere. I can't properly describe how it feels to me when I'm in that place, it's almost like a wormhole in to a different reality; the real world slip away. People are all there for the art of tattooing and mixed in is the spiritual side of things. It's situated on a busy main coast road; on one side are all the restaurants, bars, hotels, apartment blocks and cafes bustling with tourists. The side on which the studio is has car lots, mechanics, newsagents, vets, nightclub and hairdressers; above which the studio nestles. Usually when I climb the flight of stairs up the outside of the studio I can hear laughter, music and conversation punctuated by the wind charms hanging in the trees on the terrace. At the top of the stairs you enter a little outside space with a sofa, armchairs and table surrounded by potted plants. There are small stone statues of Buddha and foo dogs in the pots too. People sit out here in the sun waiting for their tattoo appointments, drinking coffee, smoking nervous cigarettes. Some people are friends or relatives of the people who are getting tattooed and they just sit out here and relax, others are part of the tattoo tribe that come up here just to have a chat. You enter the studio through some patio doors into an area with two sofas, bookshelves full of design folders and a reception desk. There are more eastern statues and a photo gallery of tattoos done by the artists. Off this room are a kitchen, bathroom and a doorway into the actual studio where the tattooing takes place. Everyone says that there is a really nice atmosphere here. It is an interesting space to be in because of all the art and spiritual objects and photos but I think the atmosphere is mostly due to the people who work there. Sarah and Toby are the married tattoo artists who run the show.

Sarah is a very strong woman; she always has an opinion and is very vocal; sstraight shooting and direct. Being half-Chinese, half-English she looks very striking and has a unique style. She dresses like a gothic geisha, long curly hair decorated with jewels, big goth boots, colourfully patterned clothes and long painted nails. Her character is feisty and powerful. She always interrogates her clients whilst they're in her chair being tattooed, like a kind of therapy; finding out their stories and offering advice or solutions to their personal problems. Even the most unlikely customers pour their hearts out to her. She believes in a lot of new age spiritual stuff - pendulums, psychics, crystals, reiki and all that; often she refers customers to people she knows in that field who can help them. She doesn't suffer fools and isn't a girly-girl, but above all she is a wife and mother and her family is very important to her. She works with her husband Toby. He's English, a body builder, covered in tattoos; he has braided hair and a goatee, if Sarah is a fierce geisha Toby is a strong and silent samurai or Viking. Toby is quiet, polite and friendly. He holds similar beliefs to Sarah but is a bit more open to exploring them for himself. I've been fortunate enough to get to know them over a few years as a customer of theirs but this summer I feel very lucky to be their 'gimp'. Each year they pick someone to work the busy season with them and this year it's me. So in exchange for tattoos I get to experience the amazing world of Bagwa Tattoo.

Today the studio is reasonably quiet, Toby has someone booked in for the whole day but Sarah has a couple of hours between appointments and is sat with a woman who has popped in for a coffee. Her name is Victoria and I recognise her as part of a big loud family who come in for tattoos whenever they are over on holiday from the UK. She always dresses very 'put together', made-up and her dark hair is bobbed immaculately. She's tall and slim and I think it's odd that she blends into the background when she's with her family because she is quite striking, she reminds me of Cameron Diaz but with dark hair. I don't remember her ever actually being tattooed herself but now that she has moved over here she pops up for a chat with Sarah and Toby every now and then. Loads of people do that, pop in to the studio for a coffee and a chat. I grab a coffee for myself and check everyone is okay for beverages then settle into the reception chair (gimp station). Sarah and Victoria are sat on the sofa in front of me and Sarah immediately gets me involved in the conversation.

"Kristoff, Victoria's just been for a reading with Noelle over the road." Sarah sits back and gestures at Victoria to carry on talking as if she's just introduced a guest on a chat show, she starts to interview her.

"So did Noelle make you cry? She's really good at that, it's almost her trademark. When me or Toby have been she's made us cry and I never cry."

"Yes she did! I thought she was very good and spot on with things. Thanks very much for sending me to her because it was accurate and made sense. It's helped with the decisions I was thinking about. I've been to a lot of mediums through my life and Noelle was good and helpful." I think that's the most I've heard Victoria say as she's normally drowned out by her relatives. But she seems a nice and intelligent woman; beautiful and coherent. In fact she really reminds me of Kris Jenner in the way that she talks. I feel comfortable enough in the environment of the studio to ask questions and obviously with my flashbacks happening all morning they are playing on my mind.

"Can they help with like - mental issues?"

"Yeah they can. Most people go because they want questions answered, problems solved or guidance in a situation. I always say that I use them as a form of counselling." Victoria opens up and it's one of those situations where a person you've noticed on the periphery starts to come into focus. Sarah then explains to me that Victoria has moved here because she had an operation on her back and is slowly recuperating.

"Yeah, I'm trying to do some walking and heal myself as best I can."

"Have you been to see Melody?" Sarah interjects "She does reiki healing and all sorts of therapies, from her house, and she does teaching and classes. That might help?"

"I'd certainly give it a go; do you have her card or something?"

Sarah gets a leaflet of Melody's and they carry on talking about Victoria's operation and how she ended up moving over here. A couple of tourists come in to look at designs and check out the studio; I help them out with ideas and do them a quote. Just at that point Melody's husband Gavin walks into the studio. Sarah looks surprised, does her double-take face and shoots her hands out as if to stop him in his tracks.

"No bullshit Gavin we were just talking about Melody! Victoria wants a session for her back, she's had an operation. Call her! This is a sign, it's this place. I always say be careful what you say in here because it'll happen. Go on call Melody, Gavin!" She hands him her phone.

"Okay, will do - hello by the way." As with most people Gavin is used to the way things work in the studio; connections are made and solutions found and rapidly set into motion I make him a coffee (a builder's – milk and two sugars) as he goes out on the terrace for a rolly and rings Melody. It turns out that Melody is available so he and Victoria set off to go and see her. That's how quick things happen here, Sarah and Toby always know someone who knows someone and whatever problem it may be no-one leaves without some sort of next step.

Next person in through the door as Gavin and Victoria are descending the stairs outside is Penny. She works in a bar on the next urbanisation down the main road, she is also a psychic. She's come for a catch up with Sarah and they sit in the relative privacy of the kitchen. I'm sat at my desk which is next to the beaded curtain doorway to the kitchen and therefore am again privy to this conversation. To begin with Penny is chatting about her work, family and communal friends; but then she starts to tell Sarah that her visions are bugging her. Spirits keep coming to her when she's at the bar and trying to work, they keep pestering her. It's really fascinating to hear someone talk about spirits and ghosts and stuff in such a matter-of-fact way, like it's completely normal. Penny is describing how ghosts are getting in her way at work trying to get her attention so that she can deliver messages to customers that are connected to the ghosts.

"Wow! That is soooo cool, I love all that scary stuff about ghosts and the supernatural." Adonai waves his hand in the air as if he's locating the ethereal beings in the space just above his head. "What an interesting place to work. Go on, go on!"

Well I take this opportunity and tell them about the flashbacks that I'd had all day, just to see what their opinion would be of the phenomenon. I actually felt really nervous and stupid telling them as if they were going to look at each other and burst out laughing. They did look at each other but just exchanged some sort of knowing smile. Penny asks me if I have ever had a psychic reading done because it seems like someone is trying to tell me something. I say that I never have so Sarah decides that a reading by a psychic medium would be beneficial. They think that Penny shouldn't do it now that I've told her about the flashbacks so Sarah grabs the mobile and an appointment was swiftly made on my behalf; apparently the availability of an appointment is a sign that the reading is 'meant to be'. It was promising stuff as I was booked in for the next day so I must be a psychic emergency. I must admit that my stomach kind of turned when I watched Sarah booking the appointment, I don't know why but it just made me nervous.

The rest of the afternoon was pretty quiet and ordinary which meant that all that was whirring around in my head was the reading and what might happen. Will there be some ominous message? Will she make some cryptic theatrical predictions about my future? It felt so odd that I was booked in to actually see a psychic, a bit scary. We closed up and I rode my scooter home and it felt as if I was being magnetised towards something. I knew that I just had to read through the journals I had written, to revisit the things that had happened to me because I felt as though something was about to change. So that night I picked up my pile of notepads that I'd kept as journals and started reading. I have a freakily good memory so as I read I was transported back through the years.

I look at Adonai and it does seem really odd that I'm actually saying this stuff out loud, here on this beach, now; sharing the intimacies of my life and thoughts with a stranger. He's listening intently but I'm really not used to talking to somebody about myself.

"So how good is your memory Mister Kristoff? Because already this sounds like an amazing story - don't leave any details out! Do you need a gigglestick break to get you into the flow of these journals of yours?"

"Um yeah, I think I do. Yeah my memory has always been really weirdly full-on. I can remember almost everything if I just take a moment to concentrate or like if I'm looking through the family photo albums." He starts to roll another joint.

"Well that's perfect for storytelling." He smiles "It sounds like you've experienced a lot; I'm looking forward to all of the gory details ha ha! Carry on while I roll. Start with the first journal."

18th Birthday/January 1997

I've just turned 18 yesterday and now that I'm an adult I've started to do a few things to start my life. The first thing that I did was to have my hair cut. I had been growing my hair since I was 12 and it had caused a massive problem for my parents; my Dad ended up grilling me at the dinner table in front of my brothers asking me if I wanted to be a girl. I didn't see how me growing my hair would hurt anyone else. At school boys weren't supposed to grow their hair past the bottom of their shirt collar so I had a pony tail and undercut. We didn't go to the local school but to one in a city 20 miles away. It was quite a posh school; my brothers and I were sent there because Nanna (my paternal grandmother) had been Head of the Art department and Head of House there. All the teachers knew of her and our surname preceded us everywhere. I didn't get on with her at all; she wasn't a cuddly, caring grandmother. She was all pomp and circumstance, fur coats, hats, strong perfume and lashings of red lipstick that stuck on you when she kissed your cheeks - a Hyacinth 'Bouquet/Bucket'. Last summer she sent me one of her poison pen letters. She would sit at her desk in her National Trust Gatehouse at Anthony House in Devon and send members of the family letters criticising them and giving them her advice on what they should do in their lives. Weirdly enough I just visited Anthony House with my Dad, his wife and my Aunt and Uncle. I was really surprised to find out that had been used in the filming of Tim Burton's Alice in Wonderland. I had watched the film loads of times but not recognised that it was filmed where my grandparents used to live. Ironic that Alice had fallen down the rabbit hole in a place that I knew from my past. My gran had invited my parents to go and stay with her in the summer holidays. My brothers and I were left at home alone because we were all working. I received a letter from her quoting the bible and telling me to respect my parents and basically get myself on the straight and narrow. She thought I would be best suited to working as a chef in a country hotel. I had absolutely no idea what she was going on about, sure I had long hair, a pierced ear and smoked but other than that I still attended church, was at college and had a job too, I hadn't done anything bad at all. I didn't know what I had done to draw her attention, but it really annoyed me. So I decided to fight fire with fire and I wrote right back to her quoting scripture that said you shouldn't judge other people and that I was actually choosing my own path, she should keep her nose out and concentrate on her own life. I had never had much respect for authority, especially when people 'pull rank' - respect should be earned by the way in which you act not arbitrarily demanded due to age. On my Mother's side of the family the elders are all so wise and gentle and we beg them to tell us their stories and quietly learn from them. But my Father's parents are all fanfare and ego, it seems that they want you to bask in their enlightenment rather than actually connect with you and communicate with you in particular. So I was surprised by receiving her letter also just because it was directed at me personally. My letter to her arrived whilst my parents were still there with her and caused quite a stir I reckon. She showed my letter to my parents as if I had spontaneously written to her to have a go at her off my own back. Well thankfully that backfired on her as they knew I wouldn't have bothered doing that sort of thing so she had to admit that she had written to me first. When they got back and spoke to me about it my parents seemed sort of proud that I'd stood up for myself, maybe because they had never had the courage to. But I do wonder what my Father was telling his Mother about me for her to see fit to pick up her pen in the first place. You should be wary when people feel comfortable enough to criticise you from within a group like a family or circle of friends - it usually means that there is a pretext of criticising you in that group. She must have known that there wouldn't have been a backlash from my parents, so reading between the lines my parents must have criticised me to her. I felt betrayed. All that her letter had achieved was giving me a sense that I had to look after myself and make my own decisions, hence the changes I am making now. Some actions are small and would seem insignificant to a bystander but to the doer the action is implanted with meaning that makes it bigger to him. I think it's pretty difficult to be a rebel without a cause because rebellion is about the mindset of how you see that which you are rebelling from or against; it needs a reference point, a cause. How you see that is based on their actions and behaviour. It's a snowball from feeling different to them and then realising that there is a 'them' and 'us'- an inside and an outside. I feel like I have more in common with the singers on the radio that I listen to late at night in my bedroom. I've got a tiny transistor radio and headphones that I listen to under the covers at night, every night for as long as I can remember. From deep within that secret cocoon in the middle of my family's nest I clandestinely connect to a world that seems so distant. That world of rock music and songs packed with emotions that are foreign to me plays right into my head in the darkness. There's a big world out there.

Well I went and had my hair all cut off on Friday and

it felt weird but I liked the way in which doing something so simple could be so easy yet meant a lot to me. I looked different and felt clean and new. It'll confuse my Mum too because she said to me earlier in the year when I had my ear pierced "Have you got anything else stupid left to do?!" So they'll think I'm starting to become normal. It felt liberating having all my long hair cut off, like I was going to emerge as a new version of myself. Little do they know that I found something else stupid to do…a tattoo!

There's a tattoo shop in Hereford that I'd passed for the last few years on the bus to school and college. It's a tiny little dark place on the roundabout next to the cattle market. Last week I plucked up the courage to go in, choose a tattoo and book the appointment. I chose to have it done on my birthday as a present to myself and as a physical marking of the start of my adulthood. The bloke in there looked at me like I was a silly little grunge kid. He was an old school metalhead with long greasy greying hair and an 80s band t-shirt. I chose a Celtic knot arm band which he thought was too big for my first tattoo, probably thinking I'm a weed who will bottle it half way through or something. But I really liked the way it was all intricate and intertwined yet technically it was just a complicated line, a circle weaving in amongst itself; a glorified number 8. I didn't tell anyone that I was doing it; I just wanted to surprise people. A girl who I sit next to at college has tattoos and I want to show her I'm not the dork she thinks I am. She's all gothy and into vampires and that stuff. When she leant me the video 'Interview with a Vampire' she decided that I needed to be re-named. So instead of Christopher she called me Kristoff. She reckoned it's the same as her being called Teri but her name is Theresa or like Peter becoming Pete - I had just dropped the R. All I know is that she made sure it caught on by telling everyone my new moniker as if I was Louis to her Lestat. Now my friends have started calling me it too and it has spread to people at work as well. I like it; somehow it makes me feel like I have a new identity and goes along with the changes I've wanted to make.

So my birthday arrives and I have changed my shift at work so that I can sneak off for my appointment. It's Saturday so my Mum is out and about, Dad is closed in his office working, my twin brother Pete is off to the farm to help out and so I can just get ready and go. When I get into my car it always reminds me of the day I passed my test. None of my family expected me to pass first time and so when I arrived home from the examination they were ready to console me. I just walked over to my Fiat Uno tin can and ripped off the L plates and drove off. I got to the end of the road and then started to panic trying to concentrate on the 20 mile drive to college to show my friends I had passed. The blue Fiat Uno wasn't a very trendy car so spurred on by my grandmother's letter I had sold it, got a bus to London and bought an old red VW Beetle and drove it back; much to my parents' shock and despair. I love my car, it's 26 years old and represents freedom to me. I like how it's old and loud and quirky, not your average vehicle. I have taught myself how to fix it up and do maintenance on the engine, which came in handy when the gear stick came out of the floor when I was chugging down the main road or when a spark plug blew out like a shotgun. It has its problems but I love that car, it just needs a bit of t.l.c and attention. And today we're going on a secret mission.

I am nervous about the tattoo, how much it's going to hurt and being in the shop. I smoke as I'm driving and listen to a cassette tape 'jagged little pill' by Alanis Morrisette. Her sound is different to the usual Britpop stuff about at the moment, very emotional and dramatic. My friend Amelia had given it to me because she'd bought it but it was too 'heavy' for her, but I like singing along to it as I drive. Songs and singing are so major to me; it's amazing how they make you feel things. I always get a wobble on when I have to turn the cassette over at the same time as driving. I get into the city and park up, having a couple of cigarettes round the corner from the shop to psyche myself up. Eventually I enter and thankfully there's no-one else in the shop other than the moody tattoo bloke, smoking a cigarette. He sits me down in the chair and asks where I want the tattoo positioned. I want it on my left arm just low enough so you can see it when I've got a t-shirt on. He has made a transfer of it and shaves my arm then presses the transfer on. It looks bigger on my arm and I'm now anxious about the pain this bloke is about to inflict on me. He recommends that if I have any chewing gum it will distract me whilst he tattoos, luckily I do have some and quickly pop a few strips into my mouth; but I chew frantically as I anticipate…the PAIN. The first thing I notice is the noise of the tattoo gun – it sounds like it will hurt. It has a mean metallic growl. He leans on me and makes surface contact and the sensation makes every single nerve in my body jangle. It hurts, but after a few seconds my body seems to be getting used to it. Now it feels as if someone is pinching me or poking me over and over with a pin. It just feels intense but irritating rather than painful. I don't know whether it's the adrenaline or pain but I feel kind of puffy headed - you know that feeling when you've broken something that you can't fix or said something you can't take back? Or even like when you're riding downhill on your bike and the brakes have broken. There's no going back now, it's done. Even having my hair cut off wasn't like this feeling because you know you can always just grow it again. This is permanent. I think I can smell blood; it makes me think of Teri the vampire from college.

The actual position of being tattooed is uncomfortable to me, I'm lay face up on a kind of dentist chair contraption with a big bloke wrapped around my arm, gripping my bicep in one hand and pushing the tattoo gun into my skin with the other. I feel awkward but he says it'll take at least an hour and a half to do the tattoo so I am going to have to just suffer it. The physical closeness of the bloke is making me squirm way more than the feeling of the needle needling me. There isn't any conversation but I don't want to break his concentration with idle chit chat and I can't think of anything to say. I start to look around the studio; it's just a gloomy box that is covered in weird symbols and designs. From the chair I can look out of the dirty window of the shop-front and see the traffic trundling around the roundabout. I can hear the radio coughing out some tinny cassette of what I think is 80's heavy metal. Judging by the tattoo bloke's band t-shirt I reckon he must have had a massive perm back in the day and been really into all that. I keep on looking at my arm as he tattoos, it's so weird thinking that the ink is actually going in, under my skin. I have no idea how it works but don't want to ask because he'll think I'm stupid. Time is ticking by and the outline is taking shape, it's a really intricate design and he seems to just be doing it in tiny little bits; you can't draw it like with a pen. Just as I'm starting to feel restless the cassette clunks to a stop and he slides across on his wheelie office chair to turn it over and we both whip round as the bell tinkles as the shop door is opened. My heart sinks as I recognise the two girls who are trotting in. They're a pair who I was in the same tutor group as them all the way through secondary school. They didn't go to Sixth Form College so I haven't set eyes on them for about 18 months. They were always really bitchy to me, taking the mick out of how I looked and calling me a swot because I was in the top sets of all my subjects. The last time they spoke to me at school was stopping me as I was walking along to tell me that they had been out to Marilyn's, one of the night clubs in the city. They thought that they had achieved something amazing because they were underage and getting in to nightclubs. They stopped me just to tell me that I would never get into the nightclub because I was too ugly and boring. I had been fat, long haired, and spotty and wore glasses all through school. I could see their point but thought they seemed pretty desperate to find someone who gave a shit whether they'd been clubbing if they needed to stop me to tell me about it. I remember that moment well because they looked like the heavily made-up 'ugly-sister' characters from some St Trinians version of a Cinderella Pantomime, convincing themselves that they're gorgeous and desirable by belittling someone else. So here they are, dressed as Slag Spice and Rough Spice, in market couture - all scrunchies, shiny polyester and lycra; I'm a kind of surprised that they're not in Union Flag dresses. What's more I can't even move or hide because my arm is attached to tattoo-geezer, great. They start to look at the tattoo designs on the walls, pointing and pulling faces at them. He asks them if they need help.

"No, *they* don't, but I could really use a cloaking device right now." I whine at him in my head. They just stare at him, Terminator-scanning him and then start giggling to each other. Then one of them squints at me hands on hips, her face broadens and her mouth drops open like a bin lorry and she starts jab pointing at me.

"You're him from school aren't you? Umm – Ayrton…Chris! Oh my god! What happened to you? Did you get a life?" She seems startled. It kind of takes me aback that she thinks I've changed, I've lost the glasses, spots, long hair and the weight but that doesn't change who I am to them. Surely I am still the swot from school, but she's speaking differently to me?

"Where have you been hiding?" The other one chirps.

"Haven't seen you out."

"I don't live in town."

"Oh, Shame" They look at each other and I'm sure telepathically decide to leave; they turn like it's been choreographed and with a tinkling of bell they go clacking out the door.

"Do you know them?" He asks.

"No not really, we went to the same school."

"Why were they so surprised by seeing you then? What's changed?"

"Well I was fat and had glasses and long hair so they just used to take the piss."

"Oh nice. That's the trouble with people they don't believe that people can ever change." With that he flicked the radio on; Babylon Zoo's Spaceman came squealing out. I thought he was going to change station but he just wheeled himself back to my arm.

"Ready." It wasn't a question rather than a warning as he started the gun buzzing and the pain reignited. I decided that I would concentrate on the music. Next was "Firestarter" by The Prodigy, I always want to say The Progidy; I glance at tattoo man and think this song suits him right now. Next up is the late Take That which people are grieving over with "How deep is your love?"

"Classic" Says tattoo man. I think he means the song not the band though. I remember seeing the video for "Pray" by them and feeling a bit confused, I didn't know whether I admired their bodies as something to aspire to or just to touch. I think it's a phase though, like everyone goes through that stage, in development. Thinking about other guys.

"The brothers Gibb."

"What? Oh yeah. Nice song"

"What music are you into?" He asks, I never know what to say to this question because I listen to real extremes of music. Do I say Fleetwood Mac? Nirvana? Blur? Red Hot Chilli Peppers? Joy Division? The Spice Girls? Because I listen to all of them. Do I pick the one he'll be impressed by?

"Well when I was a kid the first album I had was Joy Division 'Closer' when I was like 7 one of my older cousins gave it to me because he didn't like it. Then when I was about 13 the first girl that I proper liked got me really in to Fleetwood Mac."

"Oooh" He shrugs. "Not bad. There's a load of rubbish around at the moment. It's all about the marketing now. Manufactured groups, they're not even bands. It's Madchester and Brit Pop." He pauses on the tattooing for a second then starts again. "You know those girls? You should always remember and I've always thought this; things change." I hesitated for him to continue but he didn't.

"True" I answered.

"And even when things aren't changing you still don't know which side of the story you're getting. People usually can't see the woods for the trees. Sometimes things are changing and you just don't see it yet. It's like that one about the elephant. There are four blind men and this elephant stood in this room. So each of the blind men is told to feel out in front of them and tell them what it is. The first on goes up and feels the tail, he reckons it's a rope. The second one goes up and feels the leg; he says it's a tree. The next one goes up and feels the belly; he says it's a wall. The fourth one goes up and feels the trunk and he thinks it's Linford Christie. He he he!" He stops tattooing whilst he laughs at his own joke. As he settles back down he looks at me and says

"In all seriousness, you're a young fella, how old are you?"

"I'm eighteen, today actually."

"Jeez, really, well all the more reason to think on then. Oh, so you're commemorating today with the tattoo then? Good idea, I like it when people do them for a reason. Now you'll always look at that and remember what it was like to be eighteen. Many happy returns by the way. Have you been taking stock of yourself then?"

"Well yeah, I suppose so, more like looking forward to being grown up I suppose."

"Woah! You're not grown up! Ha ha, some people never grow up. Especially if you don't look back and take stock of yourself. It is the only way to see if you've changed. I always think like that on days like Christmas or New Year or birthdays, I think everyone does. What was I doing last year, or the year before? Wander where I'll be this time next year? Strewth! I hate this song" Gina G's 'Ooh Aah Just a little bit' had popped up on the radio. "This is what I mean, this rubbish. All spin doctored and sexed up crap that's all it is. What I do is spend a day writing down what happened the year before, so I can remember the next year when I look back and I'll know what's changed. How are you ever going to know if you're doing well or bad if you never think about it? I reckon that's what you should do today. It's your eighteenth birthday and you're getting a tattoo, you should write all the things you can remember from last year up to now then next birthday you can do the same with the year that's coming up now and so on."

"That's a good idea actually, I really like writing too, thanks" I'm waiting for his response, not to me but to The Spice Girls singing "Say you'll be there" on the radio. I love them and the superhero video to this song with all their alter egos, Scary is my favourite. Ginger and Posh look amazing as well though. Tattoo man must like them too because he hasn't disapproved. I don't think I'll start a conversation with him about them though. I love the idea of having an alter ego, creating a new identity; I suppose that's what I'm doing at the moment too.

"For instance, what are you doing now?"

"Well I go to Sixth Form and I work in the supermarket, evenings and Saturdays."

"What do you do at Sixth Form?"

"Art, Psychology and Theology."

"That's a bit of a strange combination, why them?"

"Well I did well at Art so I wanted to carry it on. Psychology seemed really interesting and my family is really religious so I chose Theology."

"Why is that then?"

"I suppose to study it properly and know more about it. I've always gone to church and read the bible but I don't know if I know the actual history behind it all like from not in the bible. You know, the factual side to it all."

"Good idea kid, I think you can only believe the things that you know not just what you get told by someone else. Especially if it's pot luck whether you got born here, where you're Christian and not somewhere else where you'd have been a Muslim or somewhere else where you'd be a Buddhist, or a Jew or an Aborigine or in a tribe worshipping the weather and the tree-hugging and all that. What you going to do after that?"

"I want to go to university and do Psychology."

"Ooh good luck to ya, scratching around in people's heads, messy job but someone's got to do it I suppose."

We didn't speak again for another hour until the tattoo was finished. But it did occur to me that in his job he must do his fair share of scratching around in people's heads, he'd already done that to me. He selotaped some tissue on me and cling filmed it over, there was a bit of blood. My arm feels very sore and swollen, sore like a burn kind of sore. I thank him and pay him, he advises me not to wash it for as long as I can but change the tissue and wash it then. Luckily I had already gone to the library and found a book on tattoos that told me how to look after it while it heals. I thank him again and leave the shop. I think I'm walking as if I've just received a gun-shot wound to the arm, but it is sore.

I drive straight back to work in lovely Ross on Wye, I work in a supermarket in the precinct. Saturdays are always busy and all of the staff are in so it's a good laugh. I have been working there for about a year and half so I know everyone now. The shift goes fine and people are wishing me Happy Birthday and asking me if I'm going out tonight. It seems weird that I'm hiding a secret tattoo under my uniform - my body is permanently altered but no one knows! My mate Leo is excited because I am old enough to buy us a stack of alcohol and take it to his house, he's 17 so this will be our first 'own' alcohol - he's more excited about it than I am. He works in the butchery department but keeps wandering to the other end of the shop floor to the beers, wines and spirits aisle trying to decide what we should buy. We fetch a basket at the end of shift when the store is closing but the tills are still open and grab a variety load of hooch. I tell him about my tattoo as we are walking off the shop floor and into the warehouse heading for the stairs up to the staff area.

"No way! You is shitting me mon?" Although Leo is mixed race and both his parents come from London he always speaks in a Jamaican accent when he's excited. Then he goes all gangster if he's annoyed. No idea why. It actually sounds weirder when he speaks normally and seriously. He insists I show it to him right there and starts tugging at my sleeve. So I take off my grey tunic, unclip my bow tie, open my white shirt, pull off the sleeve and start to peel the tape off.

"Aah! Ouch… ffuuhh… that hurts!" I have to close my eyes as I keep peeling back the tape to reveal the slimy tattoo. It looks sore too.

"Oh my God, you did mon!" Leo's hopping up and down and pointing. Ally from the delicatessen counter comes out into the warehouse and skips over to have a nose. We get on really well; have lunch together and cigarette breaks. Everyone thinks we're having an affair but she's 33, married, with one kid and pregnant. We just talk loads and have a laugh, she doesn't seem older to me but I get on well with older people anyway.

"Kristoff? What have you done? Wow!" She winces. Now Felix off the checkouts is walking past I know him from the bus and college but only to say hello too.

"What's up you guys?" He comes and has a look too, which is a bit embarrassing because I'm stood here with my shirt half-off. "Nice ink. Did you get it done at Scotties?"

"Yeah."

"When?"

"Earlier on before work."

"Damn that looks well sore but fair play. Nice one." He pushes past us and heads up the stairs. I cover up and we all follow on up as well.

"So what are you doing tonight for your birthday? You and Pete having a joint party?" Ally asks

"Nah, I'm going round to Leo's so I can drink alcohol. We'll have a meal and cake at home tomorrow. Pete's on the farm anyway." I jingle all the bottles together in the plastic bags as I talk, as if they're proof. We swipe our name cards to clock out, go in to the locker rooms to change and we are free!

Leo's family live in a massive cottage, miles away in the middle of nowhere. We just basically hang out in his room, smoke weed; I listen to music whilst he plays Final Fantasy. But tonight we also have alcohol! It's pretty much the same atmosphere we're just louder and more talkative. I reckon I can see colours of smoke all coming off of Leo's head and then when I look in his mirror I can see different coloured smoke coming off me. Leo makes me draw them with crayons and thinks I can see auras, whatever they are. I just think it's the weed or the computer game. We talk about girls, famous ones and real ones that we know, tattoo designs and aliens. Eventually we go to sleep, him on his top bunk and me on the sofa bed. This morning when I woke up with a throbbing head and a throbbing arm, I remembered that I had dreamt a recurring dream that I've been having for as long as I can remember. It only lasts a minute or so. I'm inside the big black gothic carriage being drawn by four horses, sometimes they're black, sometimes they are white; it's speeding over the draw bridge of a castle high up on top of the mountain. It is as if we are making an escape away from the castle. Either side of the road is a deep canyon, its night time, there's a full moon, loads of stars and a few little white clouds. Sat next to me, holding my hand is Blue 'as' Cinderella, she seems frantic and is trying to comfort me. She then grabs my hand opens the carriage door and we jump off the speeding carriage into the canyon. In mid-air she starts to fly and takes me up with her. Then she flies over to a grassy hill with a single tree on top of it and gently places me down on the grass. She then flies off and I wake up. I have a throbbing head and a throbbing arm. I made my way home to a family meal and birthday cake. Oh, I also decided to take tattoo man's advice and started writing stuff down. Hello.

I pause and look at Adonai "That's year one. Are you bored yet?"

"Hell no! I notice you were on the reefer with your mate at 18 - it's going to be a trippy story. Love it! What's it like being a twin?"

"Umm, people ask me that all the time, the honest answer is that I have two brothers one is 5 minutes older than me and the other is 2 and a half years older; it doesn't feel that much different. Obviously we are close because we experienced stuff at the same time and we knew the same people or were in the same classes at school. There's a special connection because we do get treated as a set and other people think it's significant. It pushes us together sometimes, especially when we both worked at the supermarket at the same time. But we were really different as children - he's really athletic and macho and I'm .. er.. Not." We both laugh for what seems like ages, I think the weed has properly kicked in and my nerves are going. Adonai is actually clutching his stomach rolling around laughing, an actual belly laugh. He sighs to catch his breath and urges me to carry on.

Being 18/ 1997-1998

Well the first half of the year was pretty normal stuff. I went to open days for universities, applied and got offers that were doable to go on and study Psychology. I stopped going to church because I thought that what I'd learned in Theology threw up a lot of questions about the bible and whether it tells an accurate version of what actually happened in the synoptic gospels. It's difficult having questions like that when your whole family is so into it and believe it completely. Especially when their religion is such a massive driving force in their behaviour and our family life. We basically learned to read with the Bible, reading it every night together after the family dinner. So I've gone from being very involved in church and even considering working in the ministry to not really knowing what I think because the answers aren't out there. The bible doesn't agree with itself so it's difficult to listen to it being preached when it might as well be a collection of novels as far as I'm concerned. I don't think I've lost my faith it's just a few things have made me look at it all more personally. Like I remember being at Bible Camp last year when I had just started Theology and one of the speakers made a statement that kind of blew my mind - God is not British. I remember thinking "Oh my god, yeah" I'd always thought of god as a kind of Santa Claus figure who was pretty nasty in the Old Testament and then got nicer when Jesus was around. But he was always an old man with a beard who spoke English. That statement just suddenly made me realise that I had accepted something and followed it without really thinking about it or questioning it I hadn't thought outside the box. In my extended family my paternal grandparents are Nanna who's Anglican and Poppa who's Christadelphian; my maternal grandparents are Grampy who's Methodist and Grandma who's Born Again Christian (happy clappy, swing from the chandelier types according to Grampy) My parents are both Baptist and that's how me and my brothers were raised but we went to a Church of England school. So even within my family they all have chosen different paths of Christianity that suit them with slightly different doctrines and ideas. They take it seriously and Grampy and my Dad were both lay preachers at one point. My Dad then went on to lead a youth group in the church whilst my Mum does the cooking for a lunch club for the old people. I used to be involved in it all but now I feel like I just need some time to think for myself, find my own answers.

I started going out with the people from the supermarket. That's another part of the thing about not going to church. We were preached to when we were growing up that the world outside of church is evil. The people who are all straying away from the right path, they are all doomed and everything to do with worldly stuff is bad. They can only find salvation by welcoming Jesus and the Holy Spirit into their hearts and repenting their sins. Well for a start I'm not really that sure who Jesus is anymore after studying the bible in Theology and so I'm also not sure if everything the church says is accurate. The church is in the High Street of town and is opposite a pub called The King Charles. The minister used to talk about the evils of alcohol and people's wasted lives in his sermons. Well I had my first pint of lager in that pub surrounded by a group of workmates; and the whole experience was nice. Apart from feeling awkward at being in new surroundings and dealing with the banter of the lads from work it was refreshing and different. I remember taking that first ever sip of lager and thinking it tasted disgusting but I've got to drink it because everyone is.

It's the most lively, interesting atmosphere I had ever been in and I couldn't see why the church thought it was so bad. Sure enough I couldn't imagine any of the straight-laced people from church being in the pub and enjoying themselves but no-one was doing anything wrong; they're just having a nice time together. Everyone was laughing and joking, singing, messing about; but most significant to me was the fact that people were actually talking to each other and interested in each other's lives. People wanted to get to know each other and ask questions and have discussions and are allowed different opinions. I liked it and they asked me out the next Saturday and from then on I went out every weekend with them. There are a lot of pubs in town and a lot of people work in the supermarket so when the big group of us went around the other pubs we'd bump into other workmates. Then everyone would pile out of the pubs at closing time and head to the town's only nightclub - Jax Nite Spot. It's a proper dive, sticky carpets, 80s décor and cheesy music but by then everyone has had enough drink to hit the dance floor. It was loads of fun and I felt more confident in myself, it made work feel different too because I knew everyone better. In a strange way I fitted in, or at least I knew my place in the scheme of things. My friends from college were doing similar things in Hereford and occasionally we'd get taxis over there or to Gloucester to go to a better nightclub. It was just all new experiences and new interactions with people. I still felt like a nerd and out of place a lot of the time but being part of a group meant I could just be along for the ride. I had zero social skills and spent most of the time just observing my mates and how they dealt with things. I have a few girl mates and I can talk to them really comfortably; although Teri got even more obsessed with the vampire thing and kept on wanting to actually bite me. I didn't let her. I've had a few girlfriends at church and stuff but never had a proper relationship; I remember when I was younger that was all I wanted was to be in a relationship with someone who chose to love you. I was proper hung up on it and didn't think that I would be a real person until I found that girl. But now out 'in the wild' there is female attention but I look like the younger dorky brother of the group and the women from work want to mother me. I'm a bit of a joke I think. They don't mind me being around because I'm just harmless; but I still really want to be in a relationship.

I'm still really close to Ally at work and she's been out on a few nights out too. Over the last couple of years she's been having problems in her marriage. As we got to know each other at lunch or having a cigarette she opened up to me about it. I think I must be a good listener because more people say I'm easy to talk to and share their problems with me. That makes me feel grown up, me and my Mum have been like that for years; it's just nice to be wanted though. I think my family are a bit surprised by the amount of friends I have who are phoning the house. But I've always been the one out of us brothers who went to other people's houses for dinner when I was at school, or parties and sleepovers; even at primary school. Also I can't remember my brothers having girlfriends. I was always the social one. But I think they're surprised because there are a whole variety of women ringing up to speak to me or organise meeting up for a chat. They ring the phone and then drive and park outside the house to chat or go off for a drink. Ironic really because I'm not in a relationship with any of them, they're just my friends and they need me. I don't know if my parents wonder whether there is anything going on with them; they never did the whole 'birds and the bees' conversation with us kids or rather they haven't done so yet. Perhaps they just presume I won't have sex before marriage? I remember getting told off at church when they discussed the whole 'sex before marriage' and its sacredness. I asked what they did about it before marriage was invented, or about times when they had more than one wife – surely the husband has already sex with the first wife before the marriage to the second. What about if you're not compatible? You'd wait to find 'the one' get married and then be frustrated and unhappy? Surely if sex is such an important part of the union of two people then you should have some idea about it before making that sort of commitment to marriage? It would be like buying a house before you've seen all the rooms in it. I keep thinking about things like I lived on a desert island or in an uncorrupted trib, deep in the jungle somewhere; what would humans do naturally? What would our behaviour and relationships be like if we weren't taught morality?

That sex before marriage subject was all brought to the forefront with Ruby, one of my friends from church. Me and her have hung around together since I was about 16 and she was 15. We go to the same school as well as going to church and our families know each other. In the holidays we'd spend time together and usually on a Friday night we'd go to the Video Shop and choose a film and then to the supermarket to get ingredients for a meal, we'd cook together at her house and watch the film. She's so sweet and pretty and much cooler than me. She's been going out with Mark from school for as long as I can remember. Well when she was doing her GCSEs she fell pregnant by him. It actually happened at Bible Camp which makes it even more controversial. I guessed she was pregnant because she was always being sick. We talked about it before she told her parents and she had a little boy just as she turned 17. Thankfully everyone has been alright about it and she's a great mother. We still see each other as much as possible; she's been out with me and the people from work a few times when her mum baby-sits. Like tattoo man said in Hereford - things change. Ruby's life changed because now she is someone's mother, forever. Life is changing around me, to other people. I'm having fun, meeting lots of people and helping people talk through their stuff but still I'm not actually *doing* anything. I'm just trotting along in the rat race. Education for 14 years already and another 3 mapped out ahead of me at university mixed with being a worker to support myself. I don't even know what I want to be when I've studied Psychology. Do I just decide what interests me as I go along? Is my life being mapped out already by the decisions I make right now? I'll have a degree in a subject and have to follow that pathway to 'use' it and make it a worthwhile thing to have done in the first place. People around me are living with the consequences of their decisions and actions. Ally in her marriage and Ruby having a child, their lives are permanently changed.

I'm also still hanging around with Leo, he wants to be an actor; I went to see him in a play at his college. He has a plan or at least a goal and a reason to guide his future. My best friend from school and college is Andi, throughout sixth form we've spent loads of time together. We drive to is house for lunch and free periods, watch TV, play Worms on the computer. He bought a Land Rover and we went to Eastnor to do the off roading with the Land Rover club; with his girlfriend's family. Although I felt like a gooseberry it was really cool to just laze about on the hills watching the clouds whilst they daydreamed about their future. They talked about getting married and the songs they'd have at their wedding. I can still remember that moment so well, us lay on the grass on that hill just innocently staring at the clouds drifting past and making plans for the future. They were together a few more months but split when he went off to uni. He knows that he wants to be a teacher like both of his parents are. He's someone who I've grown up with and we like the same music - Nirvana, Red Hot Chilli Peppers, Foo Fighters. Hopefully we'll stay in touch. I feel like I have several different worlds in my life, College is in Hereford with one set of friends, some I've known for 7 years now others who I met at Sixth Form. I live and work in Ross on Wye where I know a lot of people through church and now I know more people through work and going out in town. My Grampy and Grandma live on the farm about 10 miles away and that place is somewhere I've known all my life. My twin Pete is going to be a farmer, he's always idolised our Grandfather and has always known what he'd be when he grew up. I have absolutely no idea. I'll probably come back and work the holidays like everyone else does but it will all be different again.

At work they've started training me up on all the different departments so that I'm 'multi-skilled', it's fine by me because it means I can get loads more overtime. It's really interesting learning because I know all the people already so I'm not nervous. It's a nice feeling getting more involved and doing different stuff. The store manager is an idiot though, no-one likes him. He told me I had an issue with authority when I first started doing more hours when I was 17. He did these shop inspections where he'd march around and check the shop floor and there was always something wrong. But he was rude about it. I remember him having a go at me as he marched past with my department supervisor that I had black trainers on rather than shoes. I said my shoes had worn out and I could only afford these ones until payday the next week because I had just paid my car insurance. The back of his neck went red that I had even dared to address him directly.

"Ayrton - I think you need to get your priorities right. There is a dress code for uniform, whilst you are at work that is more important than fucking about with your car, don't you think?" He barked right up to my face, then swiftly about-turned to start trotting off. I couldn't stop myself from replying.

"Well my car's next to yours in the car park, would you be worried about what shoes I'm wearing if I crashed into it?" My department head just looked at me open mouthed as the store manager swung round and stared at me as if I'd just spat at him. For a moment we were just locked eye to eye. I bricked myself thinking he was going to hit me or fire me. I could see a glimmer in his eyes that he was impressed rather than seething; but he still had to hold his own in front of the department supervisor. He leaned in really close to my ear and made out that he was telling me off, pointing his finger into my chest and all. But in my ear he whispered

"You'll go a long way. But repeat what I just said to anyone and you're out of here quicker than a sheep legging it out of Wales. And I'll deny it."

That was the trouble with management they kept using phrases that half made sense or didn't quite add up. I had soon realised that the people in authority had got there by some means other than their intelligence. But there is a hierarchy and you just have to stick to it. Now that I'm getting trained up he is being nice to me; he probably has a quota he needs to meet of 'multi-skilled' workers or something. Come to think of it I have always questioned authority when I've felt that I don't agree with them. I used to get into trouble with my parents for that; not just accepting their views but wanting an explanation of them. There were a couple of times that I stepped out of line for what I thought. We were the generation that got reared on smacking; the last few years they all say it's not allowed and it's cruel. At school we were the first year that they weren't allowed to give the cane or slipper as a punishment. But it was just part of life; you did something bad and that was a punishment. But when I was about 10 I remember my Mum smacking me and my twin for something and then turning to march out of our bedroom. In an instant I just spontaneously smacked her on the back of the leg as she turned - without even thinking. "See how you like it." I had said, but I felt awful at the same time. She just carried on walking. No-one was ever smacked in our house after that, except maybe the dog. Then there was that issue with me growing my hair.

"Hey Adonai do you ever have an argument and then ages later you spontaneously think of the perfect reply? That happened to me with the whole long-hair argument. It wasn't until years later that I realised that I should have pointed out that there are loads of photos in the family albums of my Dad with long hair!"

"Ha ha, yeah how annoying and the moment's passed so you cannot do anything about it. This is all good scene-setting stuff. It's weird trying to picture you back then." He chirped.

Then when my older brother did his GCSEs they had a go at him because he hadn't done as well as they had hoped. They made him cry at the dinner table in front of us because they thought he should have done better. I felt so hurt for him and started crying too and again couldn't stop myself from speaking up.

"He's done his best and you're telling him off because it's not enough? How can he do better than his best? He's tried hard enough and you've just made him feel horrible about the results." Both my parents turned to me and rolled their eyes, my Mum held her hand up to me.

"Don't you start. This doesn't concern you."

"It does if we're going to do our exams soon and you're going to tell us if our best is good enough for you! He's really upset. You made him cry." I knew I had overstepped the mark so I got up and left the dinner table, a cardinal sin in our house if you haven't been excused; and come to think of it only me out of my brothers has ever done it on a handful of occasions. My point is that I question authority when I feel it's being unfair or inaccurate.

Luckily for me I had done well in my GCSEs and now they have big hopes for me being the academic one and getting a good degree. Now that I have sat my A Level exams it's just a matter of waiting and seeing what results I get. I also sat around one day thinking about what an odd but good combination of A levels I had done. In Art I had studied surrealism, optical illusions, Escher and Dali. They really interested me because they were translating their imaginations and what was going on in their heads into real images that we can look at. In Psychology I'd learned about so many different theories and ideas about how the human brain works and the 'science' behind it. My tutor was a younger teacher called Jo and one day she'd pulled me and Amelia aside to chat after the lesson and told us about an article she was studying. We were learning about the unconscious mind and she'd read an article about meditation and the soul. Apparently you can lie down and calm your mind and then you'll see this flight of stairs and walk up it and go through a door to higher levels of consciousness. It seemed odd that she would tell us that when Psychology is all about studies and experiments. I sort of half tried it that night but thought I was just imagining a flight of stairs and all that, like in a dream. I fell asleep before anything happened.

In Theology we learned all about the Bible and Christianity and theories of altruism and morality and all that. It felt so strange, this book that I'd been reared on had lost all its power and now I was looking at it as a collection of books bunched together after the fact; a compilation of different people's stories, from ancient cultures that were really out-dated. It just seemed really ropy - how could so many people base their entire lives on this stuff? If there is a god he certainly hadn't been represented very well in the 'Holy' book. Even in Psychology when they are covering an idea like the mind there are several different schools of thought and different theories; but in religion they group the ideas together and treat them as sacred. It's so myth guided, magic fruit, parting seas, the ark, burning bushes, angels appearing, miracles, the undead, monsters and all that. Once I'd taken a step back from it and examined it properly I realised that I didn't believe in it at all. I don't know about whether I think there is a god or what the meaning of life is but I don't believe, for me personally, that it's to be found in the bible. My A level education had really all been about different aspects of my mind; imagination, science and belief. I hadn't planned it that way at all. Maybe one day it would make sense to me and I'd find the answers about 'life' and god and stuff but for now it all just swirled about in my head. A lost religion, an awakened imagination and scientific theories about human behaviour and how our minds work.

I went full time at the supermarket to start saving through the summer for university. With my 'multi-skilledness' I can cover in a lot of departments and get lots of overtime. I start doing loads of hours and really long shifts; I can be in all afternoon and evening and then stay on for the night shift. Or one day I'll be totally on tills, another on the dairy or deli or bakery. It's fun because I feel like I belong and have a purpose and skills. It has taught me a lot working with the general public and being part of a team in each department and socially a part of the supermarket crowd. I reckon it should be made mandatory that people have to work in customer services with the general public, they would learn how to still be polite and smile and be courteous to people even when they are treating you like a nobody piece of shit - it's a very important skill to learn, you can take it to the bank.

There are different groups of people who socialise

together in the supermarket workforce, the supervisors on the shop floor all get on, the 'upstairs' staff in the offices stick together, the workers all talk to each other but tills are like the divas who think they're special. Nobody likes the managers. I find it funny because I fit in with all of the different groups because of working in all of the departments. I've got to know Felix a bit more because he started coming out with all of us. Turns out he went away to boarding school up to GCSEs then came home to do Sixth Form, he knows Andi from Sixth Form too. His parents are really posh and own the hotel on the way to Hereford which the bus goes past. He's doing more hours at work like me now that we've done our exams and left college; he's now a supervisor on the checkouts. In June Felix ran away from home because he didn't get on with his family and got a flat in the town centre just up the road from the supermarket. He was supposed to be sharing with another guy from work and a mate of theirs. I'm good friends with Felix now from going out at weekends so I stay round at the flat when we go out so as not to wake my family by getting in late. They all go to bed at 10.30 and I'd have to creep in trying not to make any noise, not these easy when you're pissed. So I've got into the habit of phoning them from a call box to let them know I'm staying out at the flat, I don't think they'd even notice but it's just polite to let them know. I always have fun when we hang out together and we like the same stuff. He's really into the Manic Street Preachers and Mansun, cool bands and I've started listening to their stuff too. He's saving up for a year and then going off to Australia to find his real parents - he was adopted but apparently his family is in Australia. It got me thinking that I'd like to go travelling and actually do something rather than just follow the crowd and carry on to university. So one night at work I asked him if he'd mind me tagging along on the whole travelling plan; he was well excited about it and so I decided to take some time out and delay from going to uni for a while. The guy from work is dragging his feet on moving in and when we all went into Hereford to get our A-level results I went home to my house and my Mum just asked me straight out when I was going to move out. I think she just presumed I was going to but I hadn't even thought about it, so I packed my things right there and then. I felt hurt that she had asked me like that. But I suppose I've never really fitted in, my brothers are both sporty and athletic; then there's me the singing and dancing weirdo who just shuts himself away in his room. I just didn't think that they felt that way too. It all happened so quickly like ripping a splinter out of your finger. I'd literally just got my A-level results and moved out of home in one foul swoop.

It is a very basic flat above the chemists; kitchen and lounge downstairs a big bedroom, bathroom and tiny box room upstairs. A bloke called Ritchie has the lounge as his bedroom, he's the mate of the guy from work who didn't move in and is a weed dealer. Me and Felix are now sharing the big bedroom upstairs. There's a single bed that Felix has, a mattress on the floor that's mine, a sofa, TV on a bookshelf and a chest of drawers. There are posters all over the walls of bands and an Australian flag as a curtain. Now it always makes me think of that lyric from 'Common People' by Pulp 'Rent a flat above a shop, cut your hair and get a job.' We call it the Lad Pad, it's already a kind of 'open house' where all of our group of friends just drop-in and hang out. Our friends from work just turn up with their dinner or with drink if they're going out or smoke if they just want to sit and chill. At some point we got fed up of going downstairs to answer the door so we just left it on the latch so now everyone literally just appears. We're fine with that, there is zero privacy but it's just a great, fun, crazy place.

We're in the centre of town and are the centre of attention, a very new place for me to be. Me and Felix are very comfortable with each other and just talk all the time, telling each other about our lives. I suppose that nowadays it'd be called a bromance. I was seeing a girl I'd met whilst out and about in town, it wasn't very serious and she was quite sweet and normal. All the girls fancy Felix and we have a laugh, we've turned into a kind of double act. He wants to get into the army but can't put any weight on; he's also really into Star Wars and Star Trek, not my kind of thing at all. The summer was spent working and making the most of our free time. We'd go down to the river and sunbathe with a load of friends, go out drinking, singing karaoke, smoking weed in the flat. Some nights we'd play about with a gang of friends on the swings and go streaking around the graveyard, just mucking about and having fun. There are no taboos and no inhibitions. I really like the punky bands we listen to and now I can dye my hair and wear the daggy clothes that go with that image and scene. Bands like the Manic Street Preachers and Mansun are playing constantly, they're new to me but I like the atmosphere. The Manics sing about rebellion and small town life and Mansun are all about telling stories, characters and emotions.

Me and Felix have decided we want to be in a band – he's going to learn bass guitar and I'm going to be the singer songwriter. I've always written songs and loved singing, recording myself sing into my stereo onto cassette tapes. I've always admired singers and bands, ever since being a kid listening to my transistor radio; it seemed an amazing world that they lived in. We've also started keeping a scrapbook of photos we've taken on disposable cameras, tickets of places we've been to and all that; we've named them the Spice Books because I'm still obsessed with the girl band and their imaging, branding. It's always funny picking up the photos from the chemist when they've been developed and the woman just looks at us funny because she's seen all the crazy photos we've taken. On the night of payday we all walk out of town about a mile to get to the garage for midnight when our pay goes in the bank and get a feast of junk food when we get money out of the cash point at the earliest opportunity. Then we all go back to the flat and sit watching rubbish late night telly. Felix keeps making us watch all of the Star Wars films together in one session, he's obsessed with all that sci-fi stuff. One time we just stayed up watching an Open University documentary on rainbows. They have shadow rainbows that are fainter, that's all I remember, but every time I see a rainbow I look for its twin.

Princess Diana died in a car crash; everyone was shocked and kept going on about conspiracy theories about her having been killed by the establishment. I just remembered that I had a poster of her on my wall when I was really young and always thought she was really beautiful. Me and Felix watched the funeral in the flat and had a cry then we had to go to work with black ribbons pinned to our uniform.

"I'm too young to remember her but I've read about her." Adonai pulled a sad face.

"Oh my god, are you trying to make me feel ancient? Ha ha - I grew up with her as an icon who was always on the front pages or on the news. She was beautiful. I've often wondered since what would have happened if Dodi and Diana had lived and had a public relationship. If they had got married and had children would that have changed the way that people look at Islam? If it was part of the establishment how different would the world be now?"

"We'll never know, if there's anything that I have learned about journalism it is that it's a matter of perspective. People look at events through the prism of their own point of view and position in society. Stories are spun and loaded to the conclusions that people are trying to make. History is just that - perspectives." Again Adonai's face was sad. It seemed to me that he may be thinking that his chosen path may be a futile one, trying to find the truth in events and telling that story to the world. What is truth?

"Yep, just like this - my story, I can only tell it from my point of view; it may be completely different from someone else's. A bit like a photograph just from my perspective, I can share it but no-one else may see it from that position."

"Well your version is captivating so far, so go on."

The sweet girl dumped me and I was upset when she called it off, taking a bouquet of flowers to her house but she refused to see me. She just told me she didn't want to be in a relationship at the moment. I was really gutted because I want a girlfriend more than anything. I want to fall in love. I want to experience the stuff that people are singing about or I had seen in the movies. But to be honest I had also sort of just gone along with it because she was the first girl to pay me any attention. I didn't really fancy her. At the same time I came down with a severe chest infection and was off work for a week, the doctor did blood tests because I'd had pneumonia as a child and he was worried I'd got it again. I was spaced out and delirious. I didn't really eat for a couple of weeks; I just went to work and then collapsed into bed the rest of the time, shutting myself away. When I was feeling better I started trying to eat but every time I did I would feel like food was stuck in my throat. I started to make myself sick after every meal, I couldn't stop myself, and it was like some kind of compulsion. I remember every time I ate all I could think about was getting the food back out again. When I made myself sick I felt a sense of relief, release. It was almost like a control thing, I was obsessed by it. It wasn't about losing weight, I just felt that physically there was something inside me that I didn't want there, I had to get rid of it. I would sneak into the bathroom, turn the taps on to disguise the noise and stuck my fingers down my throat. I even started doing it when I was at work.

This went on for a couple of weeks and people started to ask me about it; I was working on the delicatessen counter full-time with all the older ladies and they were all clucking round me like mother hens. I was losing weight rapidly and looked ill. I was going out walking by myself at night just round and round in circles. I'd walk up in to the graveyard that's on top of a cliff looking down over the river; I remember looking at the moonlight turning the river into this glistening silver water. I imagined just swimming into it and letting it take me away, floating away from here. I'd walk around all the streets of the town late at night when it is all quiet and imagine all the people in bed dreaming. It was as if I could sense this big cloud of emotions from all the people inside the houses as I walked alone out on the street. I felt like an outsider, an observer but I wasn't entirely alone because on those nights I was walking by myself there was this female voice in my head talking to me and having massive long conversations. She'd be talking to me as if she was walking along with me, coaching me about my life. It was as if I had some sort of female voice acting as my unconscious mind or superego. I tried staying indoors but it was worse when there were people around because the voice was like a running commentary on my surroundings and I couldn't concentrate or sleep. My dreams had become very vivid, fantastical stories that played on my mind during the day. I really didn't know what to make of it at all, I wasn't creating it myself with my imagination, so it must be a construct of my brain, an imbalance. But it felt real, like a separate entity with a character all of her own, completely different to mine. I didn't tell anyone about it.

"Holy shit Kristoff! This is way out - are you okay?" Adonai sounded fascinated and concerned at the same time.

"Yeah man, it's weird talking to someone about it all but at the same time it feels quite cathartic. You're not bored or weirded out yet are ya?"

"Oh my god no! Just as long as you are okay telling me - it's your story man."

"Yeah I'm fine." And I was, it felt like I was talking about a different person and a time that seems so far removed from this sunny beach.

"Well keep going Mr Kristoff." Adonai shrugged and smiled a smile that was genuine and caring.

"I lost my virginity."

"What!? I wasn't expecting that to be next, ha ha, sorry - carry on." He giggled.

It wasn't the way I had hoped it would happen with someone that I was in love with. Actually I don't know why they say 'lost' my virginity, I know exactly where it went. These two girls just turned up at our door, Felix had met one of them out and about. One was pretty, tall and slim; the other was short and tubby. They came in with the intention of sleeping with us both; Felix was all up for it because the pretty one was after him. I was not so keen because I didn't fancy the short girl and none of them knew this would be my first time. They all kicked off with foreplay, all of us in the same room and I just kept making excuses and Felix's girl kept teasing me. She and Felix started having sex and in the end I couldn't really refuse because I had nowhere to go. They just kept asking me what was wrong with me, teasing me and pressuring me. We did it doggy style, without any kissing and I burst out laughing because she was facing the wall and smacked her head against it. I can't really say that I enjoyed it but I suppose it was an experience. Felix and the other girl were noisy and went on for ages so it was awkward lying in bed with a random stranger whilst my best mate shags her best mate a few feet away. In the morning me and the short girl left when I went to work. She came to visit me on the deli counter later in the day, saying weird stuff trying to chat me up. When I got home Felix was in a right state saying his day had been a nightmare. The girl he'd been with had sent him out to buy some tights for her and whilst he'd gone she'd nicked a load of our stuff! He was really gutted and apologetic – it wasn't his fault though, she's obviously just a clepto-nymphoslut!

Lesson learned, don't sleep with strangers. A few weeks later the sex girl came to see me at work saying that she had been pregnant and had had an abortion. She said she didn't know whether it was mine or her boyfriend's! I had no idea what I was supposed to do with that information or why she was telling me. I hadn't known that she had a boyfriend, not that I had asked her either. What a headfuck. I could have had a child? How weird would that have been? It did play on my mind for a long time afterwards. What if it was mine? I didn't know how I felt about it, like if it was mine and was already alive or conscious as a foetus; I don't know what I think about all that abortion stuff and when the baby can feel things or *is* a little person. In a way there could have been a little child of mine that I didn't even know about who has now vanished.

Felix then started seeing this cool girl called Ella. She's physically the opposite to him, he's tall and dark, she's small and blond. She dresses all punky but is really pretty and a lovely person; we all got on really well. I just kept crying all the time. Partly because I feel lonely when I see them together, I don't have anyone who loves me. I started to get really panicked when we went out to the pub and in large groups of strangers. My emotions were just all over the place. We go out and have fun, but I want to hide away in the corner, merge into the background. We get drunk and sing duets on the karaoke, 'White Wedding', 'California Dreaming', 'Charmless Man'- I feel okay on stage with a microphone in my hand but the rest of the time I just want to be invisible. Random people have started to notice it and ask me if I'm alright. I look like the walking dead because of the whole not eating/puking up thing and now my nerves are all out of control - I'm proper freaking out and losing it. Then one night Felix confronted me and asked me what was wrong because people were asking him. I explained what I was doing with food and he said that I must be bulimic or anorexic or a combination of the two and I needed to go to the doctor and get help. It's just with the food thing it feels like the only thing that I have any control over. Feeling empty has started to feel normal and it's kind of an achievement if I have overpowered my body by not eating when I feel hungry. I usually just drink loads of coffee and eat an apple at work then if I have to eat at home I throw it up afterwards. I was fat for ages as a kid and got criticised a lot and put on diets so I suppose I feel like I'm in control of it now. I know it's not healthy and I don't have a death wish I just seem to not care about the physical effects, it's just turned into an obsession.

Felix said that he feels like he's under a lot of pressure because he wants me to be alright, like he feels responsible for me. I felt really bad, guilty that I'm becoming a burden to my friends; I just kept apologising and promising to try and be better. So the next day he and Ella walked me to the doctors and they waited outside. I remember sitting in the waiting room staring at the fish in the aquarium just swimming round and around. Ignorance is bliss; I'd love to be a fish. Although nothing 'major' has happened to me I've somehow disintegrated to the point that I hardly recognise myself; I've lost grip on my life. I feel like I'm drowning in that moonlit river, struggling to fight up to the surface for a gasp of air. I went in and spoke to a locum. I explained to her that I wasn't sleeping, wasn't eating and when I did eat that I kept making myself sick and she asked me a few questions. I knew when she was asking me if I heard messages in the radio or television that she was trying to see if I was mentally ill; she was ticking off a list of symptoms to put me in a box. I had learned all that in Psychology A-Level and knew the things that she was trying to get at for diagnosis. I didn't tell her anything about the voice in my head. She asked me if I needed counselling and I said no, I'd rather talk to my friends. She gave me a prescription and told me to return when I ran out of medication. I felt so relieved, whatever the pills were they were going to make everything better and get me back to normal. There was an answer, a solution, the magic beans. The whole thing had only taken 15 minutes and problem solved! I met Felix and Ella sat on the wall outside, I was smiling and happy, they were shocked I was out so quickly. I handed Felix the prescription saying that I had to go collect it from the chemist under the flat. He'd done chemistry at A-level and took one look at it and asked me

"Shit? Kristoff, do you know what this is?"

"Yeah- Fluoxitane."

"Did she explain to you what that is?"

"Nope she just said go back if anything else happens or I run out."

"It's Prozac." He was shocked and kind of annoyed. I felt a bit stupid that I'd been all relieved and that now I looked a bit pathetic. Ella was open mouthed as all this was going on and agreed with Felix that it was a big deal. I hadn't realised it was anything that serious. But we headed to the chemist and got the prescription. We went up to the flat and I read through the leaflet inside the box of medication. The list of side effects was scary and I wouldn't be able to drink alcohol but this was my only solution and I wanted to feel normal, better. It was Friday evening so Felix and Ella decided that they'd gather a bunch of mates and we'd all head in to Hereford for the night to the Crystal Rooms so that I could have one last night of alcohol and start the medication tomorrow. I think they just wanted to cheer me up, it felt nice that everyone cared that much. We were all really open with each other so everyone was told what had happened and why we were going. I felt like a pity case but everyone was being really nice. We were like a little family. Felix and Ella had popped out to the shops and got me a present; it was a necklace with a smiley face pendant on it - to cheer me up. In the taxi on the way to Hereford I was just staring out the window. Each set of headlights that went past looked really freaky to me. Instead of them belonging to the cars that were driving past I was seeing two big hells angel motorbikes and riding on them were these crazy looking zombie figures. First was a woman in an old-fashioned bridal gown, screaming with laughter whilst she glared straight at me, her dress and veil all in gassy blue flames behind her. On the other motorbike next to her was the groom, in top hat and tails; his neck and wrists were all chained to the handlebars. He had this manic fixed fake smile like the joker, from the tail of his coat were two bright blue smoke trails. The next pair were monkeys with big curly tails, jumping up and down, screeching. Little pointy metallic party hats on their head, one red, and the other blue. Then came a big blue angel and a red devil. Then just balls of flames like comets, again one red and one blue. They just kept on coming; I think I was just in shock, catatonic. My brain was fried. Ella kept prodding me and pulling faces to cheer me up. Everyone was excitable, I was just vegetablised.

We reached the club and queued up outside, I think everyone just thought I was quiet because of the whole doctors and pills thing. I was just terrified because I hadn't taken any of the medication yet and my mind had proper exploded or imploded and I was seeing all this crazy stuff. There is no way I could tell anyone about the voices and now I'm hallucinating too and going into a very crowded club feeling very panicky. This must be what insane feels like; I couldn't even sense myself inside my own body or feel where that body fitted into reality around me. My nerves were proper jangly. I thought back to studying Psychology and how ironic it was that so quickly afterwards I had disintegrated into this crazy mess of a person. Were all these mad things lying in wait inside my brain all the time just waiting for an opportunity to detonate? We got drinks inside and the place was packed and jumping. We'd been here loads of times before and enjoyed it; it was completely different to the night club on our town. Our local one was just a room with a dance floor surrounded by booth tables, playing cheesy chart music. Here was a purpose built night club on two floors with professional famous DJs playing house music. I threw myself into drinking, hoping that would calm me down or knock me out, whichever came first. We danced in the crowd and I just let myself go in amongst the flailing limbs, flashing lights and pounding music; you could feel the bass vibrating inside your bones. I felt alright, just part of the crowd. After a while we moved upstairs to the smaller dance floor where another DJ was playing. As I stood on the edge of the room watching my friends dance in the clouds of dry ice a completely different scene transposed itself on top of reality. The sticky carpet felt like wet tarmac under my feet and the dry ice hung heavy in the air, a fog, laden with perfume and sweat. On the opposite side of the room I was seeing not a blank black wall but a stage made up of scaffolding. The metal poles reached from floor to ceiling. On the wooden planks inside this cage of criss-crossing poles was sparkly silver box the size of a coffin. On the wall behind the box was a massive 5 pointed star made out of glowing light bulbs like you get round mirrors in a dressing room. There was a big star-shaped mirror too all aged and dusty. Strapped to the mirror was a man stood like the man in that da Vinci picture. He was beautiful, pale, slim and muscly; long bleach blond hair, blue eyes, naked to the waist. He was wearing golden jeans and no shoes. He was staring right into my eyes, I felt like he was trying to say something to me or show me something.

The lights around the star kept dazzling brighter then

fading one by one randomly. Sparks kept flaring out of them like fireworks. Then they all buzzed together in unison and it lit up like a Catherine wheel and the whole thing started to turn clockwise, the man tensed up as he moved with the rotating star. In perfect time with the movement of the star a dancer in front of me started to descend into a hole in the floor, flames started to fly up around their body and as it fell downwards it transformed into a skeleton, still dancing. A flume of smoke whooshed up as they disappeared into the floor. As the smoke touched the ceiling another hole opened up and the persons bare feet lowered down, then their naked legs all grey and lifeless. They were just covered in kind of caveman loin cloths and voodoo make-up, deadly still with their arms crossed up on their chest like a corpse until their feet touched the floor and they started dancing again. This was happening to everyone on the dance floor. Skeletons dropping down through trapdoors and these tribal people lowering down all amongst the flames and smoke; still the music blared on and the disco lights flashed. The man and the star were still spinning around inside the scaffold. I was just completely overloaded by it all but felt rooted to the spot. Ella's faced suddenly appeared in front of me, I tried to concentrate on her as an anchor to bring me back to reality. She was speaking to me but I couldn't hear her, she gesticulated for me to follow them because they were all heading back downstairs. I forced my limbs to move and felt along the wall and clung onto the banister as I made my way down the flight of steps. As you go down the stairs there are mirrored walls, plants and a waterfall straight up ahead of you and I thought I could see a jungle all around me; I'd seen that waterfall loads of times before when I'd been to this club but now it warped into something else.

I made my way to one of the bars and sat on a sofa. Ella followed me and sat down with me, I think everyone just presumed I was either really drunk or freaking out about having been put on medication and the prospect of things changing; I told absolutely no-one about the hallucinations I'd started to have. It was one thing having voices and conversations in my head and this woman-figure kind of following me through my life but this other stuff was another level all together. I was freaking out more about the fact that this was all happening before I had taken any medication at all. Why has everything suddenly gone more mental as soon as I know I'm about to start taking Prozac in the morning? I knew damn well from the couple of years I'd spent studying psychology at A-Level that what was happening to me was pretty serious. I was checking off the symptoms inside my head and they all kept pointing to some hardcore disorders. I had already decided not to tell the doctor the whole truth of what was happening to me and refuse counselling so as to avoid being pulled into the mental system. But if I think I'm crazy surely that means that I can't be? The saying goes that a crazy person thinks they're behaviour is completely normal and cannot see their own dysfunction. I'm well aware that the stuff that is going on is NOT normal but everything is pointing at me being schizophrenic or something along those lines. But if I know that then I don't know if I am crazy or not, perhaps I'm a functioning schizophrenic? Ella just tried to sit with me and comfort me and lift my spirits, she said she hated the club as well it's just not her type of place. I feel dishonest not being completely open about what's going on in my head and now all around me, especially to my close friends who are being so caring. I'm scared someone will work it out or they'll see me doing something I'm not even aware that I'm doing - like staring at empty walls, or weird facial reactions and all that sort of stuff. Someone is bound to catch me out, I've just got to control myself really well but I'm starting to panic. I do actually think at one point I was sat there rocking backward and forward keeping all this weird energy inside me, just like a proper lunatic. That's another thing I always go walking at night and look at the moon and just wander around, that's even where the name 'lunatic' comes from. At least right here and now it looks like I'm rocking to the music.

How have I become this person? More importantly if I don't know how I got to here in my crazy mental stuff, how can I stop it getting any worse? Perhaps the medication will switch it all off, from what everyone is saying it is quite strong, maybe they'll do the trick and I'll be normal. I just went through the motions for the rest of the night, concentrating on engaging myself with my friends. Don't look at anything else, don't let your mind wander, keep myself occupied making the right noises and acting as if nothing out of the ordinary was going on. I tried not to look out of the window of the taxi on the way home, just in case those crazy zombie bikers appeared again. I was so thankful and relieved when I pulled the duvet over me at home on the Lad Pad. Ella and Felix were embroiled in each other and I felt safe knowing that they were there.

The next morning I took my first pill and spent the morning watching telly. Everything was normal and I felt really positive. I got ready for work and set off to walk the few streets away to the supermarket. As I walked down the alley from the flat onto the high street I could see people walking about. My balance felt a bit funny, like vertigo and my head was sort of fuzzy like a hangover, it must be a hangover. As I stepped onto the street I could see a big bubble around myself all wobbly and oily with rainbow colours all shining about in it. Why haven't the hallucinations gone? When I looked at people their heads turned into stretchy cartoon versions of themselves with exaggerated expressions. How long does the pill take to work? It was all freaking me out and I was walking along on autopilot. I was okay when I got into work because it was familiar and I just concentrated on the exact thing I was doing at the time. Literally talking myself through every little movement or thought that I made; making my own running commentary in my head as I did everything. It was exhausting and I now definitely feel like a crazy person. People have been asking me about the medication thing, I just said it's because of not eating and sleeping. One of the women on the checkouts said she'd seen me wandering about at night. Ally gave me a lecture about being on Prozac and that she was worried about me because it's really strong and a serious anti-depressant. After work I decided to go and visit my Mum, I had an idea that she had been depressed when we were growing up and she might be able to talk to me about it and help me in some way. When I got there she was cooking dinner for the family so I stood next to her in the kitchen while everyone else was in the lounge. She was stirring a sauce on the hob. I said to her that I had been put on Prozac and asked her if she knew anything about depression. She didn't stop stirring the sauce or look at me, she just asked if I wanted a cup of tea and carried on as if I hadn't said anything. In that silence I had no idea what to say or do next so I just said I didn't want a cup of tea and politely made my excuses and left. I don't know if she didn't want to talk to me with the family there, if it was the wrong time or she just didn't want to talk about it full stop. It was never mentioned again.

Adonai suddenly started to talk. "Fuck man, that sounds like really heavy stuff. I feel like I want to go back in time and find you to give you a big hug." I laughed.

"It's strange looking back on it now and having a different perspective on things, for sure. I know my Mum probably didn't have the language to be able to speak to me about it. Maybe she had suffered in the past and didn't feel strong enough to bring it all back to the surface. Maybe she hadn't admitted it to anyone either? People in the family say that her Mum is a bit loopy too so perhaps it's in the family? Suddenly there is this crazy, punk son. I didn't just not fit in I must have appeared to be a completely foreign object amongst their religious suburban family. Maybe she hadn't had depression at all. Who knows?"

"Well this story is certainly unique Mister - please carry on, it'll probably help you by telling it. Get it out a bit like that baptism thing we just did. How do you say, catharsis."

The next hallucination I had was when I was at work doing overtime on the night shift stacking shelves. Each person gets given an aisle to do and this night I was stacking the shelves above the freezers. Our freezers are the ones where you lean over them like chest freezers and above them are all the ketchups, mayo and all that on shelves. I was filling up all those sauces. As I leant over them the clear lids on the freezers started to ripple. I kept feeling as if I was going to fall into them like they were a trough of water like on the farm. Then the water started to spill down the edges and onto the shop floor. I tried to ignore it and concentrate on the simple action of stacking the sauces. I could just see the surface of the water rising all around me like the whole place was flooding. One part of my brain was shouting at me that the water wasn't actually there, nothing is getting wet, no-one else can see it; another part was panicking because it was rising rapidly up. My senses were reacting like it was real. When it got to knee height a woman appeared at the end of the aisle, wading through the water towards me. She was dressed like Barbarella. Big, bouffant blond hair with a baby blue Alice band, the same colour shift dress and knee-high boots. Inside my head a voice was shouting 'Don't look in her eyes!' and I was terrified. She kept walking towards me and I tried to ignore her and carry on stacking sauces. As I leant over the freezer it was as if she had her hand on the back of my neck trying to push my head under the water. There was information flashing up in my brain. Destroy your existence and identity. There was this instinct rising in me towards death and destruction. Be like her so no-one knows you exist. She is a manifestation of the rebel, a fallen angel. The information was flashing up in my brain like it was on a computer like in one of Leo's games. I didn't know what was happening to me, was it her putting these ideas in my head? Where I could feel her hand on my head I could somehow see myself from behind, as if I was looking on from another position and I could see this electric blue energy emanating out from where she was touching me. When I turned to look at her she had turned into a bright silver liquid figure like in the Terminator films - made out of mercury. I wanted to scream, to fight her off. I was stacking jars of pickled eggs and as I jolted around towards her a jar flew out of my hand and smashed all over the floor. As it broke the whole hallucination immediately vanished and I was back in reality. I just looked at the eggs bouncing around in the puddle and the glass all over the place and I wanted to scream at the top of my lungs 'Leave me alone!'. One of the night shift women in the next aisle peered around to check what the noise was, rolled her eyes and shrugged. I went off to find a mop and broom to clear up the mess.

Felix and I went to visit our friends who had headed off to university, mainly coinciding with gigs that we wanted to go to. In Bristol we saw Gomez and Embrace; I had a panic attack whilst in the crowd. I started hyperventilating and everything felt really claustrophobic; it felt like if anyone touched me I'd get an electric shock. I legged it out into the corridor and the first aid people calmed me down. I cried when I told Felix and his mates about it which made me feel even more of a freak. Showing emotion in public to random strangers, one of the guys hugged me and told me everything was going to be alright. The rest of the time I just felt foggy. It was just embarrassing and I felt guilty for causing Felix to have to attempt damage limitation to our friends. In Manchester we went to see Mansun play at the uni and stayed at a hotel. I was a bit wary of the crowd again but eventually headed into the mosh pit when our favourite songs were being played. Everyone was jostling about bumping into each other whilst moshing. This beautiful gothy girl with long royal blue evening gloves on grabbed hold of my hand and we steadied each other from all the bodies bashing about around us. She moved in front of me and I put my arms around her, we kissed. It all happened like it was in slow motion; we were complete strangers and hadn't spoken a word to each other. Just this energy made us connect. She went off to get a drink and we didn't see each other again in the crowd. I did wonder afterwards if she had meant for me to follow her to the bar, I'm useless at that stuff. Felix hooked up with some mates from boarding school and we went off into the city to find some of his other mates and followed them back to their halls of residence. Again I got upset because I felt a bit disorientated and just wanted to get back to the hotel. I feel like I'm holding Felix back.

We also went to Bristol with Ella to see Tura Satana play who were a proper metal-goth band. I was fine there and enjoyed it, maybe because it was such a manic gig, a crazy atmosphere. Ella and me chatted loads all the way back home and Felix was a bit annoyed because he's starting to think she isn't really that into him. The next week me and Felix headed off to Cardiff to see one of our mates from the supermarket who'd gone to uni there and to see Tura Satana play again. I wore this see through black t-shirt and had written 'victim' in marker pen on my chest. We got to sit and have a drink with the band whilst the support act was playing. The singer Tairrie B sat and drew 'love' and 'hate' on m knuckles and we just hung out with them and had a laugh. During the show we got right to the front and Tairrie B kept touching my head and grabbing my hand and rubbing her body with it. The guitarist stage dove onto Felix and he ended up with bruises all over him for ages afterwards. It's great seeing different parts of the country, new places and being at gigs with live music. I still felt numb though, I was swinging between the worlds inside my head that was crazy and jam packed to a world outside that just seemed cold and empty; the gigs helped because they were such an assault on the senses and blew my system out. Don't get me wrong we still had fun and laughs it wasn't all doom and gloom every day. But all the time it was a proper struggle to keep people from seeing what was wrong with me. Everyone knew that I was on medication and treated me differently, pitied me, tried to wrap me up in cotton wool. I felt like I was an exhibit in the circus, the freak. A few times when I was really freaked out my body ended up sort of blacking out. I would be sat there with all this crazy stuff going on in my head and trying really hard to stop thinking or move and do something. I'd start doing these weird repetitive movements that made me feel even crazier and I'd then be trying to stop moving. In the end my body sort of went in to autopilot and I'd be convulsing and shaking and collapse, I was still aware of the movements but it'd feel like a head rush and then I'd be on the floor shaking; I was aware of what I was doing but couldn't stop myself - like it was a compulsion. Felix and Ella and people saw it a couple of times and just brought me round, I knew that they thought I was faking it for attention, but I genuinely couldn't stop myself once the compulsion took hold.

Even Ally's brother warned her off being so friendly with me because he'd heard about town that I was dangerous. I had no idea what he meant nor did she, people seem to see a punk rocker teenager who's said to be crazy and could be about to do something idiotic I suppose. I went and got my tongue pierced like Scary Spice has; it was really sore and swelled up load afterwards. I tried to hide it at work but kept talking with a lisp because of serving people on the deli counter I couldn't not talk. Thankfully it healed quite quickly and I just keep poking my tongue out all the time. Girls keep asking to kiss me to see what it feels like. Apparently it feels good, I'm also getting lots of snogging practice in!

One night me and Felix were having an Indian takeaway in the Lad Pad and Ella turned up with a friend of hers. Ella stood in the doorway of the room at the top of the stairs, shouted 'Hi' to Felix and then looked at me and said there was someone here who wanted to meet me. With that she ran over to the bed and jumped on Felix to give him a hug and a kiss. In through the doorway followed a pretty girl dressed in leopard skin high heels, skin tight blue jeans, a tiny sky-blue Mickey Mouse t-shirt, she had beautiful face and big black curly hair. She just stood there and smiled at me. She looked like a punk Betty Boop. Ella looked at me and then at the girl.

"Oh, yeah, this is Kat. Kat this is Kristoff and Felix"

Kat wiggled across the room and slowly squeezed herself down onto the sofa right next to me bursting into chatter about Indian food, the posters on the wall, the program on the telly, she was nervous, excitable, a breath of fresh air. Why on earth would she want to meet me? We all chatted for ages and it was just easy, Kat had so much energy I didn't have time for a thought or craziness to catch my attention. It felt nice that there were four of us just sitting around and being together. She had just split up with Joseph who she goes to college with and who works at the supermarket on the fruit and veg on nights and Saturdays. Felix and Ella seemed happy that the atmosphere was so 'up'. Kat and Ella eventually decided it was time to leave and Kat asked me what I was doing the next day. As it happened I had a day off from work and she said that she had a half day at college so it wouldn't matter if she skipped it so why don't we meet up and do something? We arranged to meet at 8.30 so that her parents still thought she was heading to college. I remember it was really misty and the sunlight looked really nice that morning. Kat had a long leopard print fake fur coat on and was skipping up and down in the cold as I walked across the market place to meet her. She gave me a kiss on the cheek and a hug. Whenever I think of that morning it seems like it belongs to a particular time and place; the late 90s in England, like it's from a movie like 'Train Spotting' a Brit Flick. A fucked up punk boy and a glamorous grunge girl setting off by bus and train for a daytrip to the seaside - very Sid and Nancy or Kurt and Courtney. We caught a bus into Hereford, had a coffee in the bus station café and then headed over to the train station. It felt good to be out of town and to be occupied by someone new, just going with the flow I felt comfortable with her, maybe a bit intimidated by her 'full-on'ness, I've never met anyone like her before. It was exciting; it felt like we were in our own private movie, improvising the plot as we went along. Kat had already talked about the medication on the bus and said that she had been on Seroxat before. She wanted to know what I was on it for and I just told her about the not sleeping and not eating and called it a breakdown. That seemed to satisfy her. She asked about the song writing, about bands I liked, all that sort of stuff. I got the impression she thinks I'm some sort of tortured artist, destined for greatness, like Ritchie Edwards, Sid Vicious etc. She knows a lot about all that culture and kept explaining it all to me, the music, the books, the films. It's all more or less foreign to me, but somehow that made her think I was even more punk because I hadn't immersed myself in all that culture, it had come naturally. Being accidentally punk is way better than trying to be apparently. We headed for Cardiff on the train. When the hostess came along with the refreshments trolley we got a load of kids' sweets and coffees. Kat said she loved having a sugar rush and caffeine buzz and that we would need it for the day ahead. We had refresher fizzy lollipops and Kat said she loved dipping them in vodka because the vodka turns pink and ends up tasting of sweets, so we got some miniature vodkas off the lady and did just that in the plastic white cups. I knew I wasn't supposed to drink alcohol with the Prozac but I felt hyper and happy. Somehow we got off the train at the wrong stop and were just stranded in this tiny Welsh village train station for an hour until the next train came past, it was funny. All these Welsh pensioners looking at us like aliens had just landed. We were just mucking about, singing, playing games, getting to know each other. Once we got to Cardiff we legged it all over the place, looking at absolutely everything we wanted to, every shop trying on clothes, pretending we were rich and lying on beds to try them out or bouncing on sofas. It was fun, everywhere we went we kept hearing the same song being played 'Mulder and Scully' by Catatonia. I found it funny because of the line about things 'getting crazy'. We had a great day and had a laugh. Eventually when we'd tired ourselves out we headed back on the train to Hereford and the bus all the way back home. I offered to walk her to her house but she said she was okay she'd call her Mum, we hugged and I headed back to the Lad Pad. I was exhausted and my brain was literally rattling and buzzing. If I normally felt foggy on the medication then the alcohol and excitement had whooshed that fog up into a whirlwind. Felix was excited to find out all the details about the day and what had gone on with me and Kat, he burst into interrogation mode. I told him as much as I could and must have blacked out mid-sentence because the next morning I woke up fully clothed on top of my duvet. My head was all over the place. I didn't know whether yesterday had really happened or if it was all just another hallucination, or a dream, did Kat even exist?

Well she did exist and we soon started seeing each other, I was in a proper relationship. Kat is very passionate and sexy; she has curves in all the right places. The only problem is that Prozac has taken all the wind out of my sails. So we kiss passionately for hours and fondle and foreplay, I go down on her; there's just no actual intercourse or anything going on with me downstairs. She loves the tongue piercing, she has a clit-ring and one time it got caught with my tongue bar. I was proper panicked trying to untangle them; she had the time of her life. I laugh every time I remember that. Adonai guffaws and claps.

I don't mind that I can't really get it up for a long time, but I think Kat is a bit frustrated that things are a bit limp. So I'm going overboard on everything else in the hopes that it makes up for it. Kat and Ella are good friends and have even slept together once before so it's a comfortable set up, two best friends going out with two best friends. Everyone thinks that it's just one big orgy now in the Lad Pad. We do everything together. Life is good and we're rolling on in to the deep winter.

One night the four of us were asleep in the room. I don't remember there being any drama going on in my head or anything unusual happening. I fell asleep in bed with Kat; Felix was in bed with Ella. Sometime in the middle of the night I became aware of myself standing looking at myself in the bathroom mirror. It was as if something else had controlled my body, I was on autopilot. I had no idea how I had got there. It was as if I had woken up standing there. The mirror looked like a kind of clear rippling liquid and the room reflected behind me was different to the bathroom I was actually stood in. First of all the walls of the bathroom were covered in all different styles and sizes of mirror then each wall and the floor and ceiling became just made of mirror. Then it was a dimly lit corridor with a deep red carpet and dark walls. Further up the corridor I could see a seating area on the right hand side where a flight of wooden stairs wound upwards. In the nook under the stairs was a booth and the cushions were of a deep red velvet. On the left hand side opposite the booth was a set of richly carved wooden doors. I could no longer see myself in the reflection. Then the woman I kept seeing was approaching the mirror. She had just come down the stairs and walked towards me down the corridor; there was an air of urgency about her. She looked so beautiful in a flowing sky blue silk gown. It had flowers on it like painted watercolours; her lips were poppy red and her eyes dark and immaculate. She looked almost oriental, pacific. She spoke to me slowly and calmly but her eyes were pleading for my attention.

"Come here to me now, come with me. You will be safer here." She opened her palm to show me a dark turquoise ribbon that was tied around her wrist. Then she picked up the end of it and reached out and offered it to me through the liquid mirror. I took it from her and so we were connected by either end of this ribbon. "You have to bail out, abandon ship." She pleaded. As I held the ribbon the room around me turned into a blank bright white empty space. It felt cold and stark. I just stared at her and still felt like something other than myself was compelling me to move. She put her other hand into the folds of her dress and slowly pulled out a pair of large silver scissors.

"You've got to cut the cord, only then will you be here with me, safe." She handed me the scissors. My hand reached out and took them, then my fingers gripped them and started to snip at the ribbon. Somewhere deep in my brain I could feel a screeching, ripping shock slicing through me like an electric whip cracking against my nerves. It came from the inside out to the surface then back down again to my core. The walls of the white room splintered into mirrored shards with every snip of the scissors. Each time there is a surge of pain. The ribbon that attached us both turned red. Now icicles were screaming down out of the ceiling and from the end of them were dripping bright blood red bubbles that burst when they hit the floor. My head was spinning, the reflected corridor was pitching from side to side and the white room I was in kept flashing and crackling. I looked down at the fist that was gripping the ribbon as if it belonged to someone else. I had snipped a jagged line from the outside edge of my wrist heading inwards right up to close to the vein. I could see the raw flesh and the spilling blood. The next couple of cuts would sever the vein. I watched as the blood filled the wound and seeped sideways, rolling off my wrist and dripping down into the white sink heading down the plug hole. As my brain felt like it was draining down through me to my feet it was replaced by clogging red clay. I closed my eyes and could see a miniature version of myself trapped inside my empty skull trying to claw my way out of this bloody landslide. I looked into the mirror, it was our bathroom, I was stood in it and she was stood looking over my shoulder at our reflections. She had a look of fear and hurt on her face, as if she was pleading with me, holding her breath in anticipation. I put the scissors down on the white porcelain and as they clunked she disappeared and the room was as it normally should appear. The scissors were the orange handled dressmaking scissors I'd borrowed off my Mum to cut holes in my clothes. The sink was splattered with my blood. I sat down on the edge of the bath and trailed my arm away behind me, bleeding slowly. Then reality started to burn up inside of me and a wave of shock and terror broke over me. I realised what I had done. The cut was really deep and jagged, I could see my flesh. I wrapped toilet roll tightly around my wrist, washed away all the blood and hid the scissors, covering m tracks. I crept back into the bedroom where no-one had stirred and slipped into bed, holding my wrist in my hand to my chest. I could only hope that the bleeding would eventually stop and that nobody would find out. I hadn't cut the vein so I didn't think that I was going to bleed to death and Kat would wake up next to a corpse in the morning. I fell quickly and heavily into sleep. The next morning I woke up and had forgotten about what had happened until I felt the soreness and saw the mock bandage. The others saw it too before I had a chance to hide it. They were shocked and angry with me; I couldn't explain to them what had happened. I just said I was hurting myself and had stopped before I'd done anything really bad. They were really angry with me, but self-harming didn't seem like a big shock to them. At work the old ladies on the deli noticed it as well and I just said I'd cut myself with a tin opener.

I just switched off for a while and concentrated really hard on just seeming normal and okay to everyone around me. I slept a lot; eating started to get better as I forced myself to digest food and ate just before going for a walk to distance myself from the toilet. I just had to try and be normal. Soon it was Christmas time, the supermarket was really busy. On the tills they were handing out these coupons for money off your next shop. Everyone kept throwing them away so Felix had started collecting them up. Over a few weeks he had £200 worth of free shopping but employees weren't allowed to spend the vouchers so we got my brothers to go round and do the actual shopping. We gave them a list and told them also to get whatever they wanted. On Christmas day I went home for the meal but felt like an outsider. Mum said she didn't want any help with cooking and that I should go and watch telly in the conservatory. I sat in there watching Top of the Pops, looking in on the rest of the family setting the table and interacting with each other. I was convinced that they had locked the door of the conservatory, trapping me inside like a caged animal. But I was too scared to get up and actually try the door. How has my identity so completely disintegrated into broken pieces? All the things that once held it together had lost their traction and now I didn't even know who I was. Somehow as I'd grown through my A level studies and the expansion of my mind at had stretched my brain until it broke. Perhaps you have to break to grow?

They opened the door and called me in when the dinner was served up, I couldn't tell whether they'd had to turn the key first before they opened it. I left pretty quickly afterwards and headed to Kat's house. She was in a good mood because I'd got her nice presents and she was also already drunk. I hadn't met her parents before and they were really excited to see me. They were really cool, Kat says that she reckons they are swingers or something because they are always partying. They gave us a couple of bottles of bubbly and we went back to the Lad Pad. It wasn't long before Felix arrived back from his folks and Ella did to. All four of us sat there feeling the same - we felt more comfortable together than with our families. We had a mini Christmas there and gradually all of our friends turned up from their families and it turned into a proper party, it was really fun and I was allowed to sneak a few drinks in. Then on Boxing Day my twin brother Pete had agreed to drive Felix, Kat and me to see the new Spice Girls film in Gloucester; Ella couldn't make it because she now had a part-time job helping in a hotel near to her house. I no longer had my beloved VW Beetle because my parents had decided t scrap it when I had moved out and wasn't using it as much. When we went round to my family's house before we picked Kat up, Pete turned to Felix and asked him what we'd done that morning. Felix just turned to him and said that he liked to have a wrestle with me every morning just to get the blood flowing. Pete knows Felix from when he used to work on the tills at the supermarket, so he just laughed. But it was hilarious because people keep thinking that me and Felix are gay because we're so close. He was a bit worried about what people were saying at first but we decided it doesn't matter because we know we're not and nothing is happening so it's up to everyone else if they want to think that. Now he's decided to play up to it for effect. Nowadays it would be called a bromance. I think Pete felt a bit out of place with us three in the car because he's never been in the company of a girl like Kat before and the three of us just kept mucking about. She was wearing a feather boa and tiara and kept flirting with Pete to try and embarrass him. It was a good laugh. I think it opened his eyes a bit too. The movie was amazing. I have a photo taken of me in the car on the way there and I look like a zombie, really pale and sunken eyes and you can see the scar on my wrist; but I remember it as a really fun vibrant day.

Then at New Year we went into Hereford and met up with our mates from Sixth Form who were all back on holidays from uni. My friends were shocked at how I had changed and it was funny to see their reactions to Kat. I don't know what they were expecting. It was nice to actually have someone I care about and be in a couple for New Year's Eve. My mates from school didn't recognise me at all I was just a completely different person. I think they could see how fucked up I was. Sometimes you see it more on the expressions on other people's faces than on your own when you look in the mirror.

Then on my 19th birthday in January me and Kat went on a trip back to Cardiff to get tattoos. We'd seen a place right by the train station. She had a playboy bunny symbol on her groin by her hip and I had a Chinese symbol that I had chosen off the wall, it means tiger because that was what Kat always called me for a nickname. The bloke who was doing the tattoo said he had done the tattoo for Ritchie Edwards which is the album cover of Generation Terrorist by the Manic Street Preachers. We all had drinks at the Lad Pad and then went out on the town. I am now 19 and the first year of being an adult hasn't exactly been a roaring success. I have no idea what will happen in the next year. You can have plans and hopes but that doesn't mean things will actually turn out how you expect them to.

By the way the journal I am writing is now in sort of

notes in writing pads. If something significant happens during the year I write it down ready for putting together the day after my birthday. Obviously this year there is a lot of private stuff and things I don't want anyone knowing about so when I moved in to the Lad Pad I went out and bought one of those vanity cases with a combination lock on it. I put all my personal stuff in there and lock it up. It's black and I got silver nail varnish and wrote 'Kristoff' in big letters on top of it and stars and keep sticking stickers on it.

"Wow that is just the first year? I am really interested to find more out about Blue - she must have been important for you to get the tattoo? What a fucked up teenager man? I know I can say that because you are sat there in front of me here and now." Adonai sounded quite serious now, proper involved. "Keep going."

Being 19/ 1998-1999

Well this year has been a journey in many different ways. The most literal of them being that I am writing this on my 20th birthday in a caravan, in a garden, in New Zealand. I've come a long way this year. To begin with Kat moved in to the Lad Pad after her parents separated. It turned out that her Dad had been leading a double life; he had a girlfriend and little baby which he managed to keep hidden. When it all came out Kat came to stay with us because she hated all the fighting and drama. So there were three of us now sharing the same room. We all got on fine anyway so it wasn't a problem, we just adapted. Ella would still stay over at weekends when she wasn't working. The dynamic was just slightly different.

We settled in to a comfortable existence, just enjoying each other's company. Me and Kat were okay with each other. After a while she started to ask me about kids and if I wanted them. I said that I did want them eventually but when the time is right. It reminded me of that whole abortion thing with that other girl. Kat just kept on about it; she wanted me to get her pregnant. This went on for weeks and Felix was there one time when she was getting angry about it. She said I was being selfish because I wouldn't get her pregnant and she really wanted my baby. I just snapped and said to her it was really unfair. I wasn't about to get someone pregnant and then go travelling to the other side of the world. The baby would be being born when I was in Australia. If I'm going to have a kid I would want to be there all the way through. We should wait and see what happens and discuss it again when I get back from travelling. Luckily Felix jumped in and said that he agreed with me and that Kat was being unreasonable. She was in a mood for ages. Things changed after that. Kat is a proper flirt and fun but she started to change a bit when she moved in. Her attention wasn't really on us or me but more on her being the centre of attention. I couldn't say what exactly made me think like that it was just a shift that only I could feel. I reckon anyone who's in a relationship can pick up on those tiny signals that tell you something is up and the other person is drifting away. It's the same signals that connected you in the first place, catching each other's eyes in a crowd, touching, sharing jokes, saying the same thing at the same time. It's like a dial has been turned ever so slightly and you've become blurry and out of focus. You're still catching her eyes but she's looking at someone else, touching her just as she moves away. The love bites have faded and now just look like a trail of bruises. With the medication things were still foggy and weird so I sort of just put it down to me being edgy; Kat and Felix did too, blamed the pills. I felt even lonelier, pushed back inside me head, isolated. There's nothing lonelier than feeling alone in a couple. How ironic that I'd spent years desperate for a relationship and now that I have one I feel terrible. Don't get me wrong we still had fun and laughs but as a parts of a group not as a couple. We went round to my family's house for a meal and it was hilarious. It was like I had taken an inflatable pink and green giraffe to meet the family. Kat is so different from females that my family are used to interacting with. At church dressing up is a Laura Ashley flowery dress, Kat dressed like a punk pin up girl, cleavage and curls. My Dad and brothers were transfixed and my Mum seemed really thrown as to how to act. Kat lapped it up and played it perfectly. My family was completely opposite to hers and there were a few different worlds colliding that evening. I don't think we were unhappy we were just treading water; it would hurt more to be honest about our relationship at that point. Least said soon is mended. I thought she was only with me as an 'in' to the Lad Pad crowd and that it looked cool to other people. But she couldn't split up with me because she'd lose that and also be the one who dumped the poor mental case.

Me and Felix started saving money and making plans for the big trip to Australia. First thing on the list was to go down to London. Well that was a humongous disaster. Me and Felix went down on the train to go to the Australian embassy and get our visas for travelling. We found a hotel in Victoria and dumped our stuff but when we got to the embassy it had closed, we decided we would get something to eat and go out for a drink then return to the embassy in the morning before we left to go back home. We ended up in a pub having a drink, when Felix had gone to the toilet some old bloke came over to me and just said to me "How much?" I was really shocked and told him to fuck off; I knew what he meant by the way he was looking me up and down. I was offended because I wandered what it was about me or the way I looked that made him think I was for sale like that. I told Felix about it and he said he didn't like the place either or the atmosphere. We left but when we were out on the street a bloke stopped us and asked if we smoked. He asked it in such a manner that we knew that he was on about weed, we looked at each other and I remember saying I wonder if London weed is different to home weed that we normally get off Ritchie who lives downstairs. We said yeah and the bloke told us to follow him. We went down this alley and there was this other man there who said here try this you'll like it, he handed me this little contraption that he was smoking from that just looked like a tiny bottle with a tube coming out of it like a mini bong but all see through. I smoked some and then handed it to Felix and my head went all hot and my vision went blurry and the places where there was light had like rainbow colours coming off them. Me and Felix smiled at each other and I dunno if I thought it or said it but London weed is loads different to home.

The blokes said they were going to a party and we could come if we wanted, we said yeah and they hailed a black cab and the four of us got in. They were chatting about the party and telling us there would be all these famous people there. They asked us about ourselves and I remember us saying that we were brothers and that we were in the foreign legion but we were on holiday before starting another term of duty. Felix said that I may look weedy but that there was no-one else he'd want beside him on the front line. We just kept talking and talking piling on the bullshit. I felt really confident and buzzing. The cab pulled up at a house in a terraced street and we all got out. When we entered the house there was no party but just a group of people who looked like a pretty normal family in a normal non-partying house. They greeted the two blokes and seemed to know what was going on. They were talking to us nicely but it started to feel a bit weird. They then said Felix had to stay there whilst they took me to find the rest of the party at another house and bring them back. We protested but both knew things had taken a turn for the worse and there was now a load of people telling us all what to do. They were all calm, no raised voices or anything we just knew we had to go along with it. All we could do was just look at each other and know we had no choice but to ride out whatever was going on, but we were sobering up pretty quickly. I think they sensed that because they all started to smoke from the contraption and made us have more as well but kept occupying us in conversation. The people in the house seemed alright but what was happening was just scary. The two blokes then took me out to a car that had pulled up outside. I got told to get in the back of the car. In the front seats were two black guys in tracksuits. The other men shut the door and tapped on the roof and the car pulled away.

I think the drugs and fear properly kicked in then because I was in a car with two strangers, terrified about whether Felix was safe in the house and having no idea what was going to happen next or where I was being taken. I just wanted us both to be safe and not hurt. I had this dread, not for myself but I realised how much I had connected to Felix and hoped no harm was coming to him. The car drove through a kind of estate with high-rise blocks of flats and there was a group of people drinking and shouting and hailing the two guys who were in the car. They were pointing at me in the back seat and whooping. I really thought they were just going to open the door and throw me to the mob. I knew I was in real danger and a wave came over me that I was likely to not survive the night. I'm going to die; somehow this chain of events that I have no power to stop is going to end with me dying somehow. I felt completely powerless and blank, full of fear. My life wasn't flashing before me or anything just a sense of futility. I've done nothing with my life other than go insane and now I'm going to die; my entire destiny is to be a pointless blip that hasn't achieved anything. I just hoped Felix was okay and not being hurt in any way. I felt guilty, if he didn't know me then he would have done things differently and not be where he was. It's my fault. The car drove on away from the mob after the men in the car had chatted to the people outside. The man in the passenger seat turned around to me and said not to worry. I just stayed silent. They drove around for a while then pulled up at a house. They took me out of the car and the three of us went inside. I felt a bit relieved when there was no-one else in the house. They took me into the lounge which had bare floorboards and two armchairs and a coffee table. One of the men got out one of the smoking contraptions and they both started to share a smoke, chatting to each other and talking to me saying don't worry my friend was alright and I just kept asking to speak to him and for them to let me go. They rang up on a mobile phone and spoke then handed me the phone, it was Felix he said they'd taken him to a minicab office and he was okay but going back to the hotel. He was obviously annoyed and upset about everything but concerned about me. I couldn't tell him where I was or say anything much because the men were stood in front of me. They took the phone off me and hung it up. They said I had to have a smoke now because they were and then I could go in a bit. They put the pipe to my mouth and came right close up to my ear and said "If you know what's good for you – smoke." I did and I was proper out of it. They both went out of the room and I remember looking at the window thinking I should just jump through it and run; but I knew I wouldn't get away from them.

One of them came back in the room and grabbed me by the arm and led me into another room. It was a room completely empty apart from a mattress on the floor. He pushed me in, sat me on the mattress and closed the door. Then I could hear him talking with the other man and their footsteps returning; I was completely fuzzy headed and on a kind of shut down. They both stood in front of me and started acting all gangster, punching each other's fists and slapping their chests. The one guy stepped forward and motioned for me to turn around; I was convinced I was going to be shot. I looked down at the mattress thinking that my blood and brains will be splattered all over it any second now. My whole insides coiled up in anticipation of the bullet. The man put his hand on my shoulder and gripped it tightly then knelt down behind me, then he started to pull me fleece off and I thought they must want to get rid of my clothes because they're evidence; I'm definitely being killed right now. Then he pulled my t-shirt off and pushed me face down on the mattress leaning his weight on my back; the other guy then took my shoes and socks off and ran his hand up my leg. But instead of pulling my trousers off he started to touch me. I struggled but the other guy just lay on me harder and shushed me right in my ear, as if to calm me down. Then my trousers got pulled down and the guy smacked his lips because I didn't have pants on. I could hear he was undressing. He put his hand on the top of my back whilst the other guy undressed.

Then I just felt a searing pain and his weight on me and hands clawing at me. I blanked out; all I could sense was pounding, animal pain, inside and out. I don't remember anything about it, whether my brain just switched off, paused or what I don't know. My whole body and brain just became pain, horror, I felt like a blank space. I have no idea how long it lasted, there was lots of movement and noises, it all just became abstract. It was like a physical shock, a wall of fiery pain. There was grunting and growling and grabbing at my body, I felt like I'd fallen into a river of lava flowing from a volcano, trapped underneath a breaking wave. My mind popped and there was just nothingness. I thought I had died but there was just a murky blankness. Eventually I felt a hand on the back of my head, grabbing my hair and shaking me to wake me up. They were getting dressed and calmly told me to put my clothes back on. The one guy had taken my wallet out of my trousers and took my money out then threw it back at me. I felt like I'd been beaten up, from the inside out. It hurt to move. They walked me back out to the car drove out onto a main road, stopped and shouted at me to get out. I was still expecting to be shot as they drove off.

I started to walk along the road and realised my fleece was ripped, it hurt to walk and I was bleeding so I took my fleece off and tied it round my waist to hide it. I remember some cars driving past and seeing a sign saying Shepherd's Bush. I tried flagging down a car to help me but they kept driving past. Then a black cab pulled up, I asked him to take me to the hotel in Victoria where we were staying. When we pulled up outside I explained I'd lost my money but left him my wallet with the bank cards and passport and ran in to our room and Felix was in bed. He gave me the money for the cab. When I returned he was just silent and angry. I went straight into the bathroom and got under the shower, the pain was unbearable. I stood under the shower and just cried. I got in to bed and told Felix what had happened. He was really angry and shocked and kept asking me where it had happened because he wanted to go and kill them. He said the people in the house had been alright they hadn't hurt him but they'd taken most of his money and left him at the minicab place. Eventually we slept. When we got up in the morning we just headed for the Victoria train station. We hadn't got enough money left to apply for the visas anyway. As we were walking down the street I took the box of Prozac out of my bag and threw it in a bin. I thought if this is what better feels like I'd rather just be crazy because this feels a lot worse.

We didn't really speak on the bus all the way home; I was just zonked, staring out of the window at everything passing by. When we got back everyone was at a fireworks display at the hotel in town that has big grounds. We told Helen and Kat about what had happened. I now feel like a victim, that night I went in the bathroom and ripped up my clothes that I'd been wearing in London. I was just really upset and angry. Felix wanted me to go to the police but I didn't really see the point because it's not as if they're going to be able to find them. He also said I should go and get a STD test, I pretended I had but me and Kat aren't having full-sex anyway because of the Prozac. Plus she is already acting weird towards me because of what happened. How is it that my life has got so out of control and I'm such a mess so quickly? It's just one thing after another and I feel like I'm trapped under a landslide. Now that I had stopped taking the Prozac I knew I had to get a hold of myself and sort things out. But my relationship with Kat took a nosedive as I was convinced she was cheating on me because she was paying me no attention and flirting with anything that moved, male and female. She kept telling me I was being paranoid.

I kept having this dream; it was set in the same building that I had that hallucination in the bathroom mirror – the corridor. The blue woman is dressed in a Florence Nightingale style nursing outfit her apron is sky blue and across the chest is a big embroidered X in red. She has one of those nurses' hats on like a bonnet in the same sky blue with a red number 8 on it. In her hand she's holding a candlestick which is burning with a blue flame like gas. She gestures me to a doorway and opens it. I look into the room and there is a bed on which Kat is having sex with Felix. I slam the door shut. The blue woman twirls around and opens another door; another bedroom and Kat is having sex with a girl I know, I recoil and push myself back against the wall out in the corridor. The blue woman walks past me to the left and opens another door. Kat is sat naked on a throne and our group of friends are all knelt around her; their hands moving all over her body. She looks straight into my eyes as she uses their hands to pleasure herself with. I pull the door closed and as I turn to look at the blue woman the corridor has shrunk to just a square with the three doors and a wall on the fourth side. On that wall the blue woman has turned into a painting that looks like one of those religious icons. A beautiful picture like the Virgin Mary, her robes was now of a blue silk covered in the pattern of little blue butterflies of all different types. The neckline of her dress is of red silk going down in a V in her breast and the red silk continuing under her bosom. At the crossing of the X there is a gold heart with a sapphire jewel in the centre. On her head is a beautiful red crown filled with puffy royal blue silk, right on top is a number 8 made with two tear drop shaped rubies set on a backing of gold. Her left palm is open and has a glowing blue ball hovering above it. The other hand is holding a wand as if it was a sceptre with a twinkling star on the end. For a second the whole picture appears frozen then all of a sudden she moves the wand and it extends out of the wall and taps me on the head; as it touches me a trapdoor opens underneath me. I fall down into darkness and land on a massive silver spider's web. I try to climb but the web is stuck to me and I start to struggle. At that point I wake up wriggling in the duvet, Kat asleep next to me. This same dream kept happening for 3 nights, exactly the same way. I knew what response I would get if I tried to talk to anyone about it – that I was paranoid, that it was the meds messing with my mind. But I had an inkling that something was giving me a heads up on the truth. Kat had understandably become more distant to me since the whole London thing. She didn't want anything at all to do with me physically; she was repelled away from me like opposing magnets and repulsed by me because of what had happened to me physically but couldn't break it off because of the situation. It was logical she was going to be looking for satisfaction somewhere else. But when I started to hint at that she, as expected, just got angry and told me I was being mental, imagining it, getting paranoid. But I was sure that the dream had an element of truth to it. It brewed in me for a few weeks and I just watched everything from inside my bubble. Kat started to play up to my 'paranoia' by telling people about it and then going over the top flirting and touching them as if to prove how ridiculous I was being. But I could see in the other people's eyes a certain look that was horrified and pitying me, they'd only do that if there was some truth in it. I kept getting that look. Also people were being nicer to me, protective; it was another one of those shifts so undetectable unless you're in a bubble and something scratches the surface. Or I suppose like how a spider feels little vibrations in its web. One of my friends said that when we were in London Kat had a bloke stay over in the flat. I confronted her and she said nothing had gone on – I was just being PARANOID! She then started arguing with me at every opportunity and saying she couldn't take it anymore, she started setting up situations that would hurt me then point out that I was being hard work or over sensitive. She dumped me and moved in to the little box room next to the bathroom in the Lad Pad. The next day when I came home from work the bloke who'd stayed over when we were in London was coming out of the front door, looking very sheepish to see me. A few days later when she was at college I phoned her Mum and explained the situation. I packed up all of her stuff and her Mum came and picked me up. We took Kat's stuff back to her room at home. Her Mum said that she was expecting that Kat would have gotten pregnant. I told her that she had asked me to but that I refused. When she dropped me off Kat's mum said to me that I was welcome any time to come round to share a bottle of wine with her, I was a nice guy and Kat was silly to have treated me badly. When I got back to the flat I waited for Kat to arrive. I heard her trot up the stairs and go straight in to 'her' room then she came flying in to the room where I was sat alone on the bed.

"What's going on? Where's my stuff?" She shouted at me.

"It's at your house, where you belong. You can't stay here."

"What the fuck have you done?"

Calmly I replied "I packed your things up, called your mum and took your stuff home. Now go there where you should be. It's the best thing for you." She just turned and ran out. When Felix got home he was surprised at what I had done. I could tell he was impressed that I had actually taken action and done something. That night I chatted to the people from in the dream and they all admitted that Kat had made passes at them all and they had felt bad because they wanted to tell me but didn't think I would have been able to deal with it. I didn't tell them about the dream I just thanked them for being honest with me, I now knew in myself that the inkling had been accurate and the dream had shown me the truth. I came up with an idea of what I should do; I invited all of our friends to come round to the flat that Saturday evening for drinks. Kat had no idea that I had discovered the truth about the last few months. I phoned her and invited her to come along to see everyone and she presumed I was making a move for us all to stay friends. Everyone thought it was just going to be a gathering of all of us to hang out together. Once everyone was there and Kat arrived she was acting as if nothing had happened; working the room as if she was the centre of attention. I just let it all play out for a while. I waited for the conversation and atmosphere to get settled into the usual banter and frivolity, blending into the background. I kept going over in my head what I was about to say, waiting for the right moment. Then I gradually moved until I was sat in the centre of the room and started to speak.

"What does everyone reckon about dreams? Do you think they are just random or do they tell us things?" The replies worked perfectly, a few people mentioned funny or strange dreams they'd had. Kat made a joke about a whacky dream she'd once had.

"The reason I ask is that I was having this recurring dream." In unison everyone asked me to tell them about the dream. So I started describing it in detail and as soon as I got to the part about looking in the room and seeing Kat having sex with Felix the atmosphere completely changed and everyone began to realise what was going on. No one said a word. I carried on describing the next room and the next. Then Kat stopped me.

"Is this why you invited me here? To have a go at me? You're fucking crazy."

"No, I brought you here to let you know something. You lied to me and made me think I was being stupid and paranoid. You tried to shag my friends behind my back and when I asked you about it you made me feel bad like *I* was a terrible person. As soon as I was out of the way in London you had someone over. The thing I need to tell you is that you are a shit person. You need to know that. You can't treat people like that. You put my friends in a horrible position and yet you still walk in here acting like nothing's happened. If you think you can play people like it's a game, you just lost. I had to do this in front of everyone so that you didn't twist it and change it. You can say what you want about me but I'm not going to let you think you can do that to my friends, to these people in this room and get away with it. You need to know you're treating people like shit and you're a bad person – you'll have to change otherwise you're going to wind up very unhappy and alone. That's all I have to say." She leapt up and ran out. Everyone was silent for what seemed like an age then Felix jumped on top of me giving me a massive hug. The others looked shocked and flustered. Ella gave me a big kiss on the cheek. They all started congratulating me and saying they never would have believed I had it in me to do that. The guys said they would not have had the balls to do that and were so surprised and that I was obviously not to be messed with. I just felt exhausted, I didn't want to hurt Kat I just wanted her to stop doing that to people; she needed to know that actions have effects. She can't just ride rough-shod all over other people's feelings just because she wants something.

Well for the rest of the evening the flood gates just opened and everyone started telling me all of the stuff that had happened when me and Kat had been together. It was like some sort of amnesty, all of the things I had thought I was just being silly about, turns out they had been true. Ella even said that Kat was just obsessed with having a boyfriend who was all tragic and fucked up because she thought it was some cool 'Kurt and Courtney' or 'Sid and Nancy' kind of thing. I just happened to fit the bill. She felt really bad about having introduced us. It was really weird thinking that a lot of the period in which I had been taking Prozac and dealing with the hallucinations there had been these thoughts which were accurate. There was things going on in my head about situations which were real and people around me had twisted them to tell me I was crazy. My friends had been torn because they didn't like what was going on but didn't know whether I would be able to handle the truth and deal with a break up. The only thing that I was a bit confused by was the fact that the blue woman and the dream had been showing me the truth. What mechanism of my brain is it that fuels this hallucination? What about the other stuff that I've seen, do they mean something?

I made a promise to myself that I wasn't going to get

into any kind of relationship for a couple of years. I needed to be alone and sort myself out without medication. I went out with my friends and just enjoyed my little bubble. A couple of weeks later we were all sat together in the pub and Kat came in and started talking to everyone. She was smirking at me and flirting with all my friends. She parked herself across the table from me and completely went over the top with everyone. Then she turned to me and said really loudly.

"You know your problem? You were a shit boyfriend. You couldn't satisfy me" She turned to everyone else and carried on. "You know he couldn't even get it up!" She started laughing hysterically at me, wiggling her little finger and pulling a sad face. No-one knew what to do or say. Without even thinking I just picked up my pint, stood up and slowly poured it over her head.

"I can still make you wet though." I said really calmly and just walked straight out of the pub. I went for a walk and when I got back to the flat Felix told me that she'd just completely lost it and started screaming like a banshee because everyone was pissing themselves laughing and left her on her own soggy and fuming.

Life carried on okay for a few months; we were saving hard for travelling. I got to the stage where I could afford to leave work and get the visa and then we would set off. Just as I had left work Felix came home this one evening and said he had to talk to me. He had told his step-mum what had happened in London and she had reacted really badly. She met up with him and told him that she'd been in touch with his birth parents. His adoptive parents had been in contact with them all along. It turns out they had gone on to get married and have two more kids and were in New Zealand. She had made a deal with Felix, if he went now, without me, she would pay for everything. She would go with him to meet his birth parents. She would give him open tickets to be able to fly back to the UK to visit if he wanted and other spending money. Another condition was that she bought him respectable clothes and he had his hair cut into a normal style. He was going without me. I was devastated but I knew he couldn't refuse the offer. I went straight back in to work and explained the situation and got my job back. Then I went to my parents' house to ask if them if I could move back in because I wouldn't be able to afford to live in the Lad Pad by myself. They said yes but that I would have to pay rent because I was now working full time. That was fair enough. I was gutted, Felix felt bad, and everyone was having a go at him because of the situation. It was just one of those things. He said he still wanted me to go meet him and we'd go travelling together, just to give it a few months and we'd make plans. I felt like I was just going backwards. I was really going to miss him. Ella was annoyed with him too, more about him caving in and conforming to his step-mum's conditions. She thought it was weird that he was going to present a different version of himself to his real family.

One night in the flat everyone had gone downstairs to smoke with Ritchie and I was in our room alone. One of the 'fits' started to take over me and I was struggling against it, the walls felt like they were closing in on me. I just went absolutely mental and banging against the walls and smashing my stuff up and proper maniac. Felix told the guys to just leave me to it, I knew they were all tired of me and my craziness and I felt so alone, alienated. I wore myself out and then cried whilst I tidied up the mess. Even the fact that I'm crying now makes me even more upset, when will this all end? I'm so used to looking in the mirror and seeing a pathetic loser that I can't even look myself in the eyes anymore.

In what seemed like no time at all Felix and I were saying goodbye to each other and he left. I didn't know when I would see him again. I just threw myself in to working all the hours that I could get at work. Me and Ella would meet up for a drink on a Friday night and just go and sit together at the Hope and Anchor down by the river. We got to know each other better. She reckons that I was on the wrong medication and that I should be on Lithium because I have mood swings between being happy and 'up' and periods of shutting off. It's nice to have someone to talk to properly about stuff. We just sit in the corner of the pub and chat, we also check out all of the groups of people socialising together – people watching. She knows more people than me because she's always gone to school and college in town. We watch people and how they interact. There's this group of guys who always turn up together and she calls them The Slices. A slice is her word for a good looking guy, I have no idea why it's a slice but I just went along with it.

Sometimes people come up and chat to her, she's always really polite but she has this 'direct' streak – she doesn't take any prisoners. She has an amazing personality, although she's younger than me I really look up to her; I'd like t be more like her.

At work they offered me a new job. Through the summer they were changing all the shelves around so that all of the stores have the same layout. We'd receive plans of each section that needed re-arranging, if it was just a small section we could do it when the store was open but if it was a whole aisle that needed changing we'd have to do it when the store was closed and work through the night. Luckily the guy I was doing it with, Ben, was a good mate who I'd known since I started at the supermarket. He was doing a foundation course for photography at the Art College in Hereford before going off to Uni. We would schedule the shifts around his days at college. The nice thing was that we were collaborating with a few different supervisors and had a sense of responsibility. Ben is a really nice guy and we get on well. During the summer he asked me to do some modelling for a project they had for college. It was portraits of interesting people in strange settings. He took photos of me surfing on a checkout, locked in the bakery oven and stuff at work one night shift when no-one was around. Then another night we went to his house and took a load there with different lighting and effects. Another session we did all over town, at the church in the graveyard, down by the river in the park. I even got in the river up to my waist. We also went on a trip into Gloucester and he found unusual settings to take photos in. It was good fun and just something to do. He gave me copies of the black and white pictures and I put them together in a book. At college they had to go in an exhibition that would be marked. On the day of the exhibition Ben came up to me before our shift at work and said he needed to speak to me. He looked worried. Apparently when the pictures had gone up and everyone was wandering around looking at them someone had said to him that they recognise me. They said I was the kid who had gone mental and got raped in London. I had no idea how that information had travelled so far, or who had said it to him, but I just admitted it was true. Ben was concerned as to whether I was okay. We'd spent a lot of time together and he was just surprised that it had happened. I just felt a bit sick that it had come back to haunt me. I told him I was fine. Inside I was struggling with being back at home where I didn't fit in, missing Felix, dealing with the events of the last year. I just wanted to move on; I kept focussing on getting out of there, escaping, going travelling and meeting up with Felix. I was working so many hours that I was just exhausted most of the time, this worked in my favour because my mind didn't have the time or energy to wander and the hallucinations left me alone for a while.

The next day my mum walked into my room when I was sat on my bed crying, she asked me what was wrong.

"I just miss Felix" I wept.

"Don't say that." She replied. In the way that she said

it I knew she was implying that she thought there was something gay going on. I just looked up at her.

"No not like that, he's my friend, we're like brothers, and I miss him." I was annoyed that she thought there was something wrong with me missing my mate. Why do people always twist things? She just walked back out of the room. It was so frustrating being misunderstood; it made me miss Felix and the Lad pad even more.

I applied got my visa sorted with the assistance of my mum; she wanted to help me but was really upset that I wanted to go so far away. One day she actually cried asking me why I wanted to leave and go so far away. I said that I just wanted to travel and see the world. It was only going to be for a year then I would be back and decide what to do with my life when I returned. I think she was just upset although I didn't fit in the family I was doing something that she couldn't do or hadn't done. It was almost she was crying for herself, that I was leaving her at home and she felt sad about that.

When Felix had gone he left me his bank card and pin number in case I needed anything or there was anything outstanding to pay on the Lad Pad. I was budgeting myself if I went out for a drink and made sure I didn't take my bank card in case I got drunk and decided to get more money out and over spent. One night I was out with Ben and we were having a real laugh but had both only got pennies left. I suddenly remembered Felix's card was in my wallet and decided to borrow £20 and put it back in the next day. When I went to the bank the following day they said I couldn't put money in the account with just the card, so I reckoned I would just give it back to him when I saw him. The next week when I was at work one of the supervisors came up to me and told me to make myself scarce because Felix's step mum had turned up and was out for my blood. I hid in the fruit and veg fridge in the warehouse. She went up to speak to the store manager. After she had gone the store manager called me into his office. He knew me and Felix and the situation. Turns out Felix's step mum had opened his bank statement and seen that the £20 had gone out and was saying that I was a thief and that I should be fired immediately. Apparently I was a bad influence and crazy. The store manager hadn't liked her attitude at all and was just letting me know to be careful. I asked him if he could give her the card when I wasn't there and he agreed that was the best thing to do. He was really pissed off that she had marched in throwing her weight around and telling him what to do. Everyone had been really protective of me and didn't like her. Later that night I was sat at the dinner table with my family when the phone went and my Dad answered it. I could tell from what he said and his expression that it was her. He just said to her that she had no right to call them and be saying the things that she was. I don't know what she said on the phone to my Dad, I can only imagine as he didn't tell me and I didn't ask. He was just annoyed by her attitude as well. All I said was the truth and that she hated me. The whole thing just made me feel sick. Ella's mum worked in the bank and when we met up on the Friday even she said she had heard about it because Felix's step mum had been in there kicking up a fuss. She didn't like her either.

It didn't change any of the plans though; Felix had got in touch to say that he'd spent a couple of months visiting family in Perth in Australia. There were Uncles, Aunts and cousins there, the cousins were our age and he'd had fun in the summer meeting them. We organised a date and both set off to meet up in Sydney airport. I bought a massive rucksack, I promised Ella that I'd keep in touch, she just kept telling me not to go, I gave Ben a load of my stuff that I didn't need and he could use at Uni. My parents gave me a lift to London to see me off. It was all quite surreal; I couldn't believe it was actually happening. That feeling when the plane started to accelerate for take-off was amazing. I think I was also a bit surprised by myself that I was travelling all away around the world to meet my mate in Sydney! I'd only ever been on a plane as far as Spain when I was younger to visit Nanna and Poppa who lived near Alicante. We went once when we were 6 and once when we were 9 so that was a decade ago. This is a proper long haul flight stopping off in Bangkok on the way. I couldn't sleep at all on the flight; I just kept watching all the films. It was weird flying through time zones and jumping ahead in time. By the time I got to Sydney I was a bit tired and disorientated but well excited to meet up with Felix.

We met up out in arrivals and got a bus into the city, it was a good feeling to be in each other's company again. We headed to a hostel on the outskirts and checked in. We went outside and Felix got his mobile phone out and said I should call home to let them know I'd arrived safely. I'd never used a mobile before but apparently they're quite common in Australia. I called home and then also spoke to Ella. It was such a weird thought that I'm on the other side of the planet speaking to them. Ella just asked whether I was okay and told me to get right back on a plane and come home. We then had a walk in to the city as Felix thought it would help me realise where I was. We walked right to the Opera House and stood there looking at the Harbour Bridge; I couldn't believe I was stood in a postcard. Felix brought up the bank stuff and I just told him the truth, he said that his step mum really had it in for me. He didn't have a lot of money so he reckoned we'd need to get jobs soon; I had saved up a chunk of money so I suggested we have fun for a few weeks and have a proper touristy holiday and then get jobs. So the next day we moved to another hostel closer into the city and set off seeing all the sights. We had loads of fun going to the aquarium, zoo, theme parks and cinema. After two weeks we picked up a newspaper and looked for job adverts. We phoned one up and they organised interviews for the next day. It was a company that did door to door getting people to change their long distance telephone provider; because Australia is so large then long distance calls are really frequent. We went out and bought smart trousers, shirts and ties and headed over to the offices. The interview day turned out to be shadowing a salesman whilst they did the job to see if it would be suitable for you then you'd have an interview with a manager when you returned to the office. Me and Felix were sent off with different salespeople. I was with this American guy called Mike. How the job works is that every morning at the office you are put into pairs, everyone is given an A4 sheet with a bit of map on it and your area highlighted as to where you are going to work for the day. You all leave the office and make your way to the area and then knock on all the doors in that area. Then you all just have to stop knocking on doors at 8pm and head back to the office for a 9 0'clock meeting. Sydney is a massive city you might need to take a bus or a train and it can take up to an hour and a half to actually arrive at your designated area. Mike took me on a train to a relatively close area and explained all the ins and outs of the job on the way. He is very enthusiastic and confident and driven, I think that's an American thing as opposed to an occupational thing. He explains that by no means are you allowed to enter a house even if someone invites you in, you have to be polite and accurate with your information and that when you get a sale the householder has to ring through to get a verification number and put it on the form you have to fill out to approve the sale. He reckons that out of every 10 doors 1 will actually listen to your whole pitch and not be closed in your face and out of that 1 out of 10 which actually be a sale, basically 1 in a 100 doors will be a sale. The job is 100% commission based and you get 20 dollars per sale. At the 9 0'clock meeting back at the office you get to go up and ring a bell if you reach 8 sales in one day because that is classed as a good day. I follow him around this massive housing estate as he knocks on doors and does his spiel. It seems easy enough when I'm listening to him do it but already I'm nervous about having to talk to a load of random strangers and not fluff up any of the information. We walked around this estate for hours and I really needed a pee, I kept remembering that we weren't allowed inside houses and there were no public toilets for ages away. I kept eyeing up shrubs and fences but there wasn't anywhere that would be concealed and Mike would probably flip that I intended to pee in the road he was working on just in case anyone saw me do it and blew his chances. I was proper desperate for a really long time, then I couldn't control it anymore and I just let go and wet myself, stood on the pavement, pretending to read the leaflets he'd given me. I had dark trousers on so I was praying that he wouldn't notice. He did, thought I was insane and just kindly suggested I head back to the office. Luckily it was blazing sunshine so I dried off really quickly, when I got back to the office I had resigned myself to them not even bothering to interview me because Mike said he was going to call to let them know I was heading back. I nearly didn't bother even going into the office and would just wait outside for Felix to come back and I'd look for another job. But for some reason I faced the music and the manager interviewed me, he mentioned the peeing and I was mortified but just said it was an accident, I'd drank too much water and hadn't wanted to break the rules about entering the houses. He offered me the job right there and then. I was chuffed I hadn't blown my chances but also thought that they're standards must be pretty low if pissing yourself during the interview process didn't warrant a refusal. When Felix got back he was interviewed and whilst he was in the office a couple of the other guys asked me if I had really wet myself, I managed to just laugh it off and make some joke about it. Felix also got the job and so we went out and bought smart clothes to work in and started 'live' the next day. The office was about 40 people all set up in teams, each team leader was responsible for training its members and they got extra commission on their sales too. Mike was my team leader. I got the impression that he didn't think I was going to last that long in the job because I was so quiet and a bit of a freak due to the lack of control I had over my bladder. That day I was shadowing him again in order to eventually start doing the pitch myself at some point in the afternoon. We'd memorised as much of the information as we could back at the hostel the night before and luckily I have a really good memory. I was dead nervous when Mike told me that the next house was going to be mine and he would only step in if I started to guff up. It was a little old lady who answered the door holding a fluffy white dog under her arm. Her hallway looked camp as Christmas, all chintzy. I launched into the speech. "Hi my name's Kris, I'm just calling round the area today on behalf of Optus Telecommunications. We're helping people out with saving on their long distance telephone calls." She stopped me mid-flow. I thought she was just going to say 'No thanks' and swing the door shut. But instead her head tipped to one side and she squealed.

"Ooh, young man! You're from England aren't you? What a delicious accent! "She glanced at Mike "And where are you from?"

"Well ma'am I'm from the United States." He went to carry on speaking but she broke him off.

"Oh, look at your eyes!" She'd reached forward and placed her hand on my cheek. "Like the sea! Now go on dear, what were you telling me about the phones?"

"Well we'd like to help you save money if you phone anybody long distance, interstate or international. Do you have any family you call who are a long way away?"

"Well let me tell you dear, yes I do. My boys have all flown the nest and I'm forever ringing them up to check how they're doing. I have to because they would never think to pick up a phone and call me now would they? Now where do I sign? I love a good bargain. Do come in and sit down." I looked at Mike and he looked shell shocked.

"Um, Ma'am you see we're not allowed to enter a property, it's against the rules."

"Poppycock, I don't bite and Mitzy here will only lick you to death. Come on in! I won't take no for an answer." Mike looked at me and rolled his eyes then entered the house. We sat on the sofa and went through all the paperwork and the verification call at the same time as having lemonade and being shown photos of the boys who had flown the nest. It took us another good ten minutes just to actually get back out of the door and on our way. When we finished waving and got back on to the street Mike grabbed me by the arm.

"Don't ever tell anyone that we went in to the house! That was crazy funny. I don't know anyone who makes a sale on their first ever pitch. You've gotta work that Brit-Shit that you've got going on. Ha ha." He was really psyched and urged me to carry on with the next house. I marched straight up to the door and knocked. A middle aged woman opened the door looked us up and down. I said

"Hi my name is..." And the door slammed in my face.

That first day was exhausting; by the time we all got back to the office we were ready to drop. Felix enjoyed himself too; He got on really well with Lucy, his team leader who was a Sydney girl. After work we went out for drinks at a pub nearby. It was funny to us thinking that Australia had 24 hour licensing – it seemed to make the pubs more relaxed and the atmosphere a lot nicer because no-one was in a rush to get the drinks in before closing time. Everyone at the office was really nice; it was a mixture of locals and a lot of backpackers too. A few of them asked us where we were staying and said we should move closer to the office otherwise we'd be spending a bomb on getting to and from work. The next day we had a look and found a really cheap hostel on Darlinghurst road just on tube stop away from the office for dirt cheap money, it was called 'The Mad House'. We moved in there that weekend. Darlinghurst is the red-light district and the hostel was above a takeaway doing Chinese food and pizza. The whole road is all brothels and nightclubs with bright lights and loads of people. It was a bit scary at first, dangerous and cheap but we soon got used to it. Me and Felix managed to get a room to ourselves with bunk beds, there were communal bathrooms, kitchen and dining room and also a roof terrace where everyone went to hang out and smoke. We soon got adjusted to work as well – it wasn't long before I was ringing the bell, my confidence had rocketed and I was really surprised. Within the last year I had been this kid who was paranoid and having panic attacks in public situations; terrified of being in a room with strangers. Now I was on the other side of the world being a door to door salesman. It was more than a world away. Once we had proved ourselves in the job they chose people to go on road trips all over New South Wales. A group of salespeople would be sent out of the city on Sunday to spend a week blitzing a whole town. You'd stay in caravans in the town during the week and return to Sydney on the next Sunday. It was such a great way to see the state and get paid too. We made good friends in the office and even more so when we went on road trips. I could help out with the driving and also because I always stayed awake on the long journeys the driver liked it as they always had someone to chat to. The place names really made me laugh because we'd travel around and see Newcastle, Birmingham and loads of English names that we knew mixed with

Australian names like Taree, Dubbo and Wollongong. When we working on the road trips they always put me and Felix to work the same area together and we had a good laugh. We always broke the rules when we knew that we could. It was fascinating to meet so many people, to hear the stories they would tell to us complete strangers who'd knocked on their door. We visited such an amazing variety of places, from luxurious suburbs to tower blocks, mansions to slums. We all exchanged stories at the end of the day about the things we'd encountered.

I knocked on one door at a terraced house in Sydney and very tall elderly man answered it, he had wild white hair and a long beard, he was stark bullock naked. He looked at me and shouted.

"Where's Geoffrey? It's time! The boats are here!" He pointed his finger in the air and started jumping, his little willy flapping about. "Hoist the sails!" He shouted, I just legged it. Another day I was working in the Bangladeshi quarter and it was one of their festivals. At each house there were candles by the front door. It was a tradition that the family would gather and eat some food in one house then gather the food and set off for another house. They were all signing up because they were calling their families back in the home country so eventually I had crowds of people getting me to follow with them to the next house. I ran out of forms that day. Another day I was right in the city centre working the sky rise apartment blocks. You just had to stand on the pavement next to the intercom with hundreds of buzzers and try to pitch the householder if they answered when you rang. It was just so boring pressing buzzer after buzzer just to try and get let in, then you could only go to the door of the person that had buzzed you in then go all the way back to the pavement and start again. When I worked Bondi I managed to get bitten by a spider. I was at the door of an old bungalow and was chatting to the guy; I rested my hand on the dry stone wall and felt a prick in the middle of my palm. I winced and pulled it up to look at it. The guy grabbed my hand to inspect it. There were two little dots close to each other in the centre of my palm. He announced to me that it was a spider bite. I asked him what I should do. He said that because we hadn't seen the spider it wasn't possible to tell if it was serious or not; the best thing I could do is sit down and wait to see if anything happened. If it was poisonous I would feel sick and he'd call an ambulance and they might be able to treat it in hospital or if not I'd be okay and live to see another day! He made me a cup of tea and sat me down. I remember thinking how strange it would be if I'd got so far and ended up dying sat here looking at Bondi Beach. It was the longest half an hour of my life. I was fine and the spider bite then became a war wound I showed off at the office that evening. In another really Muslim area where everyone who answered the door was wearing a bhurka and kept just shutting it in my face all day I eventually knocked on a door and it was opened by a woman in western clothing holding a baby in her arm. She explained to me that the rules dictated that women weren't allowed to speak to strange men and everyone hated her around there because she was a single mother and didn't dress in the traditional way. She was waiting for the day that she would get rehoused. In the suburbs I knocked on a door and there was no response so I set off back down the garden path; a woman shouted me from the doorway, apologising. She asked me if I was from the telephone company, one of her friends had called her to tell her we were making the rounds. She had just given birth to triplets and her parents lived out of state. The savings would really help her out as her husband was at work all day and she was desperate to be able to call her mother and get her advice on coping with the babies. I felt really sorry for her because you could tell she was exasperated, it made me think of my Mum who had had twins whilst her other son was only 2 and a half. It must have been really difficult for her. A little bit out of town I was signing someone up and her little toddler was playing about with me whilst I sat on the porch. He kept bringing me his toys; she was really surprised because he apparently never approached strangers. She looked out at the mountain range just a little way away and said to me.

"Look up there; this is a really rare day." I looked up at the mountains and in the light they looked a hazy blue colour. I turned back to her and asked.

"I know this is going to sound really dumb, but those mountains over there that look blue… are they the Blue Mountains?" She laughed.

"Yes they are, it's really rare that they look like that though, you're lucky. And I think there must be something special about you because he never gets on with strangers, especially men. You must have a kind soul."

I had a proper close shave with an Alsatian dog the one day. I was walking across this cul de sac that looked exactly like Ramsey Street and at the far end I could hear a dog start barking when it saw me. It was tied up to a boat that was parked on the drive way. I decided to stay out of its way and just do the houses on the other side of the road. As I was walking across the middle of the street it ran to the end of its rope, the rope came away and it was loose, running straight for me. It was barking and growling and just as it reached me it leapt to bite me right in the groin. I moved my waist backwards just as its teeth caught the fabric of my trousers right over my crown jewels! I whacked it across the side of the head with my bag just as the owner was coming out and calling it back. He didn't apologise or anything juts called the dog back. I looked down and there were bight marks in my trousers right over my wiener! One more second and I would have had mangled genitals. I was surprised because I was confident with dogs due to my grandparents breeding them on the farm. I didn't want to be afraid of dogs but I was shook up. I Went off to another street and composed myself, smoking a cigarette. When I told the guys back at the office they said that it is illegal for a dog to leave the property and I could have called the police.

One weekend the whole office was invited to a Barbie at the company owner's house. It was a really modern house right on the harbour and was a proper posh party; we couldn't believe we were actually there, doing that. From working in a supermarket, living in the Lad Pad to a glamorous party overlooking the Sydney harbour. The next day we decided to have a day out at Bondi just to soak up that atmosphere and enjoy the beach. When we got there it was the Nude Surfing Championships, very random. That week I was working with an English girl called Lyndsey, she was really nice and chatty, we kept skiving off for coffee and eats. She got her mobile phone out saying that she was going to call her boyfriend back in the UK. When she got through she started chatting then handed the phone to me saying.

"Have a word with Jon's flatmate, Rob" Waving the mobile at me. I had one of those moments where you think 'And why would I want to speak to your boyfriend's flatmate.' I had to take the phone off her.

"Er,hello"

"So ya working with our Lynds, she's lovely isn't she?"

"Yeah, yeah, we're just skiving having a latté."

"Ooh, naughty. So how's Sydney?"

"Yeah nice, sunny and that, nice people though."

"Yeah, they're the best." And in an Aussie accent…"So are ya out for a root? Ha ha" The last phrase was local slang meaning are you looking for a shag.

"Um, not right now."

"Nice to speak to ya, hand me back to Lynds." I handed the phone back and she carried on chatting for a bit. Then when she'd hung up she started giggling.

"So did you enjoy chatting to Rob?" She asked.

"Yeah he seems nice."

"You didn't recognise his voice or anything then?"

"No, should I have done?

"Well, he's better known as Robbie. As in Robbie Williams." When she said it I suddenly did recognise the twang.

"Oh my god, ring him back!"

"You're so uncool Kristoff."

"Ha, I'll….Take That!" It was just another random shift at work chatting to international superstars.

We were doing well surviving on the earnings from the door to door, but sometimes at the weekend I'd use my bank card for my English account and treat us to takeaway , a trip to the cinema or a night out. A few months in and when I put my card in the machine it got declined, I couldn't check my balance so I just figured it would stop giving me money when I'd run out. I was gutted that it had though because that meant we would have to rely solely on our earnings to survive. Felix was doing okay in the job but I had been made a team leader and had people to train of my own. The road trips were cool, we would get beers and the passengers would drink on the way up to the town and then we'd work all week and on the Saturday we would do a half day then all go out together to the local RSL club. They were like kind of village hall places in every town, just full of locals. Everyone would recognise us because we'd been going door to door all week so it would be a really fun party. I liked being out in the countryside, we saw all kinds of wildlife. I had seen wild kangaroos when we called at a farm, one guy showed me that we could see whales out in the ocean through his binoculars from his porch; I'd seen a koala up close in one of the campsites, the wildlife was crazy. Even the bugs that flew around were super-sized and looked like they'd been hatched out of Kinder eggs and wound up like clockwork. It was horrible going to the toilet blocks on the campsites because all the insects were attracted to the lights. You would have to swat them all away from the dunny and just have enough time to have a quick poo before they all came creeping back. It could really mess with your head. I lost it one day when I was working with an Aussie girl. The street we were working was on the very edge of a suburb, on one side were houses and on the other was the edge of the outback. I went to step off the kerb – the gutters are all open and I just saw this thing out of the corner of my eye as I was mid-step. It was a flash of blue. I hopped onto the road and as I looked down this massive lizard came lolloping out of the gutter, it was like three feet long. I legged it round in circles and the Aussie girl was laughing her head off.

"What the hell is that?" I screamed

"It's a blue tongued lizard. They're harmless, unless you wind them up!"

"This country is insane! You have dinosaurs wandering around and massive flying bugs, it's like the jungle!" I just kept jumping around and she was doubling over in hysterics. "They don't show you that in bloody Neighbours or Home and Away do they, there should be a warning or something!" She just called me a pom and walked off giggling. Luckily that was a Saturday so we were off back to camp and getting fed and heading out for drinks. There happened to be five English guys on the road trip including me and Felix. When we got to the RSL someone decided to convince the local girls that we were the boyband 5ive, they played all their songs all night and we did sequence dancing and sang along.

The next road trip was in a nice enough town. As we gradually made our way through it day by day everyone kept saying to us not to go over the other side of the railway tracks. Apparently it was a poorer part of town and that was where all the white trash and Aboriginals lived. We all thought that was an offensive attitude and on the Saturday me and Felix were chosen to go and work the area. We decided that if it seemed rough or we felt in danger at any point we'd just call the guys to come and pick us up in the car. We purposely didn't wear our ties and untucked our shirts. The first street was very pretty and well kept, the people were pleasant. We were working together doing houses next to each other rather than splitting the area up and doing streets by ourselves so that we could always be able to see each other, just to be on the safe side. The people in each street kept telling us not to go to the next street over because it was rough and there had been a lot of trouble. We kept heading up to the next street, the houses gradually got poorer. We saw one family hosing down a cowhide in the front garden and less and less people had phones at all. I called at one door and as the door opened a transvestite answered, looked me up and down and his face lit up, I could see past him into the lounge and there were at least four more guys all with long hair dressed in frocks looking at me. I just turned and walked away to a bunch of scary wolf whistles. Felix was being shouted at by a little old lady from the next door telling him to fuck off. By our maps we had the shortest way to head back to the main road was to cut through the last bit of the estate. As we walked along there were burnt out, boarded up houses and others with big chain fences all around them. It did look proper rough. As we passed one house all these guys got up off the porch and walked down the grass right up to the fence telling us to walk back the way we came. They were really scary and we were proper shitting ourselves. We went back into the other road and Felix started to get his mobile phone out. I told him to just keep walking, if they see you talking on the phone who knows what they'll do. As calmly as we could we just walked back through the estate and when we got to the main road called the others with the car. We were so relieved to see them and be driven away from that place.

I don't know whether it's the pressure of the job or always being tired but my nerves are just fucked. I'm not sleeping very well because everywhere just seems strange to me. We're either at the hostel listening to the druggies and prostitutes shouting at each other or in a random caravan somewhere out of town. I'm starting to struggle emotionally, I'm getting upset, angry, crying but I don't know why. I can't seem to get a hold on myself. The city seems really loud and menacing rather than new and exciting. When I do get to sleep my dreams are wild and upsetting. There's no privacy anywhere, nowhere that feels safe. It feels like something is brewing up inside me and I'm going to pop. There are a few local people who work in the office who, to them, the job was a last resort. They either have financial problems or a record and this kind of job is the only one they can get. Tommy and Kelly are a young Aussie couple who are really fun and we've got to know them on road trips and drinks after work. On one road trip we were sat around the campsite having a barbecue on the Saturday afternoon having a few beers before going out to the RSL when Tommy went a bit crazy. He'd been bitten on the inside of his elbow by a mosquito a couple of times. He was crying and going mental because apparently it looked like he had been shooting up and if when he gets home his mum is going to check his arms because she checks he isn't still on drugs. If she thinks he is she'll chuck him out and his dad will give him a beating. We were all trying to calm him down but he was beside himself. Something inside me tuned in to his despair and it kind of set off inside my head. I felt his pain. I have no idea why but I had gone off to have a shower and shave to get ready for going out, when I looked at the disposable razor I broke it apart and took the little blade and started to cut myself. I chose to cut myself on the top of my leg because I reckoned that nobody would see it there. For some reason I wanted to feel actual physical pain to release this pressure in my head. Seeing Tommy's pain had triggered me. I didn't want anyone to know. I was really upset and crying on my own in that toilet block because this was a breaking point. I'm still mental, this is stupid, I felt compelled to do it; but I knew it wasn't healthy or normal. I cut myself in little slashes and stood under the cold shower. The pain was awful but at least it was tangible and real. It wasn't some broken part inside my head that I couldn't fix, I could feel the pain and I could see the blood. I needed to be able to have a secret wound that I could cover up and I would know, that is the thing that is broken; I can put my finger on it. I could hurt myself to get the pain out.

Unfortunately I had cut my fingertips in the process and obviously had been gone a while. Felix came to look for me and I knew he was suspicious. I just said that the razor had snapped, it was no big deal. We all went out; I sat and chatted to Tommy. He talked a bit about his life and he said he had been in and out of prison for petty stuff. When we got back to the caravans He showed me these tattoos he had got when he was inside. They were concealed about his body and it made me think about the cut I had just given myself. By now he was feeling a lot better and quite hyper. We were just sat around the fire and he suddenly said to me that he wanted to give me a tattoo. Everyone was laughing but he was deadly serious, I said yeah and everyone then got excited to watch it be done. He asked me if there was anything in particular I wanted and I remembered this symbol that I always used to draw when I was at school. It's a triangle then off each corner this line swirls in a semi-circle with all three meeting back in the centre of the triangle. He told me to draw it on the bottom of my leg and he'd go and get stuff to tattoo with. He found a pin and a biro and announced that the prison tattooing was about to start. He held the pin over the flame and squeezed the ink out of the biro onto a spoon. He grabbed hold of my leg really tightly and started to pin prick the ink over the design. It took ages and we just sat and drank and chatted. He was concentrating so hard and everyone else was just chilled. Tommy was the third person to tattoo me. I knew at the time I would always remember that moment. By the end of the night we were all drunk and dancing. The next day we headed back to Sydney and to normality.

The next road trip they decided that they'd send me and keep Felix in Sydney because he wasn't doing so well in the job and they wanted to pair him up with some of the guys who would work him harder. I went off up north to Port Macquarie. The week went well; the town was really nice and touristy. On the Thursday Felix called one of the girls I was working with and asked to speak to me. He had fallen out with the managers and quit the job. Some girls who he'd met on another road trip were in Manly for a week so he was going to go and stay with them and then look for another job after that. I was really annoyed because although the job was okay it was a lot of pressure and hard work. It would be a lot easier just working in a bar or café or something. I decided then and there to quit too and head back to Sydney and do the same as Felix, have a week off and then look for another job. The whole point of us travelling together was to do stuff together not one of us be off doing door to door while the other one partied. I headed back on the train and got the jet cat over to Manly. The girls were staying in this amazing penthouse apartment that belonged to the parents of the one girl from Singapore. Felix was hooking up with the Aussie girl and the other girl Xian seemed to like me. I felt a bit awkward and I was pissed off with Felix changing the plans without talking to me about it. I went down to the beach and sat overlooking the harbour. Things had changed so quickly again and I just needed to chill for a while. As I was sat there and looked at the city lights all reflecting off the surface of the water I saw someone start to emerge out of the sea. It was a woman, she had blond hair… I realised it was the blue woman. It's a hallucination. I've come all the way to the other side of the world and she has followed me. It's not a geographical thing, it's me my head is fucked. Here she is coming out of the water wearing a sky blue silk nightie, walking up the beach and straight past me. I was gutted. I couldn't escape.

We had fun with the girls for the week, fooling around, going to the beach and the cinema. Xian wanted to have sex with me but I kept stopping her at just snogging; I just don't feel comfortable with full on sex at the moment - it scares me. We went to watch Saving Private Ryan and I had this really weird thing happen where I knew exactly what was going to be said and what would happen in the film before it did. I kept saying to Xian and she was really freaked. I hadn't seen the movie as it was new but I couldn't explain how I knew what was going to happen. That week we also discussed what to do next, it was early December and we had planned to go and see Felix's family in New Zealand at Christmas. He rang them and they agreed that we could go earlier. I had already booked open tickets to get to and from New Zealand the only problem was that I didn't have a visa to work there. My wages from the door to door wouldn't last that long. We planned to go there and then come back and go find some travellers work like fruit picking. We headed to the airport and jetted off to New Zealand.

Felix had told me all about his family and shown me photos, his Dad was called Max and his Mum was Julia he also had a little 6 year old sister called Olivia and a 3 year old brother called Mason. They lived in a bungalow in the suburbs to the north of Auckland; we would be staying in a caravan in the garden. Obviously Felix's step mum had talked to them about me when she had chaperoned Felix earlier in the year; but when I met them they let on that they would make their own minds up. Felix soon got a job in a local supermarket and I did my best to make myself useful around the house; helping with the kids and the cooking, gardening. Max took us on a tour to meet some of his family further up on the north island. Christmas was really fun; I got to do the whole Santa Claus thing for the kids. I helped them write a letter, leave a carrot, mince pie and tinny out for him. Then when they'd gone to sleep wrote them a reply from Rudolph, took a bite out of the carrot and made little footprints in the ash on the fire; Max had the mince pie and tinny. Christmas morning they were so excited. We went on a road trip to Jill's sisters for brunch which was amazing. There was champagne and a fruit platter then these croissants filed with cream cheese, bacon, avocado and fresh tomato, also French bread and then chocolate covered strawberries. Then we all headed up to Tauranga for dinner at the grandparents. It was a really nice time with all of Felix's extended family. On Boxing Day all the guys went fishing and we ate these massive crabs that you needed tools to get into the shells. They were all really welcoming but I knew I was a spare part. The grandparents wanted me to stay with them so that they could find something useful for me to do, but I declined, again I didn't see the point of travelling all away around the world to be staying an hour away from where Felix was working. I knew I was getting in the way. At Christmas my family had faxed little messages to the house which was nice. Pete had started going out with this girl who we'd known when we were growing up and was spending all his time with her. In the reply I joked to my Mum that she should start to knit booties. They also told me that my bank had called them to say I was overdrawn. I had told the bank I was going to Australia travelling and I definitely didn't have an overdraft but for some reason they had given me an extra £600 over what I had instead of just stopping it when I got to zero; great another problem.

Felix was enjoying work and went out socialising with the people who he'd met there. I didn't know anyone and just spent time with his Mum and the children. I'd started looking after them during the days so that Julia could do some part time work at the school. It was nice picking Olivia up from school and playing with them in the garden or taking them to the beach or to the supermarket to visit Felix. It also gave Julia some space. They were really nice to me but I know I'm just surplus to requirements purely because I can't get a job while I'm here. Felix seems really settled and this is his family, I get the feeling he would like to stay for a while. Everyone else was occupied; in the evenings I just read books alone in the caravan. The first book I read was 'Illusions' by Richard Bach and it really blew my mind; all about a real life messiah and how miracles work, but set in modern day America. I wrote down loads of quotes from it in my journal because they made a lot of sense to me. Then I read a biography about Led Zeppelin which was accompanied by vinyls of their songs. Then I read 'Communion' by Whitley Schreiber all about alien abduction. The combination of the books, the solitude, and the nothing to do is starting to get to me. This is such a random situation to be in, a family environment but yet again I don't fit in. I came all the way around the world to be out of place. New Year was nice there were a few friends who came round and had drinks on the deck. Ella sent me a package from UK with a letter and a mix tape; Felix was upset that she had written to me and not to him. I do miss her, she's still telling me to come home. On my birthday Max gave me a beer which was sweet of him, Julia wandered why my family hadn't got in contact. I sat on the curb having a cigarette that night looking up at the upside down stars. My head was completely overloaded and I was really upset. This emotion was welling up inside of me, I was remembering everything that had happened that year and the year before. It was all getting too much to think about, too much to deal with; and here I am sat alone on the other side of the planet. I'm a long way away but I haven't got very far. I went in to the caravan and I was really crying I couldn't control it. I took a razor apart and into the middle of my chest I carved the words 'TOO MUCH'. I was kind of on autopilot when I was doing it. I just wanted to feel something, to have a reason to be this upset; some expression of what was going on inside. It was as if I needed to cut myself to give the pain somewhere to be. That was my 20th birthday.

Being 20/ 1999-2000

Well we are all still alive, the millennium bug didn't crash all the computers and the world didn't end at the stroke of midnight. I am still living in a caravan but this one is on my grandparents' farm in the yard next to the barn; it's a long story but I'll get to that. First off I decided in New Zealand that the best thing for me to do was to leave Felix to it and come back to the UK. He was settled, he didn't really want to carry on travelling back in Australia. There wasn't much point and it would have been a majorly crazy move of me to go back to Australia and just try and wing it; I had my lane tickets back to Sydney and then back to the UK already so I just decided to use them. Felix knew it was the right thing to do and I think they were all secretly relieved that I made that choice. I arranged for my parents to pick me up at Heathrow. It was sad saying goodbye to Felix not knowing when or if I would see him again but I had to concentrate on getting home and starting my life again. My parents were happy to see me I think but also stressed about the whole bank overdraft thing. I arrived early on a Friday morning and was still buzzing from the epic journey all the way from Auckland to Sydney to Bangkok to London. My mum took me in to town to buy a fleece because I had just come straight out of summer in to English winter. We stopped outside the supermarket I used to work in and a load of the staff came out to see me and say hello. The deputy manager even came out and asked me if I wanted a job because there was a position there for me, I agreed and he said to go see him once I'd rested. Later on I walked up to the college and waited for Ella to come out, she had no idea that I had returned and I wanted to surprise her. She screamed when she saw me and ran up to me and just threw her arms around me.

"Oh my god! What are you doing here?"

"Well it's Friday I wandered if you wanted to go for a drink tonight?" That had been the night we always met up and went for a drink. We did go out that night and just talked for hours. It was so good to see her; I had missed her a lot. We checked out which groups of people were still around, she said she hadn't been out since I'd gone. It felt very weird being back in the small town where I had started off and it looked like I would walk right back in to a job at the same supermarket, where the same people were still working. Some things had changed but not a lot. After me and Ella had gone out to the same pub we went to all last summer and caught up I went home that night and didn't wake up for a day and a half, the jets had finally lagged me. When I went downstairs to get something to eat my Mum said that she was going to phone Pete because he had been round a couple of times to see if I was awake. He had moved out of home and was living with Alison. It surprised me that he was bothered that I was back or particularly excited to see me as we hadn't really been that close over the last few years. It's strange having a twin brother and a regular type of brother because you do really sense the difference but it's just what you have always known. Pete came round and was genuinely excited to see me; we went for a walk and just sat on a bench and had a chat. It was really weird because he had obviously been through a lot of growing up what with getting his first girlfriend, moving out, socialising and all that. He mustn't have had anyone to talk to about it all either. I felt really close to him in one way because he was opening up to me, usually I was treated as the younger brother but now he was talking to me as if I was an experienced man of the world and he was almost trying to impress me. It was a very new experience for me.

I started back at work the next week, working on the fruit and veg department as the number two to the supervisor. I was being trained up to take over running the department as they were shuffling all the supervisors about. Pete and Alison announced that they were pregnant. Mum and Dad announced that they had sold the house and that I could choose to stay in town and get a flat by myself or move with them and buy a car so I could travel to work. I pictured in my head staying in town in a one bed flat and working at the supermarket; it was a really lonely and depressing picture. I wanted a life; I just wasn't ready to settle for that one. I got a loan from the bank and bought a car. My parents plan was to convert one of the barns on my grandparents' farm; we would have to spend the summer in a rented bungalow off in the middle of nowhere until things were ready. I enjoyed the freedom that a car gave me and went off to different cities with my old friends, shopping and socialising all over the place. Me and Ella went out on a Friday night and on a Saturday I would go out with Ruby and stay at her house. Nothing much had changed in town at all and I didn't think it was ever going to. The people I knew would stay in their jobs for years, maybe find someone and settle down but their lives were pretty much mapped out for them already. I had made a deal with my Dad when he had cleared my overdraft from travelling that next year I would go to University and make something of myself. Ella would be going too and I would apply to the same ones as her and hopefully we'd stick together. I had no I idea what career I wanted to aim for so I would just choose the courses by which qualifications I had got already.

Me and Ella got bored of the same crowd of people and the same pub every time we went out so sometimes we went off to gigs and sometimes went into Hereford where there was a little rock club. It's a really bohemian place with a great atmosphere and cool crowd of people. One Friday we were there and having a dance when this rocker guy kept looking at me; I thought that he fancied Ella and was trying to work out if we were together. He came over and started chatting to her and asked if we were boyfriend and girlfriend. I left them to it and went off to go to the toilet and then get us drinks in. When I was making my way back to the dance floor he was walking towards me. He smiled at me and moved up really close to me to speak because the music was really loud. I remember thinking 'Well done' to Ella for pulling him because this guy is hot, long dark hair, smells nice and has an amazing smile. He put his hand on my shoulder and said.

"Be warned, you have three seconds to walk away before I kiss you." My heart jumped because I thought he was going to threaten me at first when he said 'be warned' then when he got to the kiss part it really threw me. I looked at him and my three seconds were up because he moved his hand to hold the back of my head and started to kiss me. I'll admit I was tipsy and the music had uplifted me, as his lips touched mine and I felt them part and his tongue slowly but firmly stroking mine I let myself go. It felt no different to getting off with a girl but kind of turbo charged and harder, more powerful. I love kissing and this was a really good kiss, it didn't occur to me in that instant that I was kissing a man; I just got momentarily lost in it. It only lasted about 10 seconds and he pulled away, flashed the amazing smile and said

"Mmm, wow!" Then he just strutted back to the dance floor and started dancing. I carried on walking to find Ella who was stood open-mouthed. She had seen what had gone on. How I didn't drop the drinks I have no idea.

"Oh my god! Kristoff! That guy's a slice, well done." She thought he was gorgeous and was actually congratulating me. I needed to sit down. We sat a table and she asked me if I was okay.

"Yeah... I think so; I'm just a bit shocked that's all."

"By what? I've kissed girls before, it's no big deal. But that guy! Woah."

" It just felt really normal, it wasn't any different to kissing a girl – I'm deffo surprised. Just don't know what made him do it in the first place."

"Er Kristoff, I'm going to have to break something to you now. Steady yourself. You are a slice, you're hot, that's why I hang around with you. We sit in the pub and discuss who we think is cool or cute but all the time I'm thinking that you really don't get how people look at you. You are cool and gorgeous; I'm sitting with you because people look at us in that way. Duh."

"Pfft, yeah whatever – people may look at you like that."

"I'm not going to argue with you about it. Just get over it… hot man smooching you in a rock club should be proof enough. I rest my case. Now drink!" We did just that, drank and danced, I kept catching the hot guy looking at me and he came over and danced with us for a bit then went off to the bar. I don't know if I felt embarrassed, or confused or just drunk. Me and Ella left, she wanted me to speak to him before we went but I didn't see the point. The kiss kept playing over in my head. I liked it. In the car on the way home we had a massive discussion about sexuality and stuff. I had always had a sort of admiration for guys, close friends and stuff but I didn't think it was attraction. Ella had slept with both guys and girls and didn't think it was a big deal, she preferred guys it was just different, it didn't really mean anything. It's like people think they have to label themselves or put themselves into boxes. Everyone always thought me and Felix were having some sort of gay relationship but we were just close friends, like brothers; Ella knew this first-hand having gone out with Felix. It was good to talk to her about all this stuff, it helped, but the kiss had got me curious. If it's no different with a guy or a girl then do I want to explore? To me it's more about the person and what vibe you get from them, I don't look at all girls and want to kiss them or find them sexually attractive, maybe that's the way it works with being gay? Perhaps it's only certain blokes you find attractive? I suppose I was lucky that the guy who had kissed me was really gorgeous and the sort of bloke I would have admired in the first place. The difference now was that before I thought I admired a good looking guy because I wanted to be him now I think I might look at someone and see if I want to kiss him?

In terms of psychology and science and stuff - I don't know if I was born 'gay' and have just taken ages to come round to the reality or whether sexuality is fluid and depends on if you are attracted to a particular individual. It can't be totally genetic otherwise my twin brother Pete would be as well and he's definitely not. But then again I was into playing with dolls, watching musicals and singing and dancing round the house as a child when my brothers were laying sports. I spent all my time with my Mum and went shopping with her or learned to cook with her in the kitchen - was more in line with being a girl than a boy in my behaviour and temperament. So maybe you're born that way, not aligned with the physical gender of your body and sexuality is a separate thing to that; but if you're out of synch with your gender then you are more likely to see the same sex as you as the opposite. Like I saw guys as exotic and interesting because I didn't fit in with them, whereas I had close friendships with girls and women but just as friends and felt equal to them, on the same wavelength. I don't think men and women are actually that different, it's more about the behaviour that we are taught is appropriate to our gender. Guys are raised to be one way and girls another. By the time we start to try and communicate with each other as a couple in a relationship we're fucked because we've been taught to be two different types of people. Guys are taught to keep their feelings to themselves and not talk about it all but that's all that women want to do. They want to talk about absolutely everything and with guys it just doesn't compute because they haven't had a lifetime of training. A group of blokes will just get on with each other and don't have much drama, but girls seem to constantly be analysing where they fit in the group, the pecking order, who's doing what - loads of drama. At school I had a group of girl mates and when I first got to know them it was amazing to me how differently they communicate with each other and the stuff they talked about compared to my group of guy mates. It was fascinating but exhausting to see how much attention they paid to things, socially. Blokes just kind of go with the flow while the girls have an attention to detail that's mind blowing.

There was so much going on in my head, I missed Felix but knew he was settled now in New Zealand, we may not ever see each other again yet I had loads of memories playing around in my mind. It was as if all the travelling and stuff hadn't even happened, the supermarket and the town seemed really small and closed in, claustrophobic. The voices, hallucinations and dreams now mixed about with these vivid memories. I was still struggling with what level of crazy I am and now I kept wandering about my sexuality. It's not as if I can talk to anyone about it, there aren't any gay people in this town; there are no bars in any city near here. It's a kind of catch 22, you can't explore if you think you like guys because there aren't any guys around here to like. I don't fantasise about famous people to see if I fancy them because it's that same thing of just wanting to be them, whether it be how they look or the life they have; they don't seem real. I keep thinking about my mind too, I know that sounds weird but bear with me; I listen to songs and admire the lyrics and how they wrote them, how they come up with the tunes. Where do those things come from, are they just sat somewhere waiting to be thought? Is there a place where fictional characters wait to be brought to life in a song, a story or a picture and then they can go and live in a load of peoples' minds instead? I read books and think how beautiful the words are and how they paint a scene in your head for you, I would love to have a brain like that. My brain is broken somehow and comes up with these amazingly ridiculous hallucinations and messages which are completely useless apart from scaring me and messing my life up. Why can't my brain do something useful or creative that is going to help me? I'm fully aware of how psychedelic my brain is; all fantastic scenes and mysterious voices, how come I get that stuff which is driving me mental and other people get 'inspiration' and creativity? Right now my skull seems like a small place that is getting more and more crammed with stuff; I wish they still did that trepanning and drilled a hole in it to relieve the pressure; let a few demons out.

I found a drawing that a Maori woman had done for me when I was doing door to door in Sydney; we'd got talking and I'd said I was going to New Zealand; she really missed the countryside and felt like she was suffocating in the big city culture. She sat there and drew this tribal symbol that was supposed to represent a spirit. She actually sat there and cried when she was explaining it to me, that happened a few times on the doorstep with different people, they opened up to me and I caught a glimpse of their lives. Perhaps if you have a spirit it just collects those moments where other people open up and show you theirs; it stores them up and you learn stuff. I drove off to Cardiff by myself and went to the same tattoo place that I'd gone to with Kat and had it tattooed on my right wrist. It was the same bloke who had tattooed the album cover, he remembered me when I showed him the tiger symbol. He asked about Kat and I just said we'd split up when I went travelling, we chatted about Australia and New Zealand. I realised I was more confident in myself now, doing this by myself and being able to hold a conversation with a relative stranger. It was a Friday and when I met up with Ella later at the pub I showed her the fresh tattoo. She thought it was a fake one, a transfer. She didn't believe me that I'd actually gone all that way and had a real tattoo done by myself. She leant on my arm and got her lighter to burn a bit of the transfer off, she stopped when she realised she was burning my flesh! I now have a little scar in the tattoo where the burn left a mark. But I kind of like that Ella has left her mark on me.

The supermarket is being refurbished so there's lots of work being done changing it around. We closed for a week and blitzed it all and then had to restock it all with a massive delivery the day before we relaunched. I was filling up the fruit and veg produce and managed to bang my head on one of the new metal price label plaque thingies. I proper nutted it because I was concentrating on the tray of tomatoes I was manoeuvring down into the back of the new layout shelving. I hit it so hard right in the hairline above my right eye that it felt like I had to yank my head off of it. I set off into the warehouse to check it in the mirror of the downstairs staff toilet; as I headed through the swing doors my vision started to go blurry with blood. A couple of my mates were sorting cages of stock in the back they took one look at me and legged it off to get paper towels and sit me down on the open loading bay. One of the supervisors came to check out the state of me and sent me off to the cottage hospital to get seen to. The nurse said I needed stitches but that because of where the cut was she would use this superglue stuff. My mate was with me and she told him to keep an eye on me just in case I got concussion. We went back to work and I had a couple of cans of energy drink and finished the night off. My parents were away for the weekend so two of my mates decided to come home with me just to be sure if anything happened. I was fine and we just had a beer and the next morning we all went back in to work for the opening day. Thankfully I was just doing the morning shift as I was really tired and just wanted to go home to bed. I drove all the way home out in the middle of nowhere; I was proper knackered now, I let myself in to the porch and then the next thing I remember I woke up on the floor of the porch and it was dark outside; I hadn't even made it to the front door! I must have blacked out and been k.o'd for about 12 hours. The porch is completely curtained so you can't see inside it; I learned later that Pete and Alison had come to visit me and make sure I was okay. They'd seen my car outside but couldn't get any response from knocking on the door or ringing the phones or see me through any of the windows; little did they know that I was lying unconscious on the other side of the door! I just let myself in and went to bed. The next day when my parents got back and Pete and Alison returned they were shocked at what had happened. I just felt a bit weird because everyone was worried about me and checking up on me because I had a bang on my head but when I had a breakdown no-one really said anything.

Travelling obviously changes your point of view in the world, especially if you then return to the small town where you set off from, it changes your perspective. One Friday night when me and Ella were sat outside Hope and Anchor in the beer garden down by the river a guy who I'd known for about 8 years because he went on the same bus to school and we were in a few classes together sat down with us. His name was Tom and I always liked him because he had long hair and was a proper free spirit, always cheerful and quite random. He'd gone off to Tibet teaching English to children there whilst I was in Australia. He was wearing a Tibetan woolly hat and just wanted to sit down and catch up. He was really enthusiastic about all his travels and what he had experienced. He'd really felt at home in Tibet even though it was really poor, the people had nothing at all. He couldn't get his head around being back home and being able to open the fridge and just pick out whatever you wanted to eat. To even have electricity and running water, television and a comfy bed had become alien to him. He had got so used to living in poverty with the people in Tibet that he felt really guilty about all the things we take for granted every day. He said he wanted to go back there and live; I told him some stories of the people I met in Australia. It was really nice to see him and talk to someone who had travelled as well; I gave him my mobile number and said to call me if he ever wanted to chat again.

At work I had moved on to running the delicatessen department which was easy because I had worked on it before and knew all the women. Mother hen is Beryl and she basically does everything with me in terms of running the department; we get on really well. The women who work on the deli live for gossip they know everyone who comes in and what they buy, they also know everything that is going on. It was only a couple of weeks after I had seen Tom that his mum and older brother were in shopping; they looked terrible, really drained and sad. Beryl whispered to me that the ladies son had just committed suicide. It was like she'd hit me over the head with a block of cheddar. I told her that I knew Tom and had only seen him recently, apparently he had gone missing and they found his car a couple of days later at Symonds Yat where there are a load of cliffs down by the river. He had thrown himself off. Ruby rang me to see if I was going to the funeral but it was the next day and I couldn't get time off work. That next day was pension day and the deli counter is packed with all the pensioners getting their weekly shopping in after picking up their money from the post office next door. As me and Beryl were serving people these two old ladies were stood gossiping with each other and they were talking about Tom. They were saying that he had gone mental after going off travelling. Beryl looked at me and knew I was really upset. I interrupted them and told them that I knew Tom and he was a really nice guy and he wasn't mental and that they shouldn't gossip about someone who can't defend themselves. Beryl chipped in too and backed me up. I felt so sorry for Tom and sad that he had done what he had done. I could relate to the suicide thing too and couldn't imagine what was going on with Tom for him to do it but I had an inkling of how he felt. Although I had had the problems with eating, self-harming and all that I hadn't ever really thought about suicide and life after death. Surely Tome must have had some idea of what he believed would happen when he died? I must admit it really affected me and kind of sparked in me how seriously the head stuff can take over your life. I had got used to the stuff that goes on with me, the hallucinations, and the voices the dreams and the feelings. I have good days and bad days but it's not going away. I decided I should try and get help again whilst I could. I hadn't managed to take control of it all happening to me in the first place and it's not as if I've done anything to 'stop' it all or help myself. It's almost as if my brain has let me breathe for a while or maybe it's because it's occupied and concentrating on other stuff in my life. All I do know is that I don't feel like it has finished and I am worried that the murmurings or remnants of whatever it was that was going on may suddenly rise up and take control again; even if I just pay attention to them by thinking about them. I know I need to get help now whilst I am on a level and 'in control' of my own mind. I kept putting it off though by concentrating on the other stuff that was happening; or rather other things kept happening that made me put it off, I don't know which way round it was.

On a night out in town I kissed another guy, it was different how it happened this time because I knew what was going on. I was out with the lads from work, a massive bunch of us as usual on Saturday night doing a pub crawl before hitting the nightclub. There was all the usual banter and fun and joking. But I noticed that the one guy just held my gaze for that millisecond longer than felt normal. His name is Dom and I've always thought that he's handsome, all the girls like him and he's really smiley and chatty. He's got big blue eyes and I keep catching his line of sight. He also has a girlfriend. Now I can remember thinking at the time – is this really happening, is it some sort of sign? Then again I can only see if he's holding my gaze longer if I'm looking at him as well, so is it me looking at him or him looking at me? Is he thinking exactly the same thing? Or is he just thinking "Why the fuck are you staring at me?" But he couldn't know if I was staring at him unless he was looking at me, right? Then I think that we both avoided looking at each other, at the same time as trying to sneak a glance to check whether the other one was still looking. Or at least that was what I thought I was doing and he seemed to be doing the same. I was aware that this was a dangerous situation, stood with the lads in a small town pub on Saturday night is not the time to be exploring my sexuality. If anyone notices then it's game over, I'm not sure if I like girls or guys but this is not the time or place to be checking that out. But I couldn't resist it because I had an inkling something was going on with him. It kept going on the whole night and when I left the nightclub he followed me and caught up with me. We chatted for a while and as we were walking down a back street we just turned to each other and kissed. Again it felt comfortable and normal, we kissed for ages, we couldn't stop. It felt right and normal and amazing. Eventually we went our separate ways, agreeing not to talk about it and making the excuse that we were drunk. As I walked home I was on a high, it had felt great. That was gay kiss number two and I definitely felt more kissing a guy than I had ever done with a girl. I should have been worried that it was wrong or abnormal but it just felt natural. I thought about my religious upbringing and how what I had just done goes against everything they believe. I've never fitted in with my family and I've questioned their religion, whatever I believe in terms of God and all that this feeling has to be a factor now. If I am feeling that being attracted to the same sex is normal and good for me then I don't understand a God who would dictate that it is wrong yet create a person for whom it feels natural. The other side of it all that I was thinking about was the small town where I live, it's so macho and closed-minded. I may have found someone who also likes to kiss blokes but that's got to be kept secret, society will not accept that around here. I felt like I had found an amazing release, a whole new freedom had opened up in being honest about my feelings. I'm like a bird that has learned to fly just before it gets put in its very own cage.

The next day at work I suffered the consequences of the night before. Dom's girlfriend is a supervisor on the checkouts. I was doing some work in the cash office and we found ourselves in there at the same time. My stomach turned as I could tell there was an atmosphere. She turned and confronted me; Dom had told her what had happened.

"Have you got anything to say to me? Dom told me what you did; I can't believe you would do this to me."

"I'm so sorry, we'd had a lot to drink. I didn't mean to hurt you."

"He said you kissed him. I don't care if you're gay or what but don't go round thinking you can kiss other people's boyfriends when they're drunk!" I realised then that Dom had told her a different version of what had happened than the one I remembered. Whether he felt bad about kissing someone other than his girlfriend or he felt ashamed about kissing a guy I have no idea. He had thrown me under the bus to save himself so I just went along with it.

"I'm sorry I shouldn't have done it, I was just really drunk and confused. I didn't want to hurt you I just wasn't thinking. It was my fault."

"Well you need to sort your head out then before you mess your life up and other people's." She stomped out of the cash office. I got the idea that she was hurt and embarrassed. I had learnt a valuable lesson, don't trust anyone, don't shit on your own doorstep, don't do anything that you're not happy with everyone finding out about, if you get found out just put your hands up and admit it – own your actions, the only damage limitation is to be honest. One of my girl mates has a tattoo on her shoulder of the Bacardi bat and underneath it are the initials F.U.B.A.R, she had explained to me that it means 'fucked up beyond any recognition'; I suddenly realised that this is a motto. Dom had fubarred me by using the excuse that he was drunk, I had too in my conversation with his girlfriend. It was like being drunk was a 'get out of jail free' card. People make crazy decisions and do ridiculous stuff because alcohol has lowered their inhibitions or boosted their confidence; Dutch courage and all that. Then they can write-off their behaviour by pointing out how drunk they were. That is a fubar. I think that when I've had a drink I'm more confident and if anything I'm more honest; I don't get in arguments but I'm more honest in conversations. I like to dance and sing and drinking lowers my inhibitions but it doesn't change who I am; I still only do the things I want to do. So the whole fubar thing doesn't make sense to me because you should just own your own behaviour. I was sorry I had kissed Dom only because he had a girlfriend and that was wrong, not because I had kissed a bloke and that in itself was wrong. Drinking doesn't make you do things you don't deep down want to do whether that be fight someone, dance around like a maniac, sing at the top of your voice or kiss someone inappropriate.

I had no idea whether Dom's girlfriend was going to tell everyone but I guessed not because she was hurt by the infidelity and was staying with Dom. But the nature of the gossiping around here she was definitely going to fuel the fire of people thinking that I'm gay. But even at this moment in time I'm not 100% sure if I'm attracted to men rather than women or whether it's just particular people and situations that have happened. Me and Ella get on really well and although nothing has happened between us I do think she's beautiful and can't say that if we kissed it wouldn't be amazing too. Time will tell, there's nothing I can do about it now. People already think that something had been going on with me and Felix so it's not as if anything has really changed in what people think about me. I would feel bad if someone had a go at me for upsetting Dom's relationship but I stand by kissing a bloke because I did that 'cause I wanted to. It just depends which bit of the gossip is focussed on.

As it happens nothing did change afterwards, me and Dom blanked each other when we saw each other at work. His girlfriend always scowled at me but I think she saw the fact that she knew info on me that I kissed blokes as a kind of trump card. None of us were going to say anything because it would make the situation worse; she wouldn't say because she wanted to stay with Dom, he wouldn't say anything because he wanted to stay with her and also not have it out there that he had kissed a bloke and I would not say anything to not break up their relationship and embarrass both of them and myself. What I didn't get is how come he could kiss a bloke and it feel natural and passionate, it didn't seem to make him question his sexuality. It's not as if I threw myself at him or trapped him or he stopped the kiss, it went on for a long while and we kissed several times that night. When I had been kissed by the guy in the rock club it had made me examine my sexuality yet Dom seemed to be just fubarring it totally. To me it was a game changer and this second kissing session had confirmed to me that it felt nice and natural. They wanted to forget about it and treat it as a drunken blip; so things just plodded on as usual. I wasn't any closer to finding out where I stood with my sexuality; it had just proved to me that this small town environment was not the best place to be finding anything out. I avoided going out on a Saturday for a bit and just went out with Ella on a Friday night as we always did.

The first exciting thing to happen in ages was that Felix had rung me to organise coming to visit. It was winter over there and summer here so he decided he would use one of his tickets and come and get some sunshine and catch up with everyone. At the bungalow where we were living mum and dad had bought a touring caravan for me in preparation for when we went to live on the farm whilst converting the barn. They had two big static caravans being put in the yard next to the barn one for them to live in and one for dad's office; my little caravan would be parked on the end but it had arrived already and parked in the garden next to the kitchen at the bungalow and they said that me and Felix could stay in that whilst he was here visiting. I was so excited to see him, I couldn't believe he was actually come all that way to catch up. Other people had mixed feelings about it, Ella didn't even want to see him. She wouldn't explain to me why so I presumed it had something to do with their relationship or when they broke up when he left to go to Australia. The only problem was that he was really excited to see her and had no idea of her feelings. People at work were indifferent to his visit, our close mates just kind of rolled their eyes that we would be out together being as mad as we always were. My parents were fine about him staying, which intrigued me considering what my Mum had said about me missing him and the hassle that his step-mum had tried to cause. Felix hadn't even told his parents that he was coming; he was just going to turn up and surprise them. I drove down to London to pick him up from the airport and it was so amazing to see him again after 6 months. He had dyed his hair bleach blond and when we saw each other in the crowd it was brilliant, like no time had passed at all. We just talked and talked all the way back home. I told him about the gay kisses and he was fine with it, he found it funny that I was still getting in the firing line of gossip. He didn't judge me, it just fitted in to the punk lifestyle we had always had together. I find it strange that with some people you can spend ages apart and when you see each other it's as if nothing has changed. Sometimes that connection is stronger than stuff that goes on in your life. We had loads of fun catching up with each other, my parents were polite to him but I found it odd that we were staying in a caravan outside my parents' house in Herefordshire England and the last time we'd seen each other we were staying in a caravan outside his biological parents' house in Auckland New Zealand. We just chilled out, he visited the supermarket and saw everyone and we went out on nights out. He went to see his adoptive parents at the hotel and I saw him a couple of days later. He said they were extremely surprised to see him and annoyed that they were kept out of the loop that he was visiting; also they were fuming that he was staying with me after all the bitching his Mum had done about me to everyone. He had called Ella but she had refused to see him so he was a bit gutted about that. We stayed at Ruby's on Saturday night in a caravan outside her parents' house so I reckon that makes us official gypsies. We all had a blast. Nothing major happened, no drama but it was just an amazing time catching up with someone who had been so significant in my life, all the way from the other side of the world. I dropped him back down to the airport and we promised to stay in touch and he said that it was now my turn to go back to New Zealand and visit him. We had each other's mobile phone numbers and would stay in touch that way.

After he left I felt re-energised with the life that I had had in the lad pad and the freedom that I had experienced then. It also reminded me of travelling and I felt the contrast of my small life back in England. In Australia we had travelled all over the place every day for work and seen so much yet here I was just driving to work and back and that was it. It made me determined to use my spare time and car to get about and experience more of what was available to me. I sometimes stayed out with my friends in town and drove home later or drove off into Hereford to go shopping or just walking around. I went to Bristol, Cardiff, Newport, and Gloucester just to expand my horizon. I decided I would do something productive and go swimming in the public baths in Hereford in the evenings. I went and swam in the massive pool doing lengths for a while and then they closed that off and I joined everyone was mucking about in the leisure pool with the wave machine. I left the pool and headed in to the changing rooms which were really crowded because the other pool had closed. Everyone was getting showered and changed. I showered and then stripped off to dry myself before putting my clothes on; all the other guys were doing the same all stood naked towelling themselves down. Instantly I had an uncontrollable erection; I immediately sat down and put my towel over myself pretending to dry my feet. I had to manoeuvre myself into my pants and jeans and then legged it as quickly as possible. Out in the car park I sat on the grass having a cigarette trying to recover from the embarrassment. There was a little hill on the grass which leads onto the busy parkland next to the river. Loads of people were in the park, walking dogs, cycling, playing tennis and all that. All these people just doing the things they do. I thought about what had just happened in the changing room I think that makes it definite that I am sexually attracted to men. It's not just that I felt comfortable kissing them now my body has told me that I am aroused by their naked bodies too. It was at that moment that I lay down in the evening sunshine on the grass and thought it all over. Am I gay? Am I bisexual? I don't think bisexuality really exists it's just a stop-off on the way to gaydom; but then again I do believe that you are attracted to the person and not necessarily their gender, race, class and all that. But then if that's the case why was I aroused by a general roomful of naked men? That wasn't about a connection to a particular person. Just as I was whirring all this around in my head a guy sat down next to me on the grass.

"That was very brave of you." He laughed and smiled. I looked at him questioningly. "I was in the changing room just now… that was brave of you." I put my head in my hands 'Please ground swallow me up!'

"Sorry, I'm really embarrassed it just happened."

"Hey don't be embarrassed it was impressive, just not the cleverest place to do it in!"

"Well I didn't know it was going to happen, I wasn't even looking or even thinking about anything. I couldn't stop it."

"So are you out then?" he asked

"In what way?"

"Gay, does everyone know?"

"I don't even know! That's the first time that's happened, I mean I've kissed a bloke but nothing like that has ever happened before."

"Woah, I see… so you're at the confused stage then."

"I dunno, how many stages are there?" he laughed and touched my arm.

"You're funny and cute; you'll go a long way whatever you 'choose'."

"I don't see how it's a choice? Either I am gay and just have to be honest with myself and everyone else or I'm not and carry on as 'normal'" I had already noticed that he was really cute too; short blond hair and blue eyes, amazing smile. I love a smiley person.

"True but some people choose to lie about it and cover it up; judging by your reaction to naked men though you may find it difficult to conceal. Ha ha."

"So are you gay?"

"Yep, everyone knows. Let me tell you – if, well when you come out you'll lose people from your life but the ones who stick around they are the keepers because they like you for you no matter what." I nodded and watched him as he spoke. This is the first gay person I've spoken to – as far as I know; well it's the first openly gay conversation I've had with a gay person.

"Thanks for talking to me, I was about to give myself a complex after what happened in there or at the very least a phobia of changing rooms."

"Pleasure mister, but I had an ulterior motive. I wanted to talk to you. You're cute." He smiled and moved closer. He quickly surveyed the car park and park next to us then he looked back at me, put his hand on my face and kissed me. There lay on the grass, in the sunshine; in a public park I had my third gay kiss. It was smooth and gentle, reassuring, calming. It felt like the world around us had kind of paused. I didn't care about anything. People were walking past us but I didn't care if they saw us or not, this was a moment I was enjoying.

"Definitely gay" He said when he had slowly pulled away, smiling at me "I've kissed a lot of guys and you do it with feeling. You're a natural." He stroked my hair. "Don't beat yourself up about the choice, just go with what feels right. Be careful around here though, there are a lot of guys who pop off into the bushes for sex. I'm sure you'll be fine, good luck in whatever happens next mister." He stood up and started to walk off into the park, merging into all the other people walking and doing the things they do.

"Thank you" I shouted after him. He turned and blew

me a kiss. Game changer.

That night I lay awake thinking about the kiss, thinking about how I had been looking for an answer to my question about my sexuality and how, by chance, I had found a clue towards it. If I hadn't have chosen to go swimming and if I hadn't chosen those swimming baths rather than the ones in the town where I worked; actually if my parents hadn't sold their house and moved closer to Hereford so I had chosen to go to the closest swimming baths, that kiss wouldn't have happened. Also it was my body having a natural reaction that I had no control over; it wasn't a thought or decision. By embarrassing myself in the changing rooms that guy had noticed me. In deciding to sit on the grass and smoke a cigarette he had come over and talked to me. I was looking for an answer and all this long chain of events had led to that particular circumstance. Had I chosen all those things or did they find a way of getting to me when I asked for an answer? I don't really believe in God and all that stuff but it did seem to me that something was driving the course of events; I hadn't prayed or directed my thoughts at anything yet something magical had happened. If that small but massively significant thing had happened because of what was going on in my head then what is all that other stuff, the hallucinations, voices and dreams? Am I mad if I think that maybe there is something going on other than just some short circuit or hormonal imbalance in my brain? I started to examine other coincidences and other chains of events. Like I wouldn't exist if my parents hadn't met and they wouldn't if all my grandparents hadn't and so on back into ancestry. I pondered a load of 'what ifs' and thought how everything is connected but I never look at the significance of the small everyday things that build the major dramas and events of life. Every little decision you make can have a massive effect on that chain of events that leads to a game changing moment. I fell asleep, feeling very disorientated and small in the universe.

I had a dream. I was lay on a red velvet heart shaped bed inside a castle tower. I was naked apart from a pair of golden trousers that looked like the metal had just been melted over my legs and set there. As I looked up I saw the circular stone tower like a tunnel above me and the ceiling was made of carved wood with golden stars painted on it. There was a stone stairway spiralling around the edge of the tower, it started right in front of me and wound around me up to a balcony with doorway behind me. The room was dark but gradually a warm light shone from the doorway and a silhouette appeared there. I was lay on my back looking upwards to it so it was upside down to me. I could tell that it was the woman that I had seen in hallucinations before. She was Cinderella, Barbarella, Florence Nightingale, The Icon Queen, the woman in the corridor, the blonde woman who I had seen so many times. She's the woman I would draw over and over again when I was a small child. She's the Barbie I would play with and now she's in this dream standing in the doorway above my head in this castle tower looking exactly like Gwen Stefani. I just observe as she emerges onto the balcony. In this dream she is wearing a bright royal blue wedding dress. She had this beautifully intricate lace veil and on the very edge of it were tiny silver embroidered flowers. The dress had a jewelled bodice and then layers upon layers of floaty taffeta; around her waist was a belt or red ribbon tied in a bow, in her hands she held a bouquet of red roses. She leant on the banister and looked straight down at me, she started to pull the roses apart and sprinkle the petals into the air and they floated down all around me. She dropped the stems at her feet and made her way down the staircase, her eyes locked onto mine. Soon she was stood in front of me at the foot of the bed, I leant up on my elbows to watch her, she lifted the veil and I saw her beautiful face, her hair was all curled up and bridal. On top of her head was a tiara, it was silver and in the centre were two round sapphires placed so that they made a figure of eight shape with the little diamonds around them. She pulled at the bow of ribbon around her waist and her floaty skirt came away to reveal that the bodice was part of a sort of leotard. She put her finger to her red lips and gestured me to be quiet, then she nodded at me and looked up to the ceiling. She blew a kiss upwards and extended her arm into the air as she did so all of the gold painted stars in the ceiling started to shimmer and one of them shot down leaving a trail of glitter. The star whooshed straight into the palm of her hand. It floated there as she moved her hand in front of her. The way she was looking at me was as if she was a magician doing an illusion and she wanted me to watch her every move. She waved her other hand in the air as if she was holding an imaginary needle and was moving to make a stitch; she brought her fingers to one of the points in the star and as she drew away a stem extended out of the star and it turned into a golden wand. I really wanted her to say 'Ta Dah' but she was still immersed in the choreography of the illusion. She held the wand with both hands and brought the star up to her lips; she looked up, closed her eyes and kissed it. A kind of light emanated out of the sapphires on her tiara and slowly descended over her. As the light moved down across her body she was transformed. Her veil and bodice glowed in such a bright electric blue that they seemed to be made of the neon light, her skin shimmered and the wand shone like lightning. She held the stem of the wand and moulded it into a circle with the star at the centre so it looked like a crown. She slowly moved right up next to my head, gestured for me to lie down flat and placed the crown in the air about a foot from the top of my head; it just floated there still glowing neon bright. She held the star and pulled it away from the crown so that it was another foot away from the circle. She moved around so that she was beside me and moved the palm of her hand over my face to close my eyes. All I could see was pitch black apart from these two tiny dots of electric blue light that somehow I knew were where her eyes were. The dots moved closer and closer towards my closed eyes until I felt her lips touch mine and when she kissed me I saw her eyes exactly where mine should be; as if they were projected onto the inside of my eyelids. I could still feel the heart shaped bed underneath me but it felt like it was floating and circling around. It felt amazing, I had lost all idea that I had a body, that my energy was confined to a structure. It was as if I had merged with her and nothing else existed, it wasn't that I was surrounded by darkness just that all the light was focussed into us two. I had never ever felt anything like this before, alive and real but external to myself, connected, no boundary of myself like I was a jug of water being poured into the sea. I felt her lips leave mine and I opened my eyes as she was moving towards the circle floating above my head. She reached out to grip it and as she did it sparked and fizzed like raw electricity. With both hands she started to stretch it so that it became a larger hoop of blue neon light, I could tell by her face that it was a real exertion, she strained with the effort. Then when the hoop was large enough she held it with one hand and started to move it down over my head like a magician does with a levitating person. As the glowing hoop moved into my vision I felt a searing pain as veins of lightning came out of the circumference of the hoop and shot into my head. She held out her hand to reassure me and somewhere deep in my mind an instinct to trust her awoke. She continued moving the hoop down my body and it moved through the heart shaped bed with my body in the centre. It was like it over rode the molecules of the bed; I could see both the structure of the bed and the hoop and veins of lightning. It hurt so much but the pain was so extreme I couldn't tell whether it was heat or cold. The part of my body that the hoop had passed over already felt different; it was like I was aware of every cell in my body and they were full of energy and functioning at their maximum. It felt like I had been ignited and the energy was burning through my body, every cell, system and organ was being brought to life and turbo charged. The part of my body that was still 'normal' felt heavy and dull just like holding a slab of raw meat; like jumping into water with your clothes still on and them clinging to you and weighing you down. She kept on moving the hoop down my body and I was just staring upwards, all the colours had got brighter, sharper and in the light I could see the spectrum flashing out like rainbows everywhere. I could feel everything about my body, it was like a realisation of my existence, I was elated, elevated to a new level of emotion. If I concentrated I could 'sense' my skin, or my heart beating, or my lungs inflating and deflating, my blood flowing, the electrical impulses in my brain making these perceptions. I could see the heat emanating out of my skin, I could see the air being sucked into my lungs and the oxygen merging into my blood. Even at the very edge of my field of vision I followed her movement as she shrank the hoop down again and placed it back above my head, I didn't need to concentrate solely on that it was like I was conscious of layer upon layer of awareness. My perception was moving so fast that it seemed like time had slowed right down. I was aware of everything on every level in that tower. As she had placed the hoop back into place between my head and the little golden star I could sense another focus of energy, it was as if something very big and powerful was stood right behind me pointing a finger right up close to my head and zapping a beam of energy out of it. The origin of this beam was coming from beyond the little golden star pointing a line through it, through the hoop and then on through the crown of my head and right down through my body. It was just a feeling though, I couldn't see the beam or sense the energy, it was just an awareness of its existing. She moved and stood beside me, observing me, I knew that she could see and sense everything in exactly the same way that I was. I could read her perception; somehow we were sharing our consciousness, our thoughts with each other. Her thought and feeling were already within my own and I could identify them. What I noticed immediately was that she was shielding me from something. I could sense only a frontal part of her 'being' the part she was allowing me to see was just a costume and a mask. I wasn't ready to see the rest that is behind, for the purpose of this moment and event I only needed to see as much as I was. If or when I was ready to experience more than the revelation would happen at a rate that I could assimilate. This was what her thought was telling me inside my own mind. I accepted this and expressed that I could sense there was more, behind her mask and wherever the beam of energy originated from beyond the golden star. She nodded even though there was no purpose to this other than to concentrate me on the physical and bring me back in the room; she could have just intimated this within her mind and I would have sensed it. I hadn't looked at her; my gaze was still fixed upwards to the carved wooden ceiling of the tower with the little painted golden stars on it. She held my wrist and kissed the centre of my palm; her grip felt real like an actual hand, I could feel my pulse beating against her warm skin. Yet I knew this was an illusion, whatever was behind this 'mortal' costume and mask was just using it as a point of reference that I could relate to. My senses were just picking up whatever signal that she wanted me to experience. This is a dream, this whole thing doesn't really exist but somehow the experience is real. She picked up my other wrist, kissed my palm and then drew her fingertip along the scar on my wrist where I had cut myself. She 'said' 'I hope you understand', I didn't need to reply because she knew I did and that her hope was for my broader and on-going understanding not just about the reason for the scar. It seemed to me that her hope that I understood was a timeless thing, that I would reach a point of comprehension that would span past, present and future. I would get what chain of choices had led me to 'now', be totally present in this moment and use that knowledge to interpret my choices right now that built my future. Now she took the veil from her hair and shook it into the air as if she was going to lay it as a sheet over me on the heart shaped bed. In mid-air directly over me it transformed into full length mirror and lodged itself hovering above me. The reflection surprised me as my brain whizzed into processing what it saw. I wasn't lay on a heart shaped bed but instead I had perfect swan white angel wings, the glowing hoop above my head was a halo and above that was the golden star. She waved me to stand up and as I did the mirror moved with me so that it was always directly in front of me. The wings felt heavy but I could also feel that they were an extension of my body, I stretched them a little and it felt just the same as stretching my arms and back. The halo and star stayed above my head, again I could sense that they were connected to me but the beam of energy wasn't permitting me to extend up into them, they are the edge of my circuit, for now. I gained my balance. She placed her palm on the centre of the mirror and it went an oily dark metallic colour, she pushed it onto the wall in front of me. When she released her palm I saw my reflection, it had changed again though. I saw the electric light body version of me, it held a human shape so that I could recognise myself but was just a load of energy flowing about, shining and sparkling. It moved as I moved, the room behind it was not the tower I was stood in either though. It was as if the 'mirror' had become a transparent face of a kind of coffin, a dark box. I was looking into some sort of tomb, a crevice or a vault made to contain this electrical version of me. I stared at it and as I did I could see the energy changing, it changed as I thought. As I started to become aware of this my consciousness started to transfer into the light body and within it I generated my human body; cell by cell as I accepted that this was part of me I built my organs and limbs in amongst it until I was fully inside the mirror. It happened smoothly and instantly, as my eyes generated and started to function I was looking back through the mirror from the other side into the tower. The angel version of me was now minus an actual body but made up of light energy with the woman stood between us looking at me inside this box. The castle room was just a massive map of the atoms and molecules that made up the different parts of it; I could see the air. She said

'I hope you understand'

I said "Thank you" and with that she blew me a kiss. The mirror clouded over and for a moment I was stood immersed in darkness inside a box, buried alive. I knew that the electrical light body was contained within the skin of my human structure and in turn that was also trapped inside this box. There was room for movement but there was a boundary. Very gradually the base of the box turned into a square of white light and I felt the motion that the box was descending. I was moving down through a ceiling into a bright white room and the box was now made of clear glass. The brightness of the room hurt my eyes and it took me a moment to focus as the box landed. It seemed to be some sort of space age all white modern kitchen or a science laboratory. The far wall was a massive pane of glass looking out onto a beautiful garden with a luscious lawn surrounded by towering bushes blooming with flowers of all kinds. In the centre of the lawn was a stone fountain shooting up spurts of water that sparkled in the sunlight. I pressed my palms on the front of the glass box, I didn't feel claustrophobic because the room was so airy and light but I did feel like some sort of weird exhibit, a sample of humanity preserved inside this glass case. It felt like there were a succession of spaces, the skin of my body contained all of me, the glass case contained my body, the room held the case beyond that was the garden and beyond that I didn't know – a world of some sort. Beyond that world was a galaxy? The universe? I felt very mortal, that this succession of spaces always exists, it's just a matter of perspective whether you see just the immediate space or think of yourself in context to an environment or country or part of the human race or the universe. Just as much as you can think about your position in terms of location you can also think about it in terms of being part of a couple, a family, a nationality, a generation, a community, a society or as part of a species. But that energy that I had felt in the tower that I was aware of being within my human body, I had the idea that that energy is connected to everything. It flows through everything and connects it all, somehow I knew in that moment that 'miracles' were possible by the way in which your personal energy connects with all that other energy flowing through everything else. It was just an inkling of a knowledge I knew a seed had been planted in my mind that once I helped it grow would show me the answers that I could not formulate at the moment but I had the feeling that I was on my way to knowing something amazing. I lifted my right hand up in front of my face and looked at the palm. I could see the energy flowing within it as if it was electricity, on the skin I could see words and patterns and pictures emerging and disappearing like magical tattoos. It looked almost like my thoughts or knowledge was appearing all over my skin. I placed my palm against the glass of the case and these images flowed within the glass, spreading all around me. I could see information I had learned at school, quotes and formulas, phrases from books I had read, scenes from films I had watched. Singers singing lyrics, memories of conversations; my whole life was flowing over my skin and onto all the walls of the glass case. I started to think things and the things that I was thinking appeared on my skin and flowed out onto the glass. I started to think of people I knew and their faces appeared, gradually all the faces I had ever seen flowed out onto the glass. Every one, real people that I had seen face to face and faces I had seen on television and films, all flowing out from inside my head out onto my skin and then whirling around the glass of the case. I could retrace the flow back into my head and it felt like there was a point right in the back of my mind from which they originated. It felt as if there should be a massive cinema screen behind me with all these images on and that there was a projector in the back of my head beaming them out but that it was working the other way; sucking the images off the nig screen down into my small head and then out of the front of me onto my skin. That feeling reminded me of the star that I had seen in the tower on the heart shaped bed. There was a point on my body just above where my skull met my neck and that was where my thoughts were coming from, it felt like that's where that star should still be hovering or it should be a tattoo like a target where my thoughts enter from external place and get fed into my brain. I could feel this beam going straight through my head from that point at the back through to a point in the middle of my forehead. Something was transmitting my thoughts into my mind and through it to that point above my eyes. As I concentrate on the shape of the star I can sense the image beaming from outside of the back of my head in through that point on my skull, through my mind to the point on my forehead and from there I see a beam coming out of both of my eyes and from the third point on my forehead. The three beams meet at a point in front of my face on the glass of the case and the shape of the star appears. From that star shape more start to emanate across the glass, floating and shooting until the glass case is filled with stars. It is as if each star has a different colour and frequency that is related to an emotion. There are different styles of star all of them whooshing out of the middle of those three beams coming through me. Just as the glass case reaches fullness, all of the stars twinkle and flash at the same time so that the glass turns into a sparkling light, I am in a box of bright light and as the dazzle fades the glass disappears.

Just as I step away from the square of light that was the base of the glass case a door opens in the sheer white wall to my right. A beautiful tall woman dressed in a white shirt dress with long curly black hair walks in. Her eyes are a lovely mixture of green and hazel with smoky eyes shadow, her face is bright and open. As she walks across the room in front of me she gestures me to follow her to the kitchen/laboratory area and a table that looks like a breakfast bar with two white stools next to it. She sits one side of the table and offers me the stool directly opposite her. There's an aqua marine coloured hospital gown folded up on the stool and she nods for me to put it on. It is like a papery oversized tee-shirt, I scrunch it down over my head; now I truly do feel like a mental patient. She calmly crosses her legs and places her hands on the table. It feels like she should be a doctor or a scientist who has been sent in to debrief me on my experiences.

"Now then Kristoff, I want you to process and assimilate the events that have you have just been through. All I need you to do is to formulate a belief around them and store it in your brain. You don't need to tell me what that belief is – I just want you to take a moment to sort it and store it." She was very matter of fact as if this had happened a hundred times before and I was just another subject that she was dealing with; just a number in the system. "Would you like a drink whilst you think?"

Suddenly I had a thirst and a real desire to quench it.

"Yes please, anything cold, thank you."

"Okay" She got up and opened a cupboard that turned out to be a fridge; it was full of glass beakers containing a blue liquid. She took one out and peeled the red foil lid off then placed it down in front of me and patted my hand reassuringly. As I drank it I could taste a fruity sweetness and feel the cold entering my body and refreshing me. She sat back down in front of me.

"So, now take a moment to attend to the information that you have just received through your experiences in the tower and in the glass case." She looked at me and raised her head ever so slightly as if she would be able to see 'the penny dropping' in my face. I thought about everything that had just happened and I did have an inkling that I understood what it was suggesting to me but that it wasn't obvious; it just made me think that I am connected to something that is just beyond my comprehension.

"Do you remember what you read in 'Illusions' by Richard Bach? 'The image is the dream but the beauty is real' think about that too, in context with what you've just experienced." I did remember that and I had written it down in my notebook at the time in the caravan in New Zealand; it had seemed so profound to me. Now I understood it on another level. This learning is real, whether it be in a hallucination or in a dream, it is real.

"Okay I understand.." She cut me off.

"Don't tell me, this understanding is just for you. This moment is for you, it is your present – for *now*."

I stared out of the window at the beautiful garden and tried to take the moment in. I knew I had learned something massive but I couldn't separate the different points up, I had this sense of the magnitude of the experience as a human being but that made me feel like a tiny blade of grass on the lawn outside. I don't know whether she could somehow read my mind, it wouldn't have surprised me at this point.

"I am lucky enough to live in this little corner of paradise, the meadows outside are luscious and beautiful…really full of beauty, a delight to behold. But if you look very closely you will see that they are made up of many constituent parts. Each petal on a flower, blade of grass or drop of water is part of that beauty. You could go deeper and look at the molecular structure of each part and deeper again to the energy that holds their particles together; all of these miniscule components are part of the beauty. Do you understand?" I nodded and her face shone with satisfaction or relief.

"Now I need you to move on to the next stage of your process, come with me." She got up and took me back through the door she had entered from. The next room was quite dark and totally made of drab concrete. She led me down a flight of stairs to a platform in front of a swimming pool; it reminded me of the baptism pool in the church I'd been baptised in when I was 13. The water looks really deep and I can see a faint light emanating from some sort of opening far beneath the surface, it makes the water have an eerie glow that reflects all over the walls and ceiling. The woman places a reassuring hand on my shoulder and stands square on to me.

"Okay, now I'm going to need you to enter the water." Her voice sounds more 'official' than before, like the atmosphere has changed. I nearly looked up to see if there were cameras watching us but realised that would be ridiculous in a place like this. Paradise wouldn't have CCTV, would it? I automatically obeyed and lowered myself down into the warm pool, it was deeper than me so that I had to tread water as I held on to the edge looking up at the woman. She crouched down and stroked my hand.

"Your way out is underneath the water. When you dive down you will see a light, swim towards that and you will find your exit. I must leave you now and the door will be locked behind me - that is my exit and as I have instructed yours is down there." She smiled and nodded as if to appear comforting or to reassure me. I looked down in to the water and could see the light. I glanced back at her and she had gone. I took a deep breath and dived down to investigate the light. It was the opening to a tunnel that the light was coming in from, but I couldn't see how long the tunnel was or where it went to. It was only just wide enough to fit myself into and I'd have to just propel myself along by kicking my legs I wouldn't be able to swim with my arms. I came back up to the surface. I was scared, I love swimming and diving underwater but being in a confined space underwater and not knowing where it led terrified me. Shit. My only way out was to face my fear. I just floated there in the water for a few moments, feeling my breath raise and fall. I took a few deep breaths and swam down as quickly as I could and pulled myself into the tube, it was just bright white and I kicked as fast I could and pulled myself along with my hands. It seemed to take forever and I was starting to panic, the hospital gown was clinging onto my skin, I needed to breathe and the tunnel just kept going on, I started to struggle and kick harder and as I did there was a current that pulled me along and out. I tumbled around and around as the current got stronger; I caught on to some weeds and kicked up a cloud of mud, I felt a hard ground that I stamped down on to push myself up and away from. I broke up out of the surface of the water and gasped air into my lungs, still being propelled along by this current. I looked around me and I was bobbing along in the middle of a river. It was the River Wye that flows through my hometown, I recognised it. The sun was shining but I knew this wasn't real. The water got shallower until I came to rest on a sand bank, the current had slowed right down. All around me were big lily pads and oversized flowers gently floating on the surface. On a rock in amongst them were stood two tall storks staring right at me. They towered above me, silently observing. One of them slowly lowered its head until its beak was able to gently splash water in my direction. The other flapped its wings and as it did it transformed into a pink flamingo. Its companion twisted its head to look at it and let out a piercing shriek and flew off. The flamingo flapped its wings and clucked as if it was giggling to itself. The flower that was closest to me started to move, rising up out of the water in amongst the petals was a woman's face with a butterfly mask over her eyes as if it had just landed there. She smiled and cooed at me, pulling herself up on to a lily pad. She leaned towards me and placed a hand behind my head and cradled me into her bosom, her gentle rocking sent ripples out across the surface. It felt nice, comforting; the sunshine on my face and her body warming mine. She let out an 'ooh' of excitement, the wings of her butterfly mask fluttered and as I followed her gaze I saw a large yellow rubber duck bobbing along. Its big fixed smile and wide eyes looked out of place in amongst this natural scene. Two colourful mallards came chasing along beside it, quacking away.

They prodded and pushed the rubber duck and then paddled of cackling as if they were laughing. On the opposite bank I saw a large black chess piece, an ornately carved horse - a knight. It was beautiful, like a majestic sculpture. Suddenly it threw back its head as if it was bucking, shook its mane and slid into the water. As it glided under the surface it turned into a sea horse and swam off downstream.

The flower lady just hummed and laughed almost as if she was singing, jiggling me in her arms. Little pink snowflakes started to fall all around us, when I retraced their path I realised that they were cherry blossom coming from the trees that lined the bank. As they melted into the water they looked like inks of all colours, bleeding down into clouds that swirled and spun with the lazy current. They were mesmerizing. In amongst the clouds I could see a form, a swooshing together. It was the delicate fronds of a tropical fish, the fin, the tail. There seemed to be a shoal of five or six large multi-coloured tropical fish writhing about in a cloud together. Then I saw a hand in amongst it all, then a shoulder, another hand - they were mermaids and mermen. Beautiful, exotic, merpeople. They were playing with each other now, pushing and shoving. Two delicate hands appeared on the edge of the lily pad and slowly a girly face rose up out of the water all patterned and colourful, she rested her chin on the pad and her mouth opened wide in excitement. She quickly dipped back down and reappeared with a merman, his face widened in surprise too. He grabbed my wrist and swiftly dragged me under the water. He wrapped his arm around my torso and pressed my hand against my chest with his; carrying me under his arm. The other merpeople hurriedly swam along beside us, he tapped my hand against my chest and then leapt above the surface of the water and I took a big gasp of air before we dipped back under. It seemed like the whole river had transformed into a flowing flash of exhilarating colours. I saw the colour of sand on the riverbed and we turned in towards the bank, the merman gripped my torso and launched me out of the water onto a small beach. I landed flat on my back to see them emerge out of the river metamorphosing into glorious birds of paradise, spreading their fins into wings and taking flight above me. They swirled and swooped in the bright blue sky. I laughed out loud at the amazing sight, holding my hands against my head in wonderment. I spread my arms and legs out around me and made a sand angel. The sand was warm and golden. A flash of fear broke my euphoria as I realised I was starting to sink; I scrabbled to get further up the beach towards the grassland but kept sinking deeper. I struggled back towards the river and grabbed onto the long weeds to pull myself back in. It felt like I was pulling between two magnets, one sucking me into the ground and the current of the river urging me back into its flow. I yanked myself back into the water, in amongst the green weeds.

I found myself in what was like an underwater field of long green weeds, billowing all around me. Then there was a long black frond, then another; they were eels slithering past me. I flowed into the upright stems of reeds and clung on to them so that I could raise my head above the surface and rest. The sky had clouded over and was a burnt grey, the air had a chill to it. I could still see the jet black eels darting by. I looked up around me and all the leaves on the trees had turned to oranges and browns and pale yellows. Their withered branches creaked and lurched over me like dark hands silhouetted as if they were the inky veins of the smudged sky. The eels were circling closer, weaving in amongst the reeds; they spun round and round. Then their grumpy faces started to poke up out of the water; as they rose slowly up against the reed they turned into big black centipedes and began clinging onto the reeds and winding up around their stems. Up every reed there was a spiralling, wriggling centipede; when they each reached the top of the reed they gripped on tighter. They seemed to be vibrating and the reeds started crackling, they melted into them transforming them into brassy tubes; the vibrating grew and grew until it broke into a crescendo of organ music. As this music wheezed out a fog spurted up and spilled down the tubes and hung above the surface of the water.

Rain started to fall, splattering percussion to the eerie music. I could hear a rumbling rapidly building and bright white light glaring behind the trees. The leaves started to fall off the trees floating down all around me. The rumbling kept getting louder and the light grew brighter until with an enormous roar of engine and screeching of metal a bus came crashing through the trees and reeds and landed in the river just downstream from me. There were no screams, no faces, nobody on the bus. I had released myself grip on the reeds in my shock and the water began to carry me. I tried to swim away from the bus but got sucked straight in through its smashed back window; I grabbed onto a seat. It was one of the old buses with the metal bench seats and leather cushions, I wrapped my arms around the metal bar on the top of the seat, the river was flowing through the bus. I looked out of the window and saw branches scattered all around, but the leaves that were falling now were pages from books. The bus began to creak, shifting under the force of the river. I held on tight and closed my eyes as it lurched away from the ground, bracing myself to be bashed and battered in the water. But with that momentum I could feel myself swooping upwards, upside down - I opened my eyes to see that the bus had turned into the waterwheel of a mill. I was clinging to the inside of this giant wheel that was slowly spinning around with the flow of the river. As I reached the summit I desperately held on as I dangled down and then gravity lowered me back into the water as it kept on rolling around. All I could see on the bank was a dilapidated, mossy stone wall and in the river this horrible soup of broken branches, leaves and pages of books. I helplessly watched as I looped around and around. The pages were still falling through the fog, being blown about by the wind - as impotent as I was. But then in amongst the fog and the paper and leaves I saw something floating. Gracefully fluttering along was a metallic blue feather. I watched it as it glided past me. Without a thought I just threw myself into the water to follow it. I splashed about in the splintered soup, leaves and pages sticking to as they fell. I held on to a large branch and looked up into the fog, the pages floated around like snowflakes.

Gradually the surface of the water was turning a mulchy white, laden with all the paper, layer upon layer. I could feel myself getting colder and realised that the layer of paper was turning into a sheet of ice all around me. The branch and I were being slowly frozen into place. I tried to clamber up on to the surface of the ice but it cracked and I plunged underneath it. The current dragged me along and as I clawed at the ice above me I could tell it was strong and solid. I could see up through it and the pages kept landing and merging with it. Suddenly there was a scratching sound and I saw a white line trail across the other side of the ice, then again another broad circle. Someone was skating on the ice; I could see a faint shadow moving with the line, round and round. Then with a thud it stopped directly above me and I saw two hand prints glowing electric blue against the surface of the ice and a blurry face lowered itself right down in front of mine. Then one of the hand prints faded away and with a smash a bright fist came crashing through the ice and grabbed around for me. I held on to the arm as it tugged me up by the scruff of my neck, dragging me out on top of the ice. He let out a guttural roar and threw me sliding along. As I came to a halt I struggled and slipped to raise myself up to see him but all I saw was a wisp of electric blue smoke trailing off up into the sky. The sun was starting to peep through the clouds.

The sunlight was making the ice sparkle a festive glittering; its warmth started to thaw my cold fear - the glow was magical. I turned and looked behind me and realised that I had reached the ancient bridge by my hometown that I had crossed so many times before. For years this bridge had separated home from away for me. Its stones are glazed with ice. I shuffled closer to it, wanting to lean against its solidity, to feel its history, a functional monument to the travellers - to the passers-by. But right now I didn't want to pass by I wanted to hold on to it like an anchor, stop this journey that the river was taking me on. As I got closer the ice that was covering the bridge had weird forms within it; there weren't stones underneath it but limbs, bodies, people. The whole bridge was made up of people frozen into its shape. The bridge was actually the people, they were all wearing these masks of different types like they were at a masquerade ball. It was as if they had climbed and held themselves together to make the bridge and then got frozen into position. The sunlight was warm and bright now and glistened through the clear ice. Every few moments I saw a rainbow bounce off the ice, a spectrum fanning out in the air. This prison of ice that had captured them all now formed prisms that set beautiful rainbows dancing in to the frosty air. I slowly wandered around looking at all their faces, it felt like some majestic mausoleum, quiet and eternal. I ran my hand over one of the 'pillars' to see the face inside; it was Blue. As I wondered why she would be frozen here she winked and her breath started to cloud up inside the surface of the ice. She glowed and swiftly the ice around her melted away and she stepped down and into my arms. We embraced and I twirled her around and around, holding her so tight to me; I'd never felt anything like this before. Warmth washed over me, I wanted to cry,

I wanted to laugh and scream. I felt like I was going to just burst into a million pieces all clattering down onto the ice beneath my feet. She kissed me and then held me at arm's length and stared into my eyes, smiling. She raised her finger to her math as if to tell me to stay quiet then pressed her finger into the centre of my forehead between my eyes. At the very moment that she made contact a flash of lightning exploded between us and everything went white. As the dazzle faded I realised that I was awake in my bedroom, in the darkness of the night.

I placed my palm flat against the wall, now I wanted to feel it's solidity; somehow anchor myself in this reality. But I could remember the dream as if it was a memory of an actual real life event. It had felt physically real. My senses had convinced me that it was genuine at the time and I'd responded to the perceived danger of drowning in the tube or in the bus or under the ice. What is real, if it is all the interpretation of electrical signals from your senses, all done within your brain - what is reality? I felt jet lagged, exhausted, yet I hadn't moved from my bed. I remembered the kiss from the man earlier at the swimming pool and it felt very distant, a lifetime ago. I knew that all I had just done was have a massively weird dream but there was a fragment somewhere inside of my head that felt changed. That miniscule seed of understanding had lodged itself deep down inside the flesh inside my skull. I could almost perceive a faint buzzing, a scratchy pushing as that seed tried to sprout. Whatever message I had 'understood' in the dream had actually, physically found a place to store itself deep inside the vaults of my brain. It felt like a tiny little domino been put in place and a giant finger was poised, hovering over it ready to flick it and send a toppling chain reaction throughout my head. It was something to do with that spot somewhere inside my skull where thoughts come from, where that beam of light had been shone and something to do with that spot on my forehead that Blue had pointed on me. I closed my eyes and I could imagine a laser like line straight through my skull linking up those two points. And where did that beam of light come from? What was it emanating from, who is its source? I looked around my room; it was all as it had been when I had gone to sleep. I closed my eyes and I could see it all like in the molecular, light energy way I had seen when I was in the castle room. Is that castle the same one that I had seen all my life in the Cinderella recurring dream? Was it the same place where I had seen Blue in other dreams? I started to realise that it was, this sort of dreamland which serves as a setting for my dream stories. Is that normal? That dreamland feels real though, but it couldn't be it's just inside of my mind. But Blue seems to exist there and somehow in this waking reality, I'm so confused. Where did that seed come from that I could feel inside my brain? Was it from the halo, the 'God-finger' beam of light, the blue drink, a kiss from Blue, the lightning or when she pointed her finger on my forehead? I placed my palm back on the wall, it felt good and solid and real. I curled up and placed my other palm on the wall too, I drifted back to sleep.

It's pitch black and all that I can see is a tiny little

teardrop diamond floating in the darkness. It becomes magnified and inside its fractals I can see veins slowly pulsing with a dark velvety blue liquid. It slowly flows up to the point of the teardrop and begins to sprout outwards, upwards. As it does the liquid starts to lighten and glow. The vein branches out in the air and begins to form the two hemispheres of the brain and downwards it forms a spinal cord. Gradually it forms all the internal organs of the body and keeps going layer upon layer, bones, tissue everything slowly appears until forms a layer of skin. But then it carries on and forms the energy field outside of the body and I can see little clusters of energy all over the body where the glands are and major organs. Outside in the energy field there are floating, moving clusters of energy orbiting the body. Above the crown of the head there is a beautiful glowing ball of energy and fizzles like a sparkler and fires a beam of energy back in to the teardrop. The teardrop sparkles and the entire scene rewinds back in on itself until it just a teardrop floating in the darkness. The teardrop falls and splashes into an invisible ocean that all I see are the golden ripples that are left when the teardrop vanishes. Golden shiny circles are expanding and vanishing in the darkness of my mind.

"Oh my God! That is one trippy dream Kristoff!" Adonai was waving his arms around excitedly. "I feel like you've mind-fucked me too, I'm trying to feel that seed in my brain too. I'm thinking what if just hearing the story does the same thing to me like a magic spell; an incantation?"

"Ha ha, I hope not, I don't want to fuck your head up for you!" I smiled. "That's all just the tip of the iceberg, by the way - it gets a whole lot freakier. So if you're stressing out then I can stop?"

"Oh no… I definitely want to hear the whole story now. I can already some of your other tattoos are from that dream too - the storks, ducks, fish, flowers."

"Yep, not necessarily intentional though, they do all weave together though."

"And what about Blue, who is she? Please keep going before I chuck a whitie!"

Well the next day I really struggled to go about my normal day, in reality. All I could think about is what had happened in my dreams. It really felt real and it really felt like it had actually altered my mind in some way. I know that psychologists have done sleep studies and all that and think it's your brain sorting through new information or dealing with conflicts; some say it's just creating stories to deal with the hormones swimming about whilst you're asleep. But these dreams and hallucinations seem to have a message, a meaning. On the way to work in the morning I had to drive over the bridge and the river, it all looked the same but I knew my view of it would forever be altered. The count of places and things that were being altered due to my madness was growing; scissors, razors, headlights, the bridge, the river. My real world was slowly being encroached upon and filled with reminders of the other world, I couldn't escape it. Normal everyday items were now reminders of a hallucination or crazy dream and when I looked at them they sparked up that same feeling from the other world. Was Blue just a hallucination, a part of my imagination; an externalisation of some part of my psyche? She appears in my dreams and in waking time too. Also another big issue was that she seemed to have been around all of my life; even when I was a little child I'd picked a blue ball gown to wear at nursery for the photo and a Barbie doll as my Christmas gift. If she was just part of my broken mind then my mind must have always been broken? After work I walked up to the graveyard that looks down onto the river and bridge, I don't know whether I expected there to be a sign to show me the dream had been 'real' or I just needed to look at it to anchor myself in this world. Even when I had exhausted myself trying not to think about the dreams I remembered the episode at the swimming pool. It was as if I was a different person now compared to a day ago. But then I suppose we all are, we are always changing; every day we wake up to being a new version of ourselves. All the things we experience from sleep to sleep in our waking hours do actually change us. Even just physically our cells are different. We age, we take on new information, assimilate our experiences, we evolve. And maybe, if we're lucky, we get to experience a life changing dream whilst we're asleep too - bonus.

As much as all this stuff was freaking me out another part of me was intrigued Blue was like an imaginary friend, drop dead Fred style, but she was helping me.

Her presence and commentary was comforting. She never said much to me, it was almost as if she was a personification of my superego, a part of my mind that I didn't have any control over; like that little voice in your head had actually got a body and moved about interacting with you. I still functioned normally at work, to the outside world; to other people they wouldn't really be able to tell anything was happening. I'd fine-tuned the way in which I paid attention to her or weird hallucination stuff; it was all about not showing any emotion or reaction when it happened. I might see or hear something odd but I'd just ignore it unless I was alone. It was like I had an earpiece in and Blue was talking to me and nobody else knew. She interacted with reality and I could see her but no-one else could. When me and my friends went dancing I could see her with me in the crowd and danced with her - being drunk was a good cover too because it allows you to act more oddly and just blame it on the drink. I'd stay at mates' houses usually but sometimes I drank and drove too, I didn't really care. We lived out in the middle of nowhere, down winding country lanes; I knew it was dangerous but I just couldn't stay at home alone and couldn't be out with my mates without drinking. I would obsessively listen to full on heavy music; it was as if I wanted to turn up the volume in my life to drown out the craziness. I'd go from being okay with the hallucinations and then realising how crazy it was to just accept them as normal when they blatantly weren't. I'd swing between the two extremes and neither one was good. I would try and tire myself out every day to the point of exhaustion so that I would have a really deep sleep. I started not eating again and making myself sick thinking that it would help tire me out. I just didn't want to have a single moment where I was just sat relaxing because that was when I'd freak out about everything. Even when I lay in the bath I'd have headphones on listening to music or I'd fall asleep with them on listening to the radio. I was getting iller; physically and mentally. It was just a spiral that I couldn't seem to pull myself out of. It isn't as if I can go to the library and find a book on being crazy or hunt out an article on hallucinations or crazy dreams. There is no information or anywhere I can go to get answers, it's not as if someone's going to magically appear with the knowledge or studies into it all. I can't go to the newsagents and find 'Crazy Monthly'. The local library is quite big but it doesn't have a massive psychology section, I looked. Perhaps Open University will put something on late night telly like the documentary on rainbows.

I decided I wanted a new body modification, I suppose I thought it would be a healthier way of feeling pain rather than self-harming. Because I was still avoiding sex I decided I'd have my dick pierced - there wasn't really any logic to it but I just had the idea and made it into a mission to achieve. The closest place that would do it was Newport so I made the appointment and Ruby came along for the ride. It was in a tattoo studio full of bikers and the two guys who did it looked like crazy stoners. They told me to get up on the table and strip down. It was so weird sitting there exposed to these two guys whilst they fiddled about with my penis. They put anaesthetic gel on the end of a cue tip and pushed it up the hole - that was so painful. Then put a little plastic tube down and pushed this needle through it then fed the ring through. It was such an odd pain but it made me feel alive. I could hardly walk afterwards and Ruby was relieved to get away from the bikers who were all chatting her up. The idea was that it would be a sort of secret piercing but when we went out that night I got really drunk and a load of girls took me into the loo to show it off to them. It wasn't very practical either because it makes you piss like a sprinkler. I took it out a couple of months later. It was another scar to add to the collection.

We moved in to the caravans on the farm as work on the barns was going along well. It was quite odd to be living in a tiny caravan back on the farm that I'd known all of my life. I had been given this little black and white telly by one of the ladies at work; it was really old with dials to tune in to the stations. I would just sit and watch telly or listen to the radio in this tiny little caravan, it was so odd. I'd pop in and see my grandparents quite a bit. It's nice seeing them more, there routine hasn't changed for like 50 years; they're a good point of reference. But it did highlight how abnormal I was in comparison to them and the farm that just stayed the same and ran like clockwork. At work I had been promoted away from running the fruit and veg department to running the systems management department which meant doing the ordering for the store. Everything had been computerised so that the tills told the ordering system when we were running out of something, SSM managed the whole computer system to make sure the levels were all accurate. I was impressed with myself that I must seem to be coping really well hiding my craziness. It was a really complicated job and lots of responsibility and I also had an assistant. I now had an office upstairs in the supermarket which meant I belonged to the 'upstairs' crowd rather than the shop floor workers downstairs. Luckily I just ignored the social rules and carried on socialising with everyone as I had done before even though I was now classed as one of the management. Faced with the challenge of the new role and in the interest of not fucking it all up big style I decided to try and sort my head out.

I went back to the doctors and saw one who I'd known for a few years, I explained that I wasn't sleeping well, I'd also slipped back in to not eating properly; either not at all or making myself sick when I did. I opened up with him a bit about my head being all mixed up and having crazy dreams. He asked me lots of questions and I avoided answering any in a way that would make him think I was proper mental. I didn't say anything about the voices but said I saw stuff more like day dreams and kept things vague. He pointed out that I hadn't carried the Prozac on for as long as I was supposed to; I said that I thought that maybe it wasn't the right thing for me. I explained about the black outs and hurting myself when I was on it last time. He said that he wanted me to try it again and stick with it this time; there wasn't any alternative that was appropriate to my symptoms. He advised me to make sure I drank plenty of liquids if I wasn't eating properly and that he was referring me to a psychologist for counselling. He could see that I wasn't keen and got really serious with me and said that if I didn't try this course of treatment that there is only one other thing they do to deal with hallucinations and that is electric shock therapy. He said that would be the next option if this didn't work out so I should try really hard because that other process is permanent and would completely change my life. I was terrified and also disappointed because I was now back on Prozac and now had to go to a psychologist as well. I went and got the prescription and then went home to my caravan and took the first pill, it knocked me out quite quickly; I was gutted to be back in that situation but just wanted to be better.

I still went out with Ella every Friday but now I'd go and visit Pete and Ally in their little house in town beforehand. It was really nice seeing my twin brother with a job, a girlfriend and home; with a baby on the way. I was quite envious of him; he had got it right and seemingly with no effort at all. He had always wanted to be a farmer and he'd just one to agricultural college, qualified and got a job. He'd found a girlfriend and now they were going to have a family - job done. The most responsible thing I've done is get a promotion and but my first mobile phone. Me and Ella always took the mick out of people with mobiles because we thought they were posers; they're so popular that they need to carry a personal phone around with them just in case someone wants to speak to them. But because we both lived in the middle of nowhere and drove cars our parents said we needed them in case we broke down. We were quite embarrassed about it though, I only ever call Ella or Ally. I got on really well with Ally it's really like having a sister, we sit and watch movies and chat. I've told her about being back on the medication and she thinks I should tell my Mum but I reckon it's just better to get on with it. After last time I don't really see the point. Ally always teases me that Ella and I must be having loads of fun and that we're going out with each other as boyfriend and girlfriend. I just laugh it off, but Ella is the most amazing girl - the perfect girl. I think now I just look at her and I'm intimidated at how together and cool she is; she's become almost sacred to me. I wouldn't want to fuck that up.

I started thinking more about exploring stuff with blokes so I used to go back to the swimming pool in Hereford. I'd swim sometimes but I was a bit nervous of getting aroused in the changing rooms again so I took to just walking in the park. I remembered that the guy who I'd kissed said that guys go in the park and do stuff together. There were public toilets there but I didn't fancy the idea of getting caught out George Michael style. They just wait until it's quieter and getting dark and go into the bushes together. You could tell who the guys were because they just sort of hung around, wandering about and they'd stare at me for a bit too long. I didn't want to have full sex because of what had happened in London but I was interested in doing other stuff. It was kind of scary but exciting at the same time, a bit of a buzz doing something naughty. I had a few 'experiences' with different guys, just fumbling really I was so nervous of being attacked or overpowered. One guy got a bit rough and kept trying to have full on sex with me but I wouldn't let him, we both had our trousers down and he just kept rubbing himself up behind me, skin on skin; hoping that I'd let him penetrate me but I just freaked out and ran off. I never went back again because it scared me so much. I want to explore sex with a man but I don't want it to be like that. There aren't any gay bars anywhere at all and I don't know any gay people. Maybe one day it'll happen in the right way, with the right person.

Pete and Ally had a little daughter at the end of November and called her Bethany. It's just amazing to watch as our family grows and another generation is 'generated'. Pete's a Dad, me and Simon are Uncles, my parents are Grandparents; life flows on. It makes you think of the future, what will life be like for this little girl? I babysat for them when they'd just brought her home - I was terrified being left alone in their house with this precious little thing. Babies are so amazing, just holding them and wondering what they're thinking and how everything is so new to them. It did make me think of that abortion and possible child from that other girl - I'm such a mess how could I possibly have been a father? But looking at little Bethany completely silenced my head - she's amazing.

The work on the house was going well, Mum and Dad were doing as much of it themselves as they could and Dad obviously knew a lot of people in the building trade to come and help on the more specialised jobs. Because the barn building is hundreds of years old they have to keep all the arrow-slit windows and where the barn doors were they are building these big two storey windows. One day when I got home from work my parents weren't anywhere to be seen which is unusual that they would both be out together. I looked around there was no not or anything so I made myself something to eat and settled down to watch telly in my caravan. I jumped out of my skin when there was suddenly a knock on my door, when I opened it Grampy was stood there in his overalls, wellies and flat cap, looking worried.

"Your Mum and Dad are off up the hospital. Seems Celia was painting the big door frames and they fell on her and smashed her nose in."

"Oh no! Is she alright?"

"She took a fair old knock by the look of it, but she's walking like. I dunno if they're off up the Cottage Hospital or in town. They'll no doubt phone up when there's owt to know. I see you've got your tea you're eating so I'll leave you to it. Come down the house if you need owt. Oh, she asked if you could make sure the lids are on the varnish and clean the brushes 'cause she doesn't want them to ruin." He'd started walking off half way through talking to me and shouted the last bit over his shoulder. I could see that he was concerned about his daughter but being a farmer he just got on with things. There was no room for drama or hysterics, it's all calm and matter of fact. I went in to the barn to find the varnish and investigate if anything needed cleaning up and there was a big pool of blood, it looked really serious. Neither of them had mobile phones yet so we'd just have to wait and see if they called from the hospital.

It was a few hours before they came home. My Mum had a big bandage over her swollen and bruised face, she seemed like she was still in shock. She'd been painting the frames of the big windows which were leant against a wall inside the barn, a gust of wind had blown one of them down on top of her. She had screamed for help for quite a while because my Dad was working inside his caravan and couldn't hear her; it had really shaken her up. Obviously he felt terrible, they'd ended up driving all the way to Hereford, about an hour away to get to hospital; she'd been stitched up and told to have bed rest and watch out for concussion. She looked like she'd been in a boxing match, I felt so sorry for her. It took her a good few weeks to recover and she had a scar on her nose afterwards. But she seemed most upset about not being able to alert my Dad when it had happened and that he had panicked on what to do for the best, getting her to hospital and that. I sensed that something had shifted between them that day. I couldn't explain it but there was a sort of distance in how they were being with each other. To me it highlighted the difference between their upbringings, she was a farm girl and you just got on with stuff and 'managed'- his family were more artistic and posh, all about the drama. Neither one is better than the other but I'm definitely glad that I'd grown up on the farm with the 'just get it done' temperament. It reminded me that I needed to get hold of my mental stuff and just 'get on' with life.

The Prozac has really zonked me out this time, I've become a bit of a robot. My emotions have seemed to level out at one midway frequency, they don't fluctuate up or down; I'm just monotone. I am not excited or anxious, happy or miserable - just one abstract frame of mind, blank but full…beige. I don't eat much but I'm not making myself sick, I can't be bothered. Work is fine I just plan out lists and list of tasks and tick them off one by one, regimented. I'm present in the moment but not totally engaged no spark. I can pretend quite well, I'm able to fake the appropriate emotional response to a story in the canteen, smile at the right time. It is just a mask; underneath I'm just a generic, beige, plastic mannequin. You know when you're really tired and cannot force yourself to be enthusiastic about something or be arsed to engage in the conversation when someone starts talking to you? That's what I felt like all the time, it was an effort just to process my surroundings and act appropriately. I think that's how Prozac works it just makes you feel too exhausted to bother being crazy. I was sent an appointment to go and see a psychologist through the doctors. I had to go otherwise the doctor would know, but I couldn't decide how much of my craziness I was going to reveal to psychologist. I wanted help, to know what was wrong with me so that I could get on with my life, but I feared if I was totally honest then that might fuck my future up too.

I went to the little terraced house in town and the psychologist looked exactly how I imagined Freud to look - grey beard, glasses, suit, etc. He chatted to me about the information that the doctors had sent him, trying to build up a background about the anorexia and bulimia. In my head I was having a screaming battle with myself as to whether to tell him about Blue and the visions.

"I see things sometimes." I said. He looked up at me and stopped jotting notes.

"Well we're going to have to cover that next time, our sessions up now I'm afraid." He smiled at me, as if that was going to make everything all right. "I'm on holiday now for three weeks so we'll arrange an appointment for when I am back." I felt so rejected and yet a bit relieved that I had been cut off, I obviously wasn't supposed to be revealing the stuff about Blue to anyone - fate had taken care of that. I never did go back and see the psychologist again, kept saying my schedule at work meant I couldn't get the time off or that I was ill. The Prozac seems to be levelling things off anyway.

The only time things got a bit colourful was if I drank any alcohol - then the crazy definitely rose to the surface! I knew I wasn't supposed to mix alcohol and the medication but I didn't want anyone to know I was on it so I just drank as normal when I went out. I never drink at home so it's only on a Friday and Saturday. It's not as if I became outwardly psychotic it was just that my brain stuff all went psychedelic. Like Blue had been waiting for me to pay her some attention or be aware of her, she was still there all the time I was just not reacting or engaging with her because of the meds. The dreams were still weird and wonderful but when I woke up I just shuffled along with my day - not bothering to pay any attention to them. But when I drank they came back in to focus, I suppose it's a bit like a pain killer; it stops you 'feeling' the pain but it doesn't actually make it go away, just masks over it. I keep getting flashbacks of previous hallucinations and dreams, like I'm actually back in them. It only happens for a few seconds, almost like the opposite of a black out. The environment around me changes into the one of the flashback, all of my senses stop taking in the actual surroundings like tuning through channels in a radio. Then the next moment I'm back in the room. I know when I think of a memory I can picture it in my head but this is different, my present moment switches off and the memory takes over all of my senses. It happened to me just before Christmas when I was driving for the first time alone in the snow at night. The road was deserted but suddenly I was back in that hallucination when the headlights turned in to motorbikes with scary beings riding them past me. There weren't even any real headlights that were 'feeding' this hallucination so they sped past me and took off and flew up all around me. Last time I was a passenger but this time I was the driver. I must have just grazed the bank of snow on the verge of the road and it sent me spinning around on the road. I seemed to take ages and I tried to steer out of it but just crashed into a rickety fence up on the side of the road, stalling the car as I came to a standstill. I looked out of my window and I'd come to rest at the top of a steep bank down a big field, if I had been going faster I'd have probably gone plummeting down the hill. I climbed over to the passenger side and got out to inspect the damage; I'd scratched the front wing of the car and ripped the bumper off. I picked it up and put it in the boot. I started the car and wiggled the steering to dislodge myself from the verge and trundled home really carefully. My parents were not impressed when they saw the damage in the morning, but organised for it to be taken to the garage and gave me a lift to work. It took a few days to fix but came back good as new - only my bank account was left with a big dent in it.

My older brother Simon was home from university for the holidays and for Christmas Eve he and my Dad were going to midnight mass so I got dropped off in town to go out with Ella to the pub. They said they'd give me a call when they were heading back home and give me a lift. The pub was packed and it was a really nice atmosphere everyone out enjoying themselves. There was a guy there called Aaron who had lived on the same housing estate as me when we lived in town and he kept looking at me and smiling. He'd grown up to be a handsome man, blonde hair and muscly body. We just kept on catching each other's' eyes - flirting from a distance. Ella wasn't staying out long as she'd been at work all day and really tired so I was left there by myself and carried on drinking. Aaron eventually came and spoke to me and asked if I wanted to go for a walk outside. We went for a walk along the riverbank and ended up kissing, it was so odd to be kissing a guy who I'd known from when I was 12 years old - he was just home from uni for the holidays and said that no-one knew that he liked guys. It was fun, kissing in the Christmas snow. I realised that it had got late and there had been no call from my brother or Dad. I called them but there was no answer. There were no taxis running this late on Christmas Eve, I didn't even think of walking to Pete and Ally's house. I walked home, eight miles with the snow falling; along the road and across the fields. It was such an odd experience the snow on the fields was really spooky in the moonlight. It took me hours and when I finally got to my little caravan the key snapped off in the lock; I had to prize a window open and climb in. Pete and Ally came round early in the morning with Beth for her first Christmas - there's a photo of us all that morning and I look like a corpse. Nobody ever asked how I got home, I didn't tell them that I'd walked home because I was busy snogging Aaron either.

Everyone is excited about the start of a new millennium; customers at work have been stock piling food because they believe all this stuff about Y2K. Apparently all the computers are going to break because their clocks will reset to zero - or something along those lines; so we'll be plunged back in to the dark ages. I've been nominated at work to be the person who has to go in during the early hours to run checks on the systems and liaise with head office if there are any problems and bug fix. Suits me fine as I'm going out in town and all the pubs are putting on massive parties I'll just hang around and sober up then go in and follow the procedure they've sent me to do. I just basically have to call HQ and then test all of the systems are working one by one and follow this handbook they've sent out for it. I hadn't actually thought what I would do if the bug did happen and everything fails?

So I went out with everyone from work, Ella was working at the Hotel. We had an amazing night, at midnight everyone gathered in front of the Market House on the centre of town and some idiot climbed the Christmas tree and fell off of it. Everyone carried on partying until bout 4a.m - this time another guy kept chatting me up - I didn't know him that well because he went to school in town and I went to Hereford but my mates said they reckoned he was gay. When everyone was piling out of the club at the end of the night he asked me if I wanted to go for a walk. We went up to the graveyard - there were quite a few people up there mucking around and he was really nervous that someone would see that we were two guys and we'd get beaten up. We found a dark corner and mucked around kissing and stuff; I thought it was such a weird place to choose because of all the graves and tombstones. There is all this death and a massive old church, the decay of all that seemed strange compared to all these couples being very alive and fleshy and passionate. To be honest he wasn't a very good kisser and it was all just a bit awkward. We walked back down in to town and I decided to go and sleep on the benches in the shopping centre for a couple of hours until I needed to let myself in to the supermarket. It was freezing so I risked it and opened up the shutters and disabled the alarm and locked myself in so that I could go up to my office and wait for the cue to do the bug test. HQ phoned in to ask why the alarm had been deactivated and I explained so they just told me to do start the testing then. It took absolutely ages and was really dull, eventually the staff were arriving to start work and we all laughed that nothing had happened at all with the whole Millennium Bug thing.

Needless to say I had the flu for a couple of weeks - probably too much time spent out in the cold! So by the time our birthday came round on the 11th I felt really rough. People are supposed to be excited about turning 21 and have big parties. At work it was a whole store stock take which meant a 12 hour work day counting very single item in the store, everyone hated stock takes. Nobody was allowed a day off to avoid them. Pete just wanted to have a Chinese takeaway round at his house to celebrate - so that was our 21st - a day of boring stock taking, the flu and sweet'n'sour!

"Well I suppose that's what some birthdays are about, taking stock of the sweet and the sour?" Adonai laughed. "Come on let's have another swim and cool down from this sun. You said that you have a good memory so tell me the next bit without the notes."

"Okay, yeah I can do." We stretched our legs and paddled into the sea.

Being 21 2000/2001

Well I suppose it was quite funny on my 21st all I was worried about was what was going on in my head but on my 22nd birthday all that I was obsessing about was what was going on in someone else's head - Dylan.

"Oh there's a guy? The first love?"

"Hmm, yeah or at least I thought it was love at the time."

"Where did you meet him?"

"At university."

"Ah, okay - back up how did you get from the supermarket office job to university?"

"Ha ha, well I'll start back on my 21st then."

"Yes please, this story is complicated enough!"

Well a couple of weeks after my birthday I had recovered from the flu and decided to have a belated night out to celebrate with my mates. I'd organised to stay at a friend's house in town so that I didn't drive, so I just left my car at work. We went out doing karaoke, drinking games and dancing. Come the end of the night we couldn't be arsed to walk to his house so I said I'd drive the short way to save us time. Well I got stopped by the police, arrested and done for drink driving. Idiot. The court date wasn't for a few weeks so I didn't tell my parents just in case I got off with just a fine or something. I told Ally and she said she'd come with me to court. I arrived home from work one day and my parents were really annoyed with me because the Sergeant had rung up to remind me when the court date was - I was totally busted. I got a fine and banned from driving for a year. My parents made use of my car and made me ride a bike to work for a few weeks as punishment; it was like a 20 mile round trip on a major B road; terrifying and exhausting. I was too embarrassed to say to people what had happened and instead just said I wasn't allowed to drive because of my medication. It was less embarrassing to admit that I was on meds than I was an idiotic drink driver. Eventually my parents started giving me a lift in to work and I'd catch a bus home afterwards.

On Friday nights Mum would give me a lift in to see Ella and then Ella would give me a lift back to the farm. Mum had started going out playing pool with one of our family friends Barry and even went to the pub. I remember her coming up to me and being really surprised how nice people were in the pub. Up until then her social life had just been church, she was just a wife or mother and she was amazed that people chatted to her and wanted to get to know *her* as a person. Dad went with her to play pool a few times but I don't think he really liked going out socialising in that environment. It made me laugh a bit because they'd always been really down on me for going out and suddenly, once she'd experienced it for herself, it was like the best thing ever. It was as if she saw me in a new light because I'd stuck to my guns and built a social life and now I was the only person that she could talk to about it. It was one of those moments where you stop seeing someone just as your mother but begin to understand that she's also a woman. I don't know what she was like when she was my age. I know she worked in a bakery and then in the Shire Hall in Gloucester, but I've got no idea about that period of her life or what she was like before she met my Dad. I can't imagine how difficult it must have been to be a mother to 3 boys under the age of 3 by the time she was 26. She had been a housewife all this time and now she has suddenly had a glimpse of the world outside of the family and outside of church. Us kids are all grown up and leaving home, she must be wondering what happens next? Dad works all the hours of the day to pay the bills and her life has been about looking after us all. What happens when that all changes and there is no-one who needs looking after? It's that whole 'empty nest' thing.

Talking of nesting I started thinking about the future and what was important to me. Ella was such an amazing person, the best person I had ever met and I loved spending time with her. I said to her one night when we were out that I wished we could just get married like in the film 'Natural Born Killers' where they just make a promise to each other to stick by each other and face the world. She hugged me and said that was an amazing idea. I know she cares about me a lot and I think she's amazing. I said to Leo about it and from there it got a bit out of hand that he thought we were properly getting married. I just went along with it, I guess I wanted it to be true and for me to be normal and have a normal life. We went off for the day to Cardiff and I got us matching rings to wear to signify our bond, but everyone else thought we were really married. It was one of those white lies that just gets out of hand - in a parallel universe I had met the perfect girl who I wanted to spend the rest of my life being close to; but the reality was that I saw her as this sacred untouchable girl - a bit like Blue I suppose. I wish that I could have just crossed that line with her but I knew deep down that I liked guys and so did she. Having the perfect woman in my life and knowing that it wouldn't be right and honest just showed me that the issue was just about the gender not the person - I needed to admit to myself that I was gay.

We applied to the same universities; I applied to study psychology or sociology depending on which uni would offer me a place. It ended up that she got offered a place at Birmingham and I got in to University of Nottingham to study Sociology. At least they weren't too far away from each other, we'd be able to visit each other and catch up in the holidays. It felt good to have a goal, going off to university where nobody would know me, I could start over afresh; I just needed to get my head right before I went. We booked up to go to Reading festival at the end of the summer just before we headed off to uni; there was lots to look forward to. At work they moved me on to running the delicatessen so that they could train someone else up to take over from me in Systems Management. It was a really good feeling to be doing something simple that I knew so well from working on there before and that the next step into the future was already planned out. I could just buckle down and enjoy the summer and get sorted for leaving. The university had sent me a load of information and brochures, I just kept reading them over again and again; imagining myself there, being a student. I had no idea what I would do with Sociology in terms of a career; I hadn't studied at A level. One of the youth leaders at church had been a social worker who had to look after Fred and Rose West's children after all that happened. I remember her saying how stressful it was but rewarding. I don't know if I'm cut out to be a social worker, but I hoped that I would just find a path that interested me and it would all roll-out in front of me. For now I just focussed on enjoying the summer and making the most of it, I figured if I did a lot of stuff that I enjoyed and just relaxed then I could wean myself off the meds in time for uni.

We moved in to the Barn and the caravans got taken away, it was quite odd sleeping in the barn that we used to round the cows up into or jump around in the hay stack. Now it's our home, it's all done out nicely, five bedrooms, 3 bathrooms, big lounge, kitchen and dining room; my parents' dream house. They still don't seem to be getting on very well; I suppose it's noticeable to me because I'm the only kid left at home. Dad spends most of his time working in his office and they seem to be sleeping in different bedrooms now; I don't know whether it's because he works 'til late or what. They put on a good show when Pete and Ally come over with Bethany or in front of other people but when it's just us you can tell there's a distance. They had a big house warming party and at the same time celebrated their 25th Wedding Anniversary, so all the family came to the farm. It was odd seeing the posh Ayrton side of the family on the farm, just didn't seem to fit. Simon has joined a Christian rock band playing guitar and they've recorded an album so everyone was chatting about that and cooing over Bethany. The funniest part of the day for me was Nerys my cousin who has Down syndrome going to the buffet that my Mum and I had made and taking the serving plates off so that she had all the sausage rolls or all the sandwiches, etc. She put up a fight when people kept trying to get her to give up her stash.

After work I'd go down to the meadows by the river where everyone meets up and sunbathes and play football and all that; meeting up with whichever mates were free to just hang around. It felt like the last summer where I'd be able to do that without any responsibilities. It was a really nice time. Work was easy, my head was more or less okay - the dreams and Blue were still there but I just concentrated on relaxing. Just as I thought everything was going alright I developed an embarrassing problem. I had piles.

"Ahaha! Haemorrhoids? Oh no!" Adonai clapped his hands over his face.

Well I went t the chemist and got cream and for weeks they just kept getting more and more painful, it was excruciating to go to the toilet. In the end I had to face my embarrassment and go to the doctors to see if they could do anything. It was mortifying having to show my bum to the doctor. He asked me if I'd ever had homosexual sex and I just said no, but could feel that I'd gone bright red. He told me that they weren't piles but warts and I'd need to have an operation under general anaesthetic to have them removed. I wanted the ground to swallow me up. It was too long ago for them to be from London so it must have been that bloke in the park rubbing himself up against me. I felt disgusting. He prescribed some painkillers and this horrible laxative stuff I had to drink. The hospital appointment was a few weeks later and I told my Mum they were just piles that were being removed - there was no way I was telling her what had really happened. I remember having to take off my earrings and tongue stud and giving them to my Mum to look after. I had to walk all through the hospital with one of those gowns on that exposes your naked backside, in my trainers carrying a pillow to get from the outpatient bit to the anaesthetists room. I'd had general anaesthetic when I was a kid and if anything I was fascinated by watching the needle be put in and feel the cold liquid going in to my veins. I wondered if I would dream and if Blue would be there. Above the bed was this olde worlde painting up on the ceiling of a landscape that you looked at while you counted down and 'went to sleep'. I stared at it half expecting a hallucination to kick off.

Waking up from the anaesthetic was really weird; I didn't feel like I had dreamed or like any time had passed at all. I just felt really groggy. My Mum had stayed and waited for me. The nurse offered me something to eat and drink and then kept asking me if I needed to go for a wee. Eventually I did and it was pretty painful to walk, when I returned to the bed she said I could leave now as I was well enough to get up and go to the loo. The doctor came round and said that they hadn't managed to get all of them so I would need another operation in a few weeks' time. They gave me morphine tablets for the pain. In the car on the way home my Mum let me smoke a cigarette out of the window; she must have felt sorry for me. The morphine tablets were really trippy. The second operation fell on the day before Ella and I were going off to Reading festival and my Mum was telling me that I shouldn't go. I said I would see how I feel, but I was determined to go!

This time when they were giving me the anaesthetic they couldn't get the needle in me and when they did and I counted down nothing happened, I didn't go under. I thought it was really funny and they just kept staring at me wondering what to do, so they took that needle out and tried the other arm and I counted down again all the way to zero but just as they looked like they were starting to panic I zonked out. My Mum hadn't waited for me this time and said for me to call them when I was discharged. When I woke up I remembered the routine from last time so I quickly asked for something to eat and drink and smuggled my mobile in to the toilet with me when I went for a wee and phoned home. My Mum was surprised that I was up and about so quickly. I dosed myself up with morphine and when I got home packed for the festival saying that I felt fine and really wanted to go.

"I'm sorry I can't stop laughing!" Adonai was

actually wiping the tears from his eyes in fits of giggles.

"Well you did ask for the full story - warts and all!"

"Stop it; I'm going to piss myself!"

I was still wearing the bandaged up nappy dressing that the hospital had put on me, carrying my big rucksack from travelling to Oz with a tent in it. Ella's rucksack was nearly as big as her. We caught the train in Gloucester down to Reading. It was really uncomfortable sitting for all that time. There were crowds of people all in procession from the station all the way through the town to the festival site, a sea of people and we just shuffled along with the tide. Everyone was in really high spirits and I hadn't really been in a crowd of that scale before - it was amazing to see the thousands of tents, a little city pitching itself up ready for the music. There were food carts, stalls selling stuff, a fairground and bars. We had a brilliant time, I'm sure I wasn't supposed to mix morphine, Prozac and lager but it was proper psychedelic. Even being that high though it was till excruciatingly painful when I had to go in to a skanky portaloo, peel off the bandage nappy and go to the toilet; I have never, ever felt a pain like that before or since. But the atmosphere was electric, the bands were phenomenal, just a great experience. We got in the mosh pit for Slipknot and Rage against the Machine; saw Queens of the Stone Age, watched Daphne and Celeste get pelted with bottles of piss, Ian Brown, Tom Jones with the Stereophonics, loads and loads of bands. I even saw

Davina McCall filming 'Streetmate' right next to me - I was really spaced out clinging on to my paper cup pint of lager concentrating on standing when I recognised this voice and turned around to see her with a camera crew behind her talking to the people next to me, random. On the last night there was a massive party/riot and all the portaloos got set on fire, it was pretty spectacular. By the time we got back home I just collapsed in a smelly heap and slept for a day.

Nanna and Poppa called round on a tour of all the family. She was typically frost with me, but pleased that I was going to a good university. They just stayed for lunch then set off to Wales to see other family then were going to the Isle of Man to stay with my Auntie at the end of the 'tour'. There wasn't any particular reason for them coming around seeing everyone, the just didn't have anything much to do I suppose. But it ended up being freaky that they had done because as they were walking the dogs on the beach in the Isle of Man, having just finished seeing all of the family; Poppa was chatting away to her and when she didn't reply he turned round and Nanna was collapsed. She had an aneurysm in her brain and died a few days later. We all went down to Plymouth and there was a massive funeral. It felt weird because I didn't like her, but I felt sorry for Poppa and the rest of the family. My Mum was really struggling because funerals remind her of when her sister died. Auntie Jen was 27 when she died, she'd just given birth to a baby girl and died a few days later. It was such a shock and tragedy, her leaving 3 young children and husband at such a young age herself. Everything changed on the farm -

Grandma and Grampy have never got over it - how would you? The priest at Nanna's funeral spoke about how earlier he had done a funeral of a young man who had committed suicide. He talked about how selfish the young man was and what a waste of life and how terrible to hurt his family, etc. I got really angry and upset at that, thinking about Tom and also about myself - that priest has no idea what caused that person to end his life, how dare he judge and condemn them. And if you go by the gospels' version of Jesus' life you could argue that he had a choice whether to die or not. In the garden of Gethsemane he begs God to let him off being killed, gets told to crack on and then knowingly goes to his death - how's that different to suicide? Is smoking or drinking or eating food that you know is harming your health and eventually causes you death a kind of slow suicide? I personally think that people commit suicide because they have got to a point where they don't think they can get through another day. They must have despaired over the pain they know that they would be causing their loved ones and that guilt probably made them feel even worse. I know when I slit my wrist that I felt a sense of terror at how that would've affected the people around me. Some people just need support and help and therapy to teach them that they can get through another day and get stronger.

Talking of learning - soon enough it was time to go to university. I had managed to dwindle myself down on the meds and would stop taking them completely when I left; I figured that there would be enough to keep me occupied and concentrate on that my brain would just tire itself out. I'd go back to work at the supermarket during the holidays like the other students do, so it wasn't goodbye forever just a few months. I was really looking forward to the new scenery, new people, and new challenge. Nobody would know me or about my past, I could start over. I would miss Ella and my family but I really needed this. Because I was 21 I was classed as a mature student, I'd be staying in Halls of Residence for the first year where most of the other people would be 18 year olds coming straight out of doing A levels. I chose Ancaster Hall where you had the option to be half board, you had an evening meal every night in the canteen but the other meals you sorted out yourself. The campus was absolutely massive with parkland and lakes and spectacular old buildings, breath-taking. Although I was kind of nervous moving in on the first day I figured that everyone was in the same position. Everybody had their parents helping them carry all their belongings and find their room. It was fun, being in the same boat as everyone else for once. Ancaster Hall was right on the edge of the campus and just by chance my room was the closest one to the edge of the Halls too - I was tucked away as far as possible, I liked it. Once the parents had all said their goodbyes everybody started to slowly venture out of their rooms and say tentative hellos to each other and introduce themselves. The other guys in my corridor were mostly Middle Eastern but right next door to me was a guy called Sam who was studying Spanish. We set off together to explore and meet other people. Each Hall has a little bar of its own so most people congregate in there first getting relaxed and sizing each other up. One of the first people I met was Jon, a really cool rocker who was wearing a Limp Bizkit band tee, he even looks like Fred Durst We hit it off right away and spent ages talking about bands and music in general.

Freshers Week was absolutely crazy. There were fancy dress parties every night in different Halls of Residence or we'd get piled on a bus and taken to a club in the city. Me, Jon and Sam stuck together, ate meals together and went to all the parties together. Sam is a devout Christian so he doesn't drink but he's the nicest, mellowest person - he looks like he should be a surfer. I suppose the mad parties are so we all get drunk, have fun and get to know each other - I loved it. Nottingham city looked really exciting and it was really random all of us moving round as a group but not knowing each other. They set up ice breaker drinking games, 5 legged bar crawls, strawpedo competitions, all sorts; lots of alcohol and dancing. The nightclubs were massive, totally different from the cheesy one in my hometown. The parties were loads of fun and we started to get to know who was from the same Halls of Residence, started to recognise each other. I snogged a guy in one of the clubs; he was a fresher too but from Nottingham and said there was a gay scene in the city. I was intrigued at the opportunity to meet guys and explore that side of stuff finally. At the Freshers Fair I kept wandering past the LGBT Society's table plucking up the courage to get some information, I picked some leaflets on safe sex and 'coming out'. A few people asked me if I was gay and I said I wasn't, I hadn't really worked that all out yet.

We had our orientations for or subjects. I noticed on the orientation day for Sociology which was dotted around the other side of the campus that there was a girl from my Halls that was doing Sociology as well. She was really beautiful, tall and Italian looking with long straight dark hair. From the roll calls at the meetings I knew she was called Stella. It was funny watching all the guys trying to chat her up. In Sociology it was mostly girls but the handful of guys were all subtly congregating around her. We kept catching each other's eyes and smiling. The last meeting of the day was to meet our tutor in a little group of 20 or so students and funnily enough we were in that group together too. After the session she came over to me and asked if I wanted to go for a coffee. We went to the student union and sat and chatted for a while. Then she suddenly put her head in her hands and said that she needed to confide in someone. She asked me if I minded but she really needed someone to talk to and by the way I had held myself all day she felt drawn to me. She explained that she had a boyfriend and he didn't really want her coming to uni but they were still together and he was coming down at the weekend to visit her. The problem was that she thought she might be pregnant and didn't know what to do about it. She burst out crying and I just hugged her and tried to comfort her. It was so random, having such an intimate conversation, someone allowing themselves to be vulnerable when she doesn't know me at all. I said to her that the only thing we can do is find out the facts, we need to go and get a test kit from the chemist and find out for sure if she's pregnant and then when she knew the situation she could work out what to do next. She settled down a bit and thanked me for helping her; we got our campus maps out and made our way to find the chemist. I said to her I would go in and get the kit if she didn't want the people who worked there to know that it was for her in case she ever needed to go back there again. She was so grateful. We made our way back to the Hall arm in arm; I could tell she needed someone to lean on. I've got to say it felt good to be helping someone and that she had looked at me and not seen a crazy person but someone who she trusted enough to have this conversation. It reassured me that even with all my mental stuff that I've been through it hasn't left an obvious air of lunatic. She asked me if I'd come up and wait in her room whilst she did the test, she just wanted to get it done quickly and to know. Much to her relief, after a nervous wait the test showed up negative. From that moment on we were good friends. All the guys seemed to look at me as if they were wondering how come me and her were so close so quickly. She decided not to tell her boyfriend about the 'scare'. Luckily there were still more parties for her to enjoy and she got really drunk and danced and I could see the weight lifting off of her.

For the first term of Sociology we had to choose two modules from other departments to make up our quota, I had chosen Developmental Psychology and Philosophy. When I went to the Philosophy orientation we were split down in to our study groups; I was shocked to find out that one of my best friends from Secondary School and College was my tutor! I hadn't even remembered that he had come to Nottingham or done Philosophy. By some humongous coincidence I had picked that module out f hundreds available to me and then also been randomly put into that group that he was tutoring. He came walking up to me in the lecture hall when the orientation had finished and he was just as shocked as I was. He just told me not to let on that we knew each other, hilarious -how fate works. I really enjoyed the mix of Sociology, Psychology and Philosophy; it suited me right down to the ground. I settled in to studying and partying and really enjoyed it all. After a few weeks I got to know all the different groups of people in the Halls; going out on nights out with them all. One night it'd be with the girls to Oceana for a pop night, another would be to Rock City for live bands and heavy music; different nights different clubs, different crowds. There was this tradition of doing a pub crawl of all the bars on campus - The Campus 18. You start in your own Hall bar and drink one drink in every bar ending up in The Ark, the student union bar in the centre of the campus. It was proper messy because most people would drink a cheap pint of lager so it ended up being 18 pints of lager. We'd order late night takeaways that got delivered to the Hall, classic student diet of alcohol and junk food. At the weekend Stella, Jon and me would catch a bus into the city and explore. I know such a big group of people from going out on different nights out that I'm hardly ever by myself, it's such a change - reminds me a bit of life in the Lad Pad. It's boosted my confidence because I realise that I must be an alright person because I get along with all these people and they actually want t hang out with me. I have my moments with hallucinations and dreams but I've filled my life up so much that they don't have room to breathe or take root. What with lectures, exploring the city and socialising I am on the go most of the time. My life back at home seems so far removed from this one. My Mum and I write to each other all the time and she send me vouchers for the supermarket or for my mobile, I speak to Ally and Ella but other than that I feel like a new person. There's a big world of people out there and I've spent so much time inside of my own head, it's refreshing to turn that focus outwards.

Obviously most nights out started in the Hall bar and one of the resident students, Emma, worked behind the bar. One night she said to me that she wanted to introduce me to her friends. She took me over to a group of people who I'd seen her with before but never really spoken to. As we sat and chatted they asked me about my sexuality, saying they were all bisexual or gay. I said I hadn't really decided yet. They invited me out with them that night as the LGBT Society was going in to the city to one of the gay bars. I instantly said yes, I was so curious to see a gay bar and be in an environment where you could at least openly talk about that stuff. They were all really well dressed and kind of glamorous so I felt a bit underdressed and dorky. They said they were meeting the others at The Ark so we walked off up there. As we walked along everyone was ribbing me that they had wondered whether I was gay or not and a few of the guys had been asking around if anyone knew me. I started to feel nervous, but just decided to go with the flow. I'd never really talked to any openly gay people before; it was all so new to me; kind of weird to be able to talk about it out loud I suppose. One of the girls called Maya was really beautiful, I'd noticed her around the Hall, she always looked perfectly dressed and made up like she was a model who'd just stepped out of a magazine. She wrapped her arm in mine as we walked.

"It's okay I'm a token straight girl, although I think I would try being bi, I just like hanging out with these guys they're a nicer crowd than the hormonal blokes or the girly-girls. You'll see." She whispered in to my ear. I laughed and thanked her, knowing she was just trying to make me feel comfortable. It's funny how walking in to a new bar is so much more comfortable in a group or with someone on your arm. It's almost as if people feel better if they are in context to something - must be the Sociologist coming out in me. I don't mind going out by myself, maybe because of all the hallucinations and Blue, I'm used to putting up a façade of 'confidence' to cover it all up. At The Ark we met up with a group of about 15 people mostly guys, you could tell they were gay, I don't know what it is but you could just see it. Maybe just because they were all herded together, if you scattered them up in amongst a crowd perhaps I wouldn't notice. We had a drink there and then caught taxis into the city to a pub called The Mill. It looked like a normal pub; I don't know what I was expecting. I had watched 'Queer As Folk' on the telly so maybe I was expecting a high octane atmosphere. It was a weeknight so it was pretty quiet but it just felt really comfortable being there with a group of people who it was okay to just chill out with. Maya introduced me to everyone and chaperoned me really. We got chatting, she was studying Art History and her family are Wiccan. I was fascinated; I didn't know anything about Wicca or all that New Age stuff. She said that the women in her family were all white witches. I was really interested to find out about magic and all that but we got cut off by the leader of the LGBT Society coming over and chatting to me. He sat down and started pointing out who all the guys were and who was going out with who. He waved a one of them to come over so he could introduce us. He was really cute, he looked exactly like Del Marquis from the Scissor Sisters, his name was Dylan. We got left alone to chat. He was studying music. We just made small talk but it was obvious that we liked each other. He said he'd just split up with a guy called Steve who was a Fresher too, we swapped numbers and he said he'd like to go out for a drink sometime.

We all headed back to campus and he text me to say it was nice meeting and invited me out with all his music course friends the next night. They were quite a high brow bunch but I really enjoyed myself and at the end of the night we kissed. We went out loads and got to know each other properly. It was fun going out to the all the clubs that I'd been going out to before but with a guy as my 'date'. We'd drink and dance together but not kiss or touch in the straight clubs; we'd just kiss at the end of the night when I walked him home. We mucked about a bit physically in his room but didn't go 'all the way'. It was really nice having a boyfriend, and being introduced as his boyfriend. I still wasn't out in general but my close friends new that me and Dylan were together. I felt really happy and comfortable. Soon it was time for the Christmas holidays and it felt so odd going back to the farm, going to work in the supermarket but having a boyfriend. I had put a bit of weight on during the term, too much beer and takeaway pizza so I decided in the 5 week holiday at home I'd lose weight and give myself a makeover. I borrowed my Dad's rowing machine and worked out every day. I got a bit silly with food though - the bulimia/anorexia kicked back in. I was just eating a bowl of cereal in the morning, an apple and black coffee at work, then at night I'd eat a meal and throw it up before working out on the rowing machine before going to bed. I went out with Ella on Friday nights and told her about Dylan, she wasn't surprised that I was seeing a guy. She was really enjoying Birmingham and we both were in really good places in our lives.

Disaster struck on Christmas Eve, Dylan hadn't replied to a couple of texts and when I was at work I got a message from him saying that he wanted to break it off because he had been spending time with Steve during the holidays and thought he still had feelings for him. I felt like I'd been punched in the stomach, really gutted. I took it out on myself by working out harder; I became obsessed about losing as much weight as possible before I got back to uni. I even threw up after Christmas Dinner. Anything that I ate I just had to get rid of again and work out as hard as possible. I just shut myself away in my room and listened to the Garbage album 'Version 2.0' over and over again. By New Years Eve I was in a proper hole. I stayed in my room with a bottle of red wine watching Jools Holland on my little black and white telly. I had all these emotions that I wanted to vent and stupidly I decided to start cutting myself. I took a razor apart and cut myself on my torso and thighs, I knew it was ridiculous and pointless. But the stupidity of lapsing back in to disordered eating habits, self-harming and all that just made me feel even more pathetic and I took that out on myself too.

By the time I headed back to uni I looked like a completely different person, I'd cut my hair and lost a load of weight. I'd bought a bunch of new clothes and basically had a new identity. I also took loads of stuff to decorate my room with. I hung up a tie-dyed bed sheet on the wall and made posters out of magazine cuttings and took my little optic fibre lamp which shone psychedelic lights rotating all over the room. There was a new me and a new environment for me to nest in. When I stood in the Hall bar that first night some of my close friends didn't even recognise me because of the weight loss and new image. It was almost as if they were seeing a different person than the one from last term. It was my birthday the next day and I invited everyone to come out with me to my favourite club - Rock City. Dylan had text me a couple of times to say he hoped I was alright and that we could stay friends so I had invited him out for my birthday too. My mates knew that he had dumped me but I still had feelings for him and wanted to see him. Everyone had congregated in my room to have drinks before heading in to town when he turned up. It was so strange seeing him for the first time since with everyone else there, but good in a way because it was a bit of a buffer. When we all started to head off to town he hung behind and it was just me and him in my room.

"Where have you gone? You've lost like half of yourself? Are you okay?"

"Yeah I'm fine, just fancied a bit of a revamp."

"Is it alright me being here tonight? I don't want to get in the way, but I do want to still be friends. I'm sorry about what happened." He started telling me how Steve had been calling him and missed him and wanted to see him. I tried to zone out, just nod and smile, be cool. Luckily Stella and Jon came in just at the right time with a card and a present for me which was Mansun's new album. We headed off and had a great, wild night at Rock City. Dylan sidled up to me at the end of the night and asked me if it was okay if he stayed with me that night because he just wanted to be close to me. So we slept in the same bed that night, nothing happened it was just nice not to be alone, even if it was him who had hurt me in the first place. That was my 22ND birthday.

Being 22: 2001/2002

Well on the Saturday after my birthday I had a proper

party with fancy dress theme of Heroes and Villains and we all dressed up and did the campus 18 pub crawl. I dressed as a Goth version of Neo from The Matrix. Some friends just made up superpowers, Stella was an angel, Jon was Superman, Maya was Lara Croft carrying a toy machine gun. We had a great time and it was odd having a birthday on my own rather than with Pete. By the time we got to the student union we were all wasted. Maya suggested we got to the gay club in town, we'd heard of it but never actually got to go there yet. No-one else was up for it so just me and her jumped in a taxi and headed to NG1. It was named after the postcode. There was a big queue of people waiting to get in and we soon got chatting to people and Maya kept 'shooting' people who she thought were cute with her gun. When we got to the door the bouncers wouldn't let her take the gun in so we left it with the cloakroom attendant. We were both amazed at how busy it was and what a great atmosphere it had. We'd never seen that many gay people all in one place before! The music was hyper pop and the dance floor was packed. We had a great time, both of us ended up snogging people and meeting loads of new people. In the taxi home we just laughed and said what an amazing night out - like no other we'd had before, we were hooked.

So this year was really about furthering my spiritual exploration, the spirit being Vodka or Malibu and the exploration being of the gay scene and nightlife.

"Ha ha, I thought you were serious then for a minute - you'd found God or something?" Adonai chirped up.

Well I had found a new religion and a new church to attend. I'd swapped the stain glassed windows and candles for strobe lights and dry ice, the pews for bar stools and hymns for pop anthems. Worship happened on a Saturday night and all you needed was to look good and dance. Everybody was welcome whether they were boy or girl, gay or straight, young or old; you just had to want to have a good time to be able to fit in. I still went to Rock City for the music I really liked but every Saturday night I'd go to NG1. I hooked up with guys and had a load of one night stands just jumped on in off the deep end. It was really new to me that guys were paying me attention and chatting me up, I'd never thought of myself as attractive; I think it's just because I look all rock'n'roll because of my style rather than all other guys who are wearing labels and posing. Everyone makes such an effort with their clothes and appearance; it's a bit of a culture shock. I started to have a look in high street shops rather than the grungy thrift shops and vintage stores I normally shopped in, just to see if there was anything that was near to my style. I got a few new tee-shirts and 'going out' clothes. Up until now I'd just worn my everyday clothes out, it felt nice to dress up to go out; it made it more of an event. I'd get ready in my room with my music on full blast and then catch a bus into town and go out by myself. The bar next door to NG1 was really cool as well, it was where most people drank before heading in to the club, it was called @d2 apparently because it was originally called The Admiral Duncan and when they'd modernised it they had renamed it. It was all glamorous inside - white leather booths, hardwood floors, big tropical flower arrangements and space age mood lighting. There was a small dance floor and then booths all up one side opposite the bar; then up a corridor there was a modular seating area and unisex toilets. It was really funky and a nice crowd of people. The bar staff all wore lilac shirts to match the walls. Once everyone piled in to the club next door the bar would close and the staff comes in to the club to party. They were treated like celebrities and danced on the stage together doing routines and showing off. I hung around on the side-lines by myself most weeks, waiting to hook up with someone, edging closer to the dance floor as the night went on and going home with someone when the lights came up. I was sort of collecting men, different nationalities and styles; I wanted to try them all.

I'd still go out with my friends on other nights but I'd always end up in NG1 on a Saturday night, to explore my sexuality and try a new man. I wasn't really that interested in having a relationship just in sex, in that initial meeting someone new and getting intimate. A lot of the guys are like that, they're well versed in the routine of waking up on a Sunday with a guy and choreographed in untangling themselves and making a polite exit back to their normal distance. It's just as much of a sequence dance as they all do on stage in the club on Saturday night. Big fish, little fish, cardboard box. They seem to all dress the same, do their hair the same, smell the same and live to the same pattern. It is like someone designed a prototype gay guy and then everyone decided to look like clones. I like going to Rock City as the antidote to that - loud rock music that you can't dance to unless you've been to a gig and everyone is messy and doesn't care about their appearance. It seems that a few people must've thought that way because I started to pull guys in Rock City too.

University was going fine, studying was all going okay. I still had no idea what I wanted to do with it afterwards and nothing was popping out at me and drawing my interest. I still hung out with Dylan even though he was back with Steve, we just all got on with it and went out on nights out. It seems to be a part of gay life - you can have an intimate relationship with someone and then remain friends afterwards, it's kind of nice. I don't look at Dylan and think that I still want to be with him, it's good to not lose someone from your life completely just because a romantic relationship didn't work out. Although I had now accepted that I was gay I hadn't really announced it to anyone else. I wasn't hiding it, it just seemed like an odd thing to need to do, proclaiming that I was homosexual. If it came up in conversation I'd tackle it then. My mates know that I sleep with guys and they're all fine with it. There doesn't seem any point telling my parents until there is actually something to tell them. Saying to them that I am attracted to men or am sleeping with men seems a bit pointless. I'll tell them once I'm in a relationship. Things with Dylan were over before they got that serious, my friends who are around me knew we were boyfriends and I spoke to Ella about it; but telling my family is a bit different because of all their religious stuff. I think it'd be better to tell them once I've been in a relationship for a while or living with someone, then it's about that rather than just my sexual orientation - it'd be about what makes me happy.

I went to a couple of weddings back home, one being Ally who I had worked with back at the supermarket and the other was my twin brother. It felt good to still feel like I came from somewhere and belonged somewhere. It was a bit of an odd feeling that Pete was married with a child but I was really happy for him, he was winning at life. He was doing the job that he had always wanted to do and had found someone and was getting on with things.

Well telling more people in the Halls of Residence about my sexuality came about quicker than I had anticipated. Once a month in one of the massive straight clubs they had a gay night called Revolution that was supposed to be amazing because people travelled from neighbouring cities to come to it and there were famous DJs and acts on. The crowd was said to be great and atmosphere electric. All my gay friends were going so I said that I would meet them there. One of my girl mates said she'd give me a lift into town as her parents had just bought her a car and she was taking every opportunity to drive it. Being a poor student I decided a good plan would be to get some wine from the supermarket and have a drink before I went out so that I'd save a bit of money. I go two dirt cheap bottles of wine and orange juice to mix it with just in case it tasted foul. So I had dinner and then cranked my music up and started drinking and getting ready to go out. I finished the first bottle way before I was due to go out so started on the second one, jumping round my room and dancing. I finished the second bottle. I set off to my girl mate's room and burst in excitedly, she just laughed at me and how merry I was. We set off in the corridor to go to her car and everyone was saying hi, where are you going out and I was just replying - "Gay!" at them. When my mate dropped me off in town she was slightly worried that I was so drunk already, but I said I'd be fine. She dropped me off opposite the club; I waved her off and concentrated on crossing the road. I was just stepping out when a double decker bus whooshed in front of about a foot from my head. I focussed on the little red man of the crossing and wandered over to the club when he turned green. Outside the club I started a conversation with the bouncer.

"Excuse me why do we have to pay to get in?"

"Er... everyone has to pay to get in."

"No I don't mean why do 'I' have to pay, but why does anyone have to pay. We buy drinks don't we?"

"Well it's to pay the wages of people who work here, the ticket attendant, the bar staff, DJ and all that."

"And you."

"Yes and me too."

"Well can't I just give you the money then I know your pages are weighed.?"

"Wages are paid. Yes you can." He took the money off me and handed it to the ticket attendant who stamped my hand - Revolution.

The club was packed and jumping, my friends spotted me and said there's a vodbull offer on 'til midnight so if I hurried I could get cheap drinks. I remember looking through the glass of my vodbull at the dance floor when I knocked it back. The very next thing I remember is waking up in a bed that I didn't recognise, in a room I didn't recognise. I rolled over and looked at the guy sleeping next to me, absolutely no idea who he was. I dozed for a while just waiting for him to wake up, he wasn't bad looking just not someone I'd particularly go for. I am never drinking ever again. He eventually stirred and leant over and kissed me.

"How are you feeling this morning? You were crazy last night."

"I'm okay thanks, a bit fuzzy." I laughed it off, wondering what exactly he meant by 'crazy last night'?

"Do you need a lift home to the University? I can drop you off."

"Yeah that'd be great." We dressed and he drove me over to uni and swapped numbers, he was quite smitten I think; I just felt awkward. I slept a while longer and lazed around that afternoon. Dylan text me and said they were going up to the student union if I fancied a drink or something to eat. I strolled up there and when I arrived all the guys from the Gay Society were there. Dylan grabbed me and took me to one side.

"Oh my God! Are you alright today?"

"Yeah, why?"

"You were so wasted last night, it was epic!"

"I remember getting in to Revolution but I don't remember anything after that 'til I woke up wih some random guy this morning."

"Well you started off dancing around like a maniac, on the podium and stage. Then you decided you wanted to snog people, because you kept going on about how much you like snogging and poking your tongue stud out at guys. Basically you got off with about fifty people, they were queuing up, guys, girls, everyone!"

"Fuck off - you're winding me up."

"No I'm serious and then eventually you vanished with that guy who was dressed as an angel."

"Oh God, did I upset anyone? Was I nice about it?"

"It was hilarious; you're a nice drunk, spreading the love."

Just at that moment one of the guys from the society

walked past and winked at me, asking how my head was. It was true, Dylan wasn't winding me up.

"Did I get off with anyone here?"

"Kristoff, you got off with everyone here."

"Oh my God." I wailed, burying my head in my hands. I got a drink and sat down with them and endured a whole evening of people ribbing me about the night before. I'm never drinking wine again or was it that one vodbull that sent me over the edge?

Adonai started clapping. "Well you're certainly a wild one, loco boy. You must be a good kisser if you had them queuing up when you can't even remember!"

"Yeah my autopilot seems to be pretty awesome"

I still stayed in contact with Ella and Felix by phone, he was still working in the supermarket in New Zealand and she was really enjoying Birmingham. We visited each other a couple of times to go to gigs or for nights out - it's really easy just catching a train and you're there in no time. Every time I see her it's like no time has passed. We saw each other in the Easter holidays when we were both back home. I worked in the supermarket for a few weeks then went to Bristol to meet up with Emma, Maya and their friends. Then I went back up north to Dylan's house for his birthday and met his family. Then I had a week before term started so I went and stayed with a guy who I'd been out with a couple of times that I'd met in Rock City.

He was called Billy, him and his mates had been in Rock City one night and were checking me out. To find out if a guy was gay or not they would dance up to him and offer him some poppers. I'd learned about poppers in NG1, they sell them in the gay bars - it's a little brown bottle of liquid. When you sniff them your body goes all warm and fuzzy and your head swirls but it only lasts a few minutes. People in the gay bars sniff them now and again when they're dancing, but I think they're something to do with sex in some way. So Billy and his mates used them as a test, if a guy knew what they were and sniffed them then it was a pretty safe bet that he was gay. On that night it was their girlfriend that they'd sent over to me while Billy and this other guy danced around watching what happened. I passed the poppers test and went and danced with them all, I was out with Jon and Estella and they just laughed at me that I could pull anywhere. Hazel was the name of the girl and she introduced me to Billy and his mate Ritchie who it was obvious was the one who had been keen to meet me. It was great dancing with gay guys in Rock City because it was the music I loved while dancing with the gender I fancied, win-win. Ritchie was quite 'rock' looking in a band tee and jeans, he reminded me of Billie-Joe from Green Day. Hazel had amazingly long dark hair and was dressed as Vampira, Billy was dressed all in black but had this amazing short peroxide hair. They were fun. Ritchie kept trying to make the moves on me but I was enjoying dancing with all of them rather than just trying to pull him. As the night went on Billy pulled me aside and said that Ritchie liked me but he also fancied me so it was up to me who I went home with. He was so confident; there was something about him that attracted me too. I said I wanted to go with him so we went back over to Ritchie and Hazel and Billy announced straight to their faces that he was taking me home. Ritchie just looked gutted but Billy just told him to get over it and grabbed my hand and we left.

We got a cab to his place which was in a rough part of the city called Donkey Hill. He lived in a terraced house that had been converted into two flats, his Dad lived downstairs. We stayed up drinking and watching 'Friends' on telly. He was such a nice genuine guy, totally direct and confident, I admired him a lot. He just announced things like 'I'm going to kiss you now' and leant in and did it, he was a great kisser. We had loads of fun that night. Then I didn't hear from him afterwards, I just assumed it was a one night thing until I saw him town one day. He shouted me and when I looked he was in crutches with his leg in plaster.

"Long time no see?" He grinned.

"Yeah, how have you been? Er I mean what happened to our leg?"

"No word of a lie this happened that night after you left. You know my aquarium in my bedroom? Well I was jumping around dancing and fell onto and mashed my leg up!"

"Oh my god! How long does it have to stay on?"

"Just another couple of weeks as hop along. I wanted to call you but didn't want you to seem me like this. Why didn't you call me?"

"I just thought when you hadn't called that you weren't that into me."

"What are we like? Yeah I like ya, we should hang out some more. Give. Me. A. Call" He laughed. I did call him and we did hang out more. We were kind of friends who fancied each other and had sex, but didn't really want a relationship. So when I was up near Nottingham and had a week to spare before Uni started I went to stay with him. He's one of these bad ass characters who shows no mercy in conversation and speaks his mind yet now and again you catch a glimpse of a softer side. Like at the end of that week I said I'd take him shopping and for something to eat at the pub and he was so excited because no-one had ever taken him out for a meal before, he was treating it like his first date. He was working in a band that were trying to get signed so most of the time they just sent practising dance routines and singing. We stayed in contact and went out every now and again, he was a good friend.

Another guy who I met at Rock City was a Spanish guy called Javier. He was stunning, spoke enough English for us to understand each other with my rubbish Spanish from GCSE, it was the only subject I failed. He was a waiter in an Italian restaurant and lived with three other Spanish guys. I really wanted to learn more Spanish because I really liked the idea of spending some time there after university. But it was evident from my conversations with Javi and his friends that my Spanish was useless. We started seeing each other; he visited me at uni and loved the campus and all the old buildings. We spent loads of time together, I was really happy to be in a relationship, it felt nice to be thinking about someone and doing loads of stuff together, going on dates or out as a couple. We just got to know each other and day dream about what we wanted to do in the future and all those things. I really fell for him. Then all of a sudden he went off the radar, he'd gone to see a mate of his in another town and just stopped answering texts or calls. This went on for about a week and I was distraught. I went out to NG1 and saw him there with his friends, I asked him what was going on and he just called me to chat with him in the toilets. He just announced that he thought I was too much of a dreamer. When we'd talked about the future I'd said that I hoped one day to have a home in the city and a boyfriend, a dog and a garden with a tree in it. I didn't really mind what job I did so long as I was happy. He said I was being unrealistic and living in a fantasy land, you can't live in the city and have trees around. It was just one of those moments where someone you thought was being genuine turns out to have been pretending. I asked him why he hadn't just text me or spoken to me to break up and he said that he thought I would get the message by him not replying. I remember being really upset and going to a cubicle and crying, partly about the break up but also because of the character assassination. Then I began to think how ridiculous it was, I could imagine whatever future

I wanted and it was possible. I went back out to the bar and I remember laughing because Destiny Child's 'Survivor' was blasting out on the dance floor. Blue whispered in my ear.

"Being a dreamer is a strength not a weakness. You *are* a survivor." I just smiled and looked at Javi dancing around with his friends and realised you can fall out of love just as quickly and heavily as you fall in to it.

Blue had always been around, not talking much just floating around in the scenery. Only when I was really struggling would she come in close and say something. It was like she was a guardian angel of some sort, but a mental hallucinatory one. There had been a few weird things happen this year which made me question what I thought about her. I had a dream one night which wasn't amazingly significant in itself, one of those in which you're going about your normal environment with the people you see every day. It was set around university and the halls of residence At one point in it I was eating a meal in the dining hall when Jon and Estella came in through the exit door and Estella said to me "How are you chicken?" then Jon started singing "I feel like chicken tonight, like chicken tonight" and doing a chicken dance; with which Estella pokes him and tells him to behave. The next day was Saturday so we'd all gone off in different directions, doing shopping, cinema, laundry, all the weekend stuff. Me and some other hall friends went for dinner and noticed that Jon and Estella hadn't turned up. The kitchen is only open for a certain amount of time so if you miss it you miss the meal. Jon and Estella went rushing past but they'd missed the serving time so they came in through the exit door. As soon as I watched them come through the door I felt nauseous, remembering the dream. I hadn't thought about it since this morning but realised I was sat in the exact place and they were wearing the same clothes and coming in that door like in the dream from last night. Then they said exactly the things they'd said in the dream, it all played out 100% as it had in the dream. I just went silent, it was s odd. There wasn't anything significant about the dream, no grand meaning or message; but I had seen this small scene play out last night. I said to them about it and they just said it was spooky and laughed it off.

I decided to ask Maya about the whole 'magic' thing that her family all believed in. She explained to me that they were White Witches and did spells and readings and stuff. She showed me her Tarot cards and said that a lot of people have the potential to do magic but that they just never explore it. I was fascinated with it all, especially because of all the freaky stuff that had happened to me but felt very wary of getting more involved in it. To me, organised religion was just too misleading, myth guided and I didn't want to get sucked in to another one. I thought about it a lot and just sat in my room listening to my music, mulling things over. Then one day when Maya and I were in Beeston doing some shopping we stumbled upon a little new agey candle shop and went in to have a browse. There were two old women running the shop and it just seemed like a place with incense and candles and trinkets. The women kept watching us and as we were making to leave they came over and said that we might be interested in the other room they had out back. They led us to this curtain and pulled it open to reveal a whole other room full of stuff. Maya went in and grabbed my arm.

"It's spells and things! Look." She said excitedly as she picked up little bags of stuff. On each bag was a label saying what each spell was for - love, luck, health, all sorts of things and there were different stones and coloured candles. "It's all the things that you would need to do a spell or carry out a ceremony. It's a magic room!" I browsed around the items and to be honest was a bit weirded out that people actually made this stuff. Obviously I'd seen movies about magic and read books with witches or wizards in them, but I saw it just as fantasy. One of the old women came over to me and touched me gently on the arm.

"You have a lot of magic about you my dear, I can see it." She cooed. Maya stopped what she was doing and stared at her.

"Oh, I know - he does doesn't he?" She looked at me and smiled. I just wanted to run out of the shop. What could they see? This was just too freaky, I felt embarrassed. The lady showed me over to a bookcase and told me to take my time and look to see if anything took my fancy. There were books about magic and new age spirituality and decks of Tarot cards. Maya came over and looked with me. "You know they say that a deck of cards will call out to you if you're meant to have them." I glanced through them and stopped dead when I saw a pack that had a beautiful blonde haired woman with glowing blue skin from the blue moon that was shining on her. It totally reminded me of Blue. I had a really dizzy feeling whirring around my head and couldn't stop staring at the pack. "You should get them; it looks like they've found you." Maya whispered. As if I was in autopilot I took the cards to the cash desk and placed them down, just mesmerised by the picture. The old women gave each other a knowing glance and rung the Tarot cards through, as I handed the money over the woman held on to my hand.

"She's beautiful, hauntingly beautiful isn't she?"

"Um, yeah." I murmured.

"She suits you; I hope she helps you dear." She placed the pack in a small flowery paper bag and I quickly put them into my satchel, wanting to get them out of sight. Maya had filled a basket with loads of items from the 'other' room and I said I was going outside for a cigarette whilst she paid for her stuff. I just wanted to get some fresh air and get out of that odd environment. The magic stuff just made me feel strange. Maya emerged a few minutes later and we waved at the ladies as we walked away.

"How weird was that? We've walked past that shop loads of times and never gone in. They just said to me that they hardly ever show people the back room but there was something about both of us that compelled them to do so; they were very interested by you!"

"In what way?"

"They said that they could see this unusual aura around you."

"I don't really get all that stuff about auras and magic, my family's religious."

"Ha ha, so is mine - just a different religion."

"Yeah, I suppose so. What did they mean then?"

"They said you look like you have gifts that you haven't used yet."

"Gifts?"

"Spiritual stuff and magical things. Okay, when we get back to halls I'm going to phone my Mum and get her 'read' you, she can sense stuff even over the phone. All you have to do is to speak to her for a bit to make a connection."

"Maya, I really don't know about all this stuff."

"Don't worry, it's just a conversation, nothing more and if you don't believe in it then it won't matter will it?"

"Okay, I suppose so." Within no time we were in her room and Emma was there too, I hadn't left Maya's side so I knew that she couldn't have given any information to her mother before she rang her. Maya put her on speaker phone and we chatted for a minute just about university and what I was studying, inane questions. Then she said to Maya that she felt that she should do a Tarot reading for me over the phone. Maya explained that we'd just got back from buying some for me, a fresh pack. Her mum told me to take the cards out and shuffle them while thinking of a question that I wanted answering. As I shuffled all I could think of was Blue, who was she, what were all these hallucinations and dreams and visions? What did they mean? Maya's mum told me to spread the cards out face down in front of me and pick one that I felt drawn to then place it apart. I did so, then she told me to pick a second and place that to the right of the first, then another and place that to the right of the second one so that I had three cards in a row. She told me that the one on the left represented the past, the one in the middle was the present and the one on the right was the future. Then she asked me to turn over the past card first. It was The Moon. She explained that the moon card represented confusion and uncertainty, I'm in a phase where the psychic and intuition are playing an important role in my life but that it may take time for thing to become clear to me, I should trust my instincts. Because it was in the position of the past it meant that the spiritual world had been trying to contact me and that I hadn't been aware of it or understood it; but that it had been watching over me. Information had been shown to me, apparently from nowhere and this had confused me. I was a bit freaked out because this did make sense, but tried to remain objective and see what else she had to say. Next was the present card, I turned it over and it was The Empress card. It was a picture of a beautiful red-haired woman with a blue hat on that was covered in stars, in a bush next to her was the world and beside that was a bird with a red berry in its beak. She said that The Empress represented feminine power and intuition; because it was in the present it meant that my intuition was trying to send me a message. I should sit alone and listen to what my 'inner voice' is saying to me. Again that made sense too; I was really freaked out now. I turned the future card over and nearly screamed, it was the picture from the cover of the pack - The High Priestess, that had reminded me so much of Blue. Maya's mum let out a little gasp of excitement. She said this was an extremely spiritual card that was connected to The Moon, feminine power and inspiration; it fits perfectly with the other two cards. Moving into the future I should pay attention to my dreams, expect synchronicities and messages from all over the place. I should explore different beliefs and spiritual experiences, move out of my comfort zone. When this card appears in a man's reading it represent s an unobtainable woman. Maya chirped up that I was gay and winked at me. Her mother just said that it didn't necessarily represent a relationship rather than contact with a female force that was outside of my reach. She recapped over the cards and summarised them together, asking me if I had any questions. I was just dumbfounded, it was pretty spot on when I thought about Blue and all the stuff that had been happening. I thanked her and she told Maya that she loved her and would call her in the coming days. We sat and chatted for a short while, Maya and Emma were excited about the 'reading' - my mind was just blown and I made my excuses and went to my room. My head was spinning; I couldn't concentrate on anything so I just put some music on and eventually drifted off to sleep.

The next day I tried to just put it all to the back of my head and get on with my normal day. Someone had stuck a load of posters up on campus advertising a Wicca group, I thought about going along to it but the whole 'magic' and new age religion thing just seemed a bit culty to me. I knew it was partly due to years of being brainwashed by Christianity but I wasn't in the right place in my life to get into all that. Even though the Tarot card meanings had been really significant I just felt scared of all that; if the message was to follow my instincts then I would do exactly that and steer clear. I didn't know whether Blue was a 'magical' thing, a spiritual thing or just a part of my unconscious mind, maybe all of the above. But I couldn't afford to drive myself crazy trying to find out, I didn't want to jump down the rabbit hole. I just got on with my routine, that was what my gut was telling me.

"I'm starting to prune up. Shall we get out and sunbathe?" Adonai asked, splashing water at me. "So the plot thickens, even I'm now more intrigued about Blue, come on." We went back up on to the beach and towelled ourselves off. He reached in his bag and pulled out a packet of crisps. "Munchie?" He shook the packet at me, I smiled and nodded. "Munchie!" He sang like aTarzan call. "Purrthee..." He mumbled through a mouthful. "Proceed."

I studied the Tarot card pack and little guidebook that came with it; it showed you different ways of setting the cards out and all the meanings of each card. I read back through the meanings of the cards I'd got when Maya's mum had spoken to me. The things she said were basically just the textbook meaning of each card. It seemed to me that you could just memorise the meanings of the cards and the positions they appear in a 'reading' and just fluff up the bits between with pop psychology; there's not really anything magical about it or skilful. You could basically just use any cards - playing cards or draw your own and assign archetypal meanings to them and go from there. I wasn't particularly impressed by the whole thing; even if by chance they had been significant to me I had probably just piled the meaning on because it meant something to me.

I carried on with my routine; sociology was pretty boring; the only part of it that interested me this term was a module on Globalisation and Consumerism. Most of the subjects were really general and seemed irrelevant to life. I was more interested in the life that the city had to offer. I started to go to @d2 and NG1 every weekend and carried on 'collecting' one night stands. Basically whenever I get drunk all that I can think about is sex, I'm still exactly the same; as soon as I start to feel tipsy I just start to think about pulling. Bearing in mind that I had never seen a porn film or knew anything about sex I was learning quite a lot!

One night in @d2 there was a group of guys checking me out, two of them were my age and the other one was older, like late 30s early 40s. Eventually one of the younger guys came over and started chatting to me. He asked me whether I fancied him and the other young guy; I said yes, they were really cute. But I couldn't work out where the older guy fitted in. He leaned in and whispered in my ear that I could go back with them and have fun with the young guys at the older guy's house. I just looked at him in a confused way. "He likes to watch, he's well off; a great party house – if you fancy it?" I didn't know what to say but I was intrigued.

"Oh my god!" Adonai laughed. "You dirty dog! So you had your first orgy?"

"Well kind of yeah, I went back with them to this guy's posh apartment and he cracked open some red wine from his cellar from the year I was born. He then let us all get relaxed and they asked me if I minded photos being taken."

"Jesus, this just gets kinkier" Adonai crossed himself.

"Basically the three of us stripped off and he was taking photos all the time. I felt a bit self-conscious because I've never thought of myself as handsome or sexy; but it was kind of a liberating experience too. I suppose that's just an ugly duckling complex, you never think that you're attractive."

"I get that, I've always had a lot of attention and I

suppose I just take it for granted. I've never been fat or had glasses or braces like you did. But now with the dreads I notice the difference; people can be really superficial. The trick is to be comfortable in your own skin and not let other peoples' attention be part of your self-esteem."

"Yeah, I get that now but it's been a long journey and I'm kind of thankful that I was an ugly duckling in a way. I'm glad that I spent all my time reading books and listening to music and watching movies; I had that time to experience the world vicariously through other peoples' stories."

"Woah, that's deep man; but I get what you're talking about. It's like you tapped in to a collective evolution, a shared experience through art. You were able to be an observer and set up your views on stuff before you were in a position to experience things and test out your views."

"Yeah as dumb as it may sound it was through music and books and films that I accessed this world out there. The characters in the books were people I'd never have access to in real life, the situations in movies or the emotions in the songs were all alien to me. I didn't realise at the time but I was slowly evolving into a protagonist rather than a passive observer. At the time I was just going with the flow and existing on the edges of stuff. Like even that night I was just stood on my own in the bar, observing everybody else having a night out; I was way too shy to actually approach someone to talk to them. I always waited for people to come and talk to me never the other way round."

"So you ended up in at the deep end that night, pardon the pun; a starring role!"

"Yeah, at uni obviously with a big group of strangers all getting to know each other I had realised that people saw as a bit of a mystery and wanted a night out with me, but I just thought that it was the environment. It still didn't register with me that I was that interesting or attractive at all. But this night was all about physical attraction and being liberated and experiencing something new. It turned out that guy was a professional photographer and afterwards he asked me if I wanted to do more modelling work and maybe help him out in his office. I was really surprised that he wanted me to and just took his information. I'll admit I did think about it and it did interest me but I was way too shy to actually contact him. I just left it as a crazy, wild night and nothing more."

"Aww, so that was then of your foray into porn then?"

"Er, no not exactly, it did come round again a few times after but that's a long story."

"Well that's what we're here for right now; do tell."

"Ahaha, well after that night my mind-set shifted a bit; I got more confident in just going with the flow, putting myself out there and hooking up with people. I wanted to explore the gay scene, the society and of course the men. I was still shy but I suppose by going out by myself to the bar and nightclub my face became known and gradually people started to approach me. I got to know a few people here and there; I can hold a conversation and make friends, I'm just too shy to make the first move. As the summer holidays were approaching I was hanging out with a cute black guy called Troy. I'd decided to stay in Nottingham during the summer and had managed to get a job as a chef in the staff restaurant at the big cigarette factory near to uni. I made fresh pizzas and cooked omelettes on one of those TV kitchen set ups in front of the customers as they waited. I've always enjoyed cooking so it was an okay job to be doing. Troy and I were kind of together but it wasn't that serious, we were more friends with benefits. One weekend when we'd been out shopping in town he took me to the gay bar for lunch. I'd been there loads on a night out and it was trendy and lively; but I'd never thought of going there during the day. We sat down to eat and the bar owner came over to chat to Troy because he knew him. I'd seen the owners before but never been introduced to them; Graham was a little camp guy, dripping in gold and like a joyous gay cherub, his boyfriend Martin was like a Scottish Freddie Mercury. Graham was teasing Troy about us hanging out together and wanted to be introduced. I said that I was a student but working as a chef for the summer, at that he said that they were looking for a chef to work their kitchen on a Monday night and offered me a trial. I jumped at it because I'd always thought that @d2 was my favourite bar and the workers were really glamorous.

My life had suddenly taken a really different direction, instead of being back home in the countryside working in the same supermarket I'd been at for years I was alone in the city. I had moved in to the house I'd be living in for the second year of uni, I knew the girls who were living there already through the LGBT Society at uni; there was a spare room through the summer so I moved in early. It was odd living with relative strangers, especially as they were lesbians and very different from me. But I had a day job and now an opportunity to make contacts in the gay scene from within, so I felt like I was kind of making my own way. I'd decided not to say anything to my family about my sexuality until I had a relationship to tell them about. To me just saying to them that I was gay wouldn't really mean a lot unless I was talking about it in context of having a boyfriend. I spoke to my Mum a lot but I just didn't go in to specifics, I never really had done about girlfriends in the past so it wasn't a conversation that was already open. Obviously with all my family being religious the idea of being gay is a sin and I've always been taught that it is wrong; but now that I'm in the midst of my journey of accepting myself as gay and getting to know more about the society on the gay scene I can see it differently. As I get to know people and hear about their coming out stories or their relationships with their family I know it's a conversation I'm going to have to have at some point. I have no idea how they will react, especially because I already see myself as the black sheep.

I was really nervous that first Monday night going to

do the trial at the gay bar; I was a nobody entering in to the eye of the storm. To me the people who worked there were really cool and I was a geeky student from the sticks, I didn't know how I was going to fit in or if I'd even survive the trial. Luckily I knew of the guy who was working behind the bar that night and he did the orientation; putting me in the bar uniform and showing me around the kitchen. He showed me downstairs where there was an office and cellar and also a dressing up room where the drag queens got ready. On Sundays it was cabaret night and the entire bar staff dressed up in drag and put on performances. I'd seen it a couple of times and it was a really fun crazy night. Tony told me that upstairs there was an apartment where Graham, Martin and another one of the managers lived.

It was a pretty complicated menu for bar food but I'd just have to work things out as I went along; Tony behind the bar was really nice and keen to help me out wherever he could. There were a few people coming in just ordering chips and snacks and it went okay; then Tony asked me if I'd ever worked behind the bar before. I said I hadn't but I was definitely keen to learn because I knew it would be a great skill to have under my belt. He showed me the ropes behind the bar and I served a few customers and just got to know more about the lay of the land in the bar. At the end of the night I helped close down and had a staff drink and thought that it had all gone okay. I was only supposed to be doing the kitchen cover on a Monday night so they said they'd just contact me during the week to let me know if I'd got it or not. When I went in for a drink at the weekend they told me I'd got the job and to see me on Monday, Tony was out on a night off so we hung out and he introduced me to everyone as the new worker. It felt really good to be getting to know more people and I was dead chuffed to be working in the bar that I thought was really cool. It was like being handed the keys to the scene because as soon as I was introduced as one of the @d2 workers people started to pay more attention, I found it really funny. The owners told me to come in on Monday and have a chat with them before doing another shift; I didn't know whether I'd done something wrong or what to expect. When I turned up on the Monday I got sent upstairs to the apartment; it was so posh and glamorous. They sat me down and told me that they'd had a few people talking to them about me being behind the bar last week; I was convinced they were going to tell me I'd done something wrong. They went on to say that everyone was asking who the cute new guy was and when I was working next so they had decided to put Tony in the kitchen and I would be behind the bar that night. I was totally shocked and worried what Tony was going to say about me being put in his place. When I went down and started Tony was a bit miffed but just said it was because I was hot fresh meat; he gave me a wink. I knew he was cracking on to me too but at least that meant that he was alright with me and there wouldn't be a bad atmosphere. I was so nervous about being behind the bar, about having to be confident and chatty; I felt like it was a baptism of fire. It actually went alright and I really enjoyed being behind the bar and learning new skills; the customers really interested me. I tried to look at that environment and the people as a social experiment. I saw myself as a newly fledged gay guy and I was suddenly in the perfect position to observe the gay scene and how it all worked; right from the inside. Being a barman in a popular gay bar meant that I could watch everything unfold in front of me. I got offered other shifts on other nights and got to know all the other staff until I felt like I was being accepted in to a little gay family. It was the best way to work out what being gay meant and the dynamics of the gay scene and the different types of people; a super vantage point for people watching.

After a few weeks I got asked to cover a Sunday night shift which meant that I would have to be dressed in drag and join the dance troupe; I was absolutely terrified. I am a grunge rocker at heart so I had no idea how I was going to transform into a drag 'queen' and dance around in front of hundreds of people. I've always thought that gender is kind of taught to us when we are kids, obviously there are differences between male and female in terms of hormone levels and physiology but a lot of stuff is just what we're told is acceptable or not. Boys are taught to behave in a certain way and girls in another. I know that in my childhood I had automatically wanted to play with dolls, watch musicals, cook and draw; whereas my brothers and cousins were all very sporty and masculine. But I'd never considered dressing in women's clothes or even developing a theatrical 'persona' at all. I got taught the dance routine that I'd be part of and given a makeover. As I was looking in the mirror piling on the make up to look like a woman Blue was looking back at me in the mirror, cracking up laughing. I had this full length red sequinned dress on and a big red afro wig; worst of all was tottering around on high heels. It was terrifying just working behind the bar in drag but by the time it came to perform I was shaking like a leaf. I had to dance as a backing singer to 'Leader of the pack' and I've never known pure fear like that. Until later on when they told me that next week I'd be performing a solo number. They christened me Penny Shove and the next week dressed me up in a Carmen Miranda fruit headdress and bikini and told me to perform Geri Halliwell 'Mi Chico Latino'- that time I was even more scared because it was just me in the spotlight with hundreds of people just staring at me. It was a sink or swim kind of thing. I can't say that I enjoyed the dressing up but eventually I did get into the dancing and lost my nerves. The staff would meet up in the bar on a Thursday and learn the routines for that Sunday and it ended up being a good bonding experience and good fun; they're great memories. We'd be The Spice Girls or Steps or Liberty X and in the end I really got in to the formation dancing. Even now I really love to watch flash mobs, there's something about people moving together that's really cool; a kind of metaphor to unity and cooperation.

By the time that the summer holidays finished and I went back to uni I was working at the bar most nights, it was like living a double life. I certainly was more of a worker than a classroom student. I'd had a lot of fun over the summer and had a few one night stands, met loads of new people and felt like I was part of something. In the autumn I'd got together with one of the other barmen who I worked with called Scott. I thought he was really glamorous, he was going to stage school and I kind of idolised him. I seem to have the habit of falling quite quickly for someone I guess I'm a bit immature like that but I'm still learning about gay relationships. It's one thing to have a one night stand but if I start seeing someone and like them then I kind of focus just on that person and overanalyse everything. Blue was still around trying to help me but even that situation was starting to worry me. I had one persona as a gay barman, one as a student, one dressed in drag, one where I was a son and all that life before, away from here; then another as a person who could see Blue and the magical stuff. I was worried that something was going to happen and I was at risk of having another breakdown; I had to take a real careful look and work out where my life was going. It's funny that at those times life throws in a curve ball and shows you a sign. Scott was supposed to be doing some porn work for an agency; he'd already done some solo stuff but was meant to be taking his ex to do some work together. I wasn't thrilled about it but I knew that it had been arranged before he and I had got together so I just let him know how I felt but let them get on with it. Well his ex was really drunk in the club the weekend before and managed to fall down a flight of stairs and break his arm; Scott didn't want to flake out and look bad to the agency so I offered to stand in for his ex. I'd had photos taken before so I figured it'd be easy enough to do. We went down on the train to the agency and I just had to pretend to be his ex because Scott thought it'd look unprofessional being boyfriends. I'll admit I was nervous being in the studio and it took a while for me to rise to the occasion but the photographer did a solo test shoot and then we did a bit together. I signed the rights off and got given some money for the travel costs; job done.

At uni the second year was okay but I was finding just pure sociology a bit hard going, I just wasn't that interested in it or could see what I would do with a sociology degree in the long run. My life outside uni was so full and colourful compared to sitting in the lecture hall. I used to sit there thinking that I've got a job already and experiencing a lot of stuff but nothing that I was learning really captured my interest. That Christmas I got the train down to the farm on Christmas Eve, it was really nice to see everybody but it felt like going back in time; like I was a foreigner in that environment even more so than ever before. Something had shifted with my Mum too; obviously she had an empty nest and had also had a hysterectomy which was a massive procedure over the summer. I could see a difference in her, my parents hadn't been close even when it was me and them in the house when I was working in the supermarket. She'd started going out on a Friday night and discovered that the world wasn't such a bad place, just like I had learned when I first started going out. Everything seemed to be changing. I wanted to talk to her about Scott but she seemed to have enough on her plate and the changes had thrown me a bit. I was back in Nottingham for New Year and we had to work in glamorous drag, it was so funny seeing the New Year in dressed up as a different persona. We were allowed to go out on a bar crawl in the early hours round the gay scene. The streets were thick with snow and it was hilarious tottering around in heels and people on the street doing double takes as a gaggle of drag queens went past.

I decided that my present to myself on my birthday would be that I left university; I just had to choose a direction and my gut feeling was that sociology and all that wasn't getting me anywhere. I'd gone to uni for the experience of going, I should probably have chosen to do psychology somewhere but I just had to go with what the situation was right now. I told my Mum on the phone that day and she took it surprisingly well; I was glad that I'd waited to be a mature student and that they hadn't had to contribute towards my tuition and all that. She just sighed and said that she understood but joked that she wasn't looking forward to telling my Dad. I broke down that night because it really hit me that I hadn't seen the course through, I felt like a failure and got really down on myself. Scott didn't know what to do to console me and I was really embarrassed to be breaking down in front of him. We went out for an Indian meal with a load of friends and then out clubbing that night, gradually I felt liberated; it was a new year and a new direction.

<u>Being 23</u>

Well Scott dumped me a couple of weeks after my birthday; he'd kind of ghosted me a bit, as much as you can when you work with someone. I knew something had shifted but what with being down on myself about leaving uni I just felt like it was another blow and I just cried and cried. I had to hold it together when we were at work but the heartbreak felt like a physical pain. He moved on quite quickly and I had an inkling that he'd fuck buddied up with Tony too. I just had to get back out there and move on too. I reverted to listening to Garbage every night before sleep, their songs always helped me through. So I decided that the best way to get the pain out and dealt with would be to get a tattoo done; I planned to concentrate all of the pain in to the pain of the tattoo being made. I found a tattooist in the city and decided I'd place it on my lower back because it wouldn't be visible to anyone else or when I was in drag. I just walked in and looked for a flash design that I could fit some words in to. There was a chorus of a Garbage song that really made me feel positive and I thought I'd get that tatted on me to always remind of moving through this pain, the divinity of falling out of love with somebody.

"C'mon show me Kris." Adonai said as he signalled me to roll over on my towel. "Oh man, a tribal circle with 'Go Baby Go' written in it?"

"Yeah I didn't quite think of the connotations of that phrase beyond the Garbage chorus that meant something really significant to me at the time. Obviously lots of guys think it means something else, it being just above my bum and all that."

 Adonai rolled around laughing and pretending to be riding a bucking bronco shouting 'Go Baby Go!' I still stand by my choice of phrase but it's a pretty shit quality tattoo, it's on my list of tattoos that I'd like to upgrade. I'd like to cover it up with a more artistic one but also keep that phrase in it somehow; just like I want to add the Japanese symbol for 'neon' next to my 'tiger' one to represent the Killers song of the same name. The back tattoo served its purpose at the time though and I drew a line under the negative way I was feeling and thinking. It became my mantra, go baby go get moving in life and explore what's out there, embrace the now rather than living in the past. After a while I started seeing another guy called Matthew; he had caught my eye at work. He had a big red Mohican and dressed really punky. He was crazy and fun and we hit it off quickly and soon started spending all our time with each other. Everyone was surprised that the clean cut barman was going for the punky bad boy but I kind of liked that. I'd got more hours at the bar so I was full time now; I was living in a completely gay bubble. In that environment things move pretty quickly and a week can feel like a month in that little world. I liked the fact that Matthew was wild and I just surfed the wave. We'd only been together a short while when I got a late night phone call from my sister in law asking me if I had read my Mum's letter and what I thought about the news. I was staying at Michael's so she told me to get to read the letter then ring me back. I phoned my flatmate and asked her to read the letter out to me over the phone as it was important. It turned out that my Mum was leaving my Dad and going off with a family friend eloping to Spain. I was so shocked, I knew that things hadn't been good between my parents for a while but never saw this coming at all. I just wanted to get in contact with them all. For some reason when I rang my sister in law back she told me that my Dad thought that somehow I'd known about my Mum's plans to leave him and that I was involved in some way. I tried calling him but got no answer. I was worried about my Mum too; I just wanted her to let me know that she was okay. I completely broke down because for some reason in my head it seemed to me that the love that created me no longer existed, the family was broken and I was helpless to do anything about it. Matthew didn't understand why it had hit me so hard as his parents had split when he was a child; I was in my twenties and not living with them so he didn't get why it had affected me. I eventually got through to my Dad and went down to see them all on the farm that weekend. My Mum had got in contact from Spain and we'd spoken long enough to see that she was physically okay and that she was glad that I was still speaking to her with what had happened. In that moment I was worried about her as a woman and my Dad as a man. They'd been married for more than 25 years and suddenly everything had changed. I couldn't imagine how they were both feeling but I wanted to show that I supported both of them. It was a horrible feeling going to the farm with them all thinking that I had been something to do with my Mum leaving; how could I prove otherwise? Because they knew I was coming the family had gathered to see me, Pete's wife Alison was heavily pregnant with their second child and Bethany was toddling around. They were really angry and said that my Grandparents were too; my Grandad called me to speak to him alone and just asked me if I had heard from my Mum. I was completely honest with him and I knew part of him was asking because he was a concerned father, I told him that I'd heard from her and that she was physically okay. Up at my Dad's house he was surrounded by the family and we sat down for a meal. They were all saying that it was just a blip and that she would return once she'd come to her senses. I knew from the conversation that I'd had with my Mum that she wanted a divorce and I knew that I had to be honest with my Dad about that for his sake. Eventually we were alone and I hugged him and told him that I loved him; he told me that he hadn't thought that he'd ever see me again. I got the message across as best as I could that I didn't have any idea what had been going on. I'd been the only son living with them when things were frosty between them and we spoke about that a little. I suppose to me it wasn't as big a shock to me as it was to my brothers because they hadn't seen the atmosphere between them over the last year or so. I told him that I had to be honest that Mum had said that she wanted a divorce but that he was my father and nothing was going to change that. It was just a really lonely time for me because I felt like I was in the middle of it, in the eye of the storm.

When I got back to Nottingham I clung to my relationship with Matthew because I felt like it was all I had. I'd grown a Mohican and embraced my punky side. We moved in together and gradually I saw the cracks, he was drinking loads and taking lots of drugs. It was a fiery, toxic relationship. I got an extra job working in Gap to try and get a career going rather than just staying as a barman forever. He was DJing and doing occasional work as a drag queen. He'd vanish for days at a time and I found out that he'd been stealing money from me, I even walked in on him having sex with somebody else yet I still couldn't see a way out of the relationship. I clung to it even though I was losing the plot, I was cutting myself and locking myself in the toilet at work and crying my eyes out. I'd dug a hole but I wanted to believe that he would change somehow and everything would be alright. I needed it to work out despite things turning violent and crazy. He would always apologise and be charming and tell me what I wanted to hear. He'd get jealous if anyone flirted with me at the bar and treated me like a possession. He really hit the roof one night when we went out to the bar on a night off. When we entered the bar everyone turned to stare at me and they were all whispering and pointing at me. The managers quickly ushered me to go down to the office with them. I had no idea what was going on. They started by asking me if I'd done anything naughty because they'd been getting phone calls about me all day. I said no, it was getting really weird. Then they handed me one of the free gay magazines that get delivered on mass to the bar each month and told me to turn to the back page. It was Boyz magazine and I knew that the back page was the backroom boy; a nude spread of a model or porn star. When I opened it I saw myself stark naked all over the back two pages. The test shoot I'd done with Scott at the agency had somehow been sold to the magazine. The managers started laughing and patted me on the back, they thought that it was great to have a nationally famous barman. I was a bit embarrassed but also quite proud that I was in the magazine it was quite a big deal. When I got back upstairs Matthew had been joined by Scott and neither of them were impressed in the slightest. Scott was pissed off that he had paid to join the agency and get headshots done but got no work and Matthew was annoyed because his possession was on display for the whole of the gay scene in UK to see. Everybody else just kept staring at me and for that whole night and the next week everyone kept talking to me about it. Matthew just vanished for a few days and turned up eventually looking really wasted. I knew whenever he vanished he was with somebody else and that was obviously my punishment.

It was a struggle holding stuff together between Gap and the bar and things at home with Matthew. The year just merged in to a succession of days that I had to get through. I was in regular contact with my Mum who was trying to build a life in Spain. My Dad got in contact to say that he wanted to come up and visit me in Nottingham because they were all meeting up at a Hotel before Christmas. I knew there and then that I would have to come out as gay to him before he came up so that I could how him my life and my friends. I wrote to both him and my Mum at the same time and told them that I was living with Matthew. Both of them said that they had always had their suspicions but that they accepted me as I was. Dad came up and I showed him the bar and introduced him to everybody, it was so weird seeing him sitting there; like worlds colliding. I didn't want him to feel uncomfortable but I wanted him to see my life. I took Matthew with me to meet the extended family at the Hotel and have a meal. My paternal grandfather and aunties and brothers were all there; Pete had a new little baby son. As we entered the room some of them were sat down reading the Bible, although everyone was polite and chatted nobody addressed the subject of being gay or spoke about it at all. I don't know what I expected to happen especially with them all being so religious. That Christmas I stayed in Nottingham to have the time as a couple with Matthew, it didn't go that well as he got really wasted and I ended up with the Christmas tree being thrown at me in an argument. Then come New Year he was asking me to get engaged to him and that he wanted me around forever. I said yes, with it in the back of my mind that gay people aren't going to legally be married for ages yet as far as I know. Even though it was dysfunctional I didn't want to fail again and I needed somebody to belong with. My birthday was just a drunken night out in the club but my Mum sent me a card inviting me and Michael to go and visit her in Spain. She and Barry had started a business and there was a job for me if I wanted it; we could go on holiday and see if we like it there. I'd always wanted to live in Spain since I was a kid and Matthew was really enthusiastic about trying out a new start.

Being 24 – 2003

I'd always thought that I'd have my life sorted by the time I was 25, that girl I worked with back in Australia who had had her 25th birthday and stressed about feeling old had stuck in my head. She saw 25 as either young or quarter of a century; it had stayed with me as an age that I thought I'd have a life all in place. So I had a year to get things together. Matthew and I went to visit Mum and Barry in Spain for the holiday to see if we liked it. He thought it would be a great new start and we'd be moving forward as a couple together on a new adventure. Barry was an old family friend who I'd known for years, it was awkward seeing my Mum and him together in this foreign place but I wanted to just roll with it and accept them as they are. They were living near Torrevieja south of Alicante. I remembered the area from when my paternal grandparents used to live over there. I loved that country; I never knew why just something about the atmosphere I'd always said that I wanted to end up living there. They had opened a private post office and internet café and had a job for me with them because the business was growing; they were sure there would be work for Matthew too somewhere. Although it was strange seeing how my Mum had changed and getting to know Barry as her partner it did feel nice and we decided to take the plunge. I wrote and told all the rest of the family, I wish I'd had the money to be able to go and visit them all to say goodbye but it just wasn't possible. On May 12th we moved over and started the new life.

The area was full of ex pats and really busy, loads of bars and restaurants; great beaches and nightlife. I knew a miniscule amount of Spanish from doing GCSE but I was really rusty. Matthew got work after a while in a new drag bar. We got to know loads of people in the local bars and even found a gay bar up the coast. But it wasn't long before I realised that nothing was going to change with him at all. We were living in a villa with Mum and Barry, over a few months Matthew went back to his old ways, vanishing all the time or not coming home at night as he made new friends whilst he was out at work in the bar. I was working 9-5 and we'd go out sometimes but he just always ended up picking an argument and I'd go home and he'd stay out all night. By the time August came around I'd had enough and one morning when he rolled in wasted I just snapped and chucked him out. He had plenty of mates he could go and crash with. I'd surprised myself that I had finally had enough, I think it was the fact that even in this dream place nothing was going to change that made me flip. Mum and Barry had seen that things were bad and I think they were relieved that we'd split. Once I had realised what had happened I lost the plot seeing that I was now in a foreign country and on my own socially. We had known people because Matthew was gregarious and chatty. I felt like a fish out of water and didn't know what I was going to do. I kept having more and more hallucinations, Blue was around but they just got more vivid. I'd go out on my own every night to The Lansdown a particular bar where I knew the staff. But I'd be sat there and see Blue come in dancing around the dance floor, or I'd see a whole scene superimposed over what was actually there. There'd be 'people' singing and dancing around me as I walked home. Even during the day when I was at work I'd look out of the window and see figures flying and floating around. I'd go the beach after work most nights and there'd be visions of people swimming around me.

I joined a boot camp run by ex-army on the beach with Amanda the lady who also worked at Mum and Barry's business. We got along great at work and went out for a drink with her boyfriend at the weekends. We decided we wanted to get in shape and the boot camp sounded like more fun than joining the gym. It was on twice a week and there was a great bunch of people going. They'd send us running in the sea or doing load of different exercises on the beach; I really enjoyed it. After a few sessions we got to know other people in the class. One time when I was walking home across the beaches one of the other young guys who went to the class came over and started walking with me and chatting. He was called Keith and was Irish, a really good looking guy. As we chatted he got round to asking where I went out and who I knew; then mentioned the village where the gay bar was and we got round to saying we were gay to each other. He asked me if I knew the guy called Matthew and when I said I was his ex he laughed and said he'd met him around and about. It didn't bother me at all Matthew and I hadn't ended things on good terms at all but I wasn't about to bad mouth him to anyone or influence anyone else's opinion about him. Already some of the gay friends who we'd met when we were together had turned round to me and told me that he was playing around behind my back. He'd told people we were in an open relationship and said he was just biding his time before he dumped me and moved on; I'd just surprised him by beating him to it. Keith and I started going out for a drink together, we got on alright as mates and because he was outgoing and handsome he was fun company to be in. We'd go out round the local bars or off to the gay bar.

At Christmas we all met up on the beach in the morning and then ate dinner in the sunshine. I'd stayed in contact with everybody back home and I did miss the rest of the family but this was life now. I'd also made contact with the porn agency and the photographer invited me to fly over for New Years and do some shooting and stay with him. I reckoned I had nothing to lose and flew over to London. It was good fun and a bit of an adventure, plus I liked the idea of doing more modelling work. I fitted in as much as I could when I was there and flew back just before my birthday.

Being 25

Well 25 had arrived and I knew I hadn't got my life sorted. Although I was in the right place and surrounded by new friends the visions were bugging me and I didn't know what to do about it. Through some Spanish guys who I had met at work who could speak English I had started improving my Spanish; we'd go out to the cinema so I gradually started to pick more up. Keith loved it because it meant I could help him pull Spanish guys too. The boot camp was still going great and I was the fittest that I had ever been I had a few one night stands and fun but I was not interested in having a relationship at all. People assume that me and Keith are together because we're always hanging around, he's a great looking guy but we're totally platonic. It seems that I always become friends with people who are much more outgoing and gregarious than I naturally am; I ride their coat tails and usurp a bit of their spotlight. Don't get me wrong when I have a drink I'm like a chimp bouncing around doing karaoke and dancing but I don't think I'm cool at all. Because there are so many tourists here the days and weeks just roll on; then season into season. Mum and Barry paid for me to go back to Nottingham and catch up with everyone. It was so weird going back and surprising them all. Whilst I was there loads of people came out of the woodwork telling me what Matthew had been up to whilst we'd been together. None of it surprised me at all, it just told me that the inklings that I'd had at the time were accurate. I did some more porn work while I was there and had loads of fun staying in a hotel but it didn't make me want to move back. I'm still in contact with the family and I like seeing what they're up to; Simon got married but said it would be awkward if me or Mum went because of the divorce. When Mum and Barry got married in Gibraltar they all stopped talking to me because they opposed the idea. I miss the farm and my grandparents but my life is here now. In Spain there's just a routine of work, then beach, then out drinking at night or off exercising. Mum and Barry had expanded the business through franchising and eventually bought a little finca way out in the countryside, they said to me that I could live with them and get a car to travel about in or get my own apartment and stay on the coast. I immediately thought of when that had happened back in Ross on Wye and I'd ended up getting in to trouble with drink driving so I took the other option this time and looked for a place of my own. Over the summer I met a great girl called Kerri, she'd seen me and Keith on a night out and fancied me and tried to chat me up. When she realised that I was gay we had a laugh and got on together over shared taste in music. She's only 18 but so fun and cool and I really enjoy spending time with her. That summer was also the time for a new inking; Keith had seen my tattoos and decided that he wanted his first one so we set about finding somewhere to have it done. I had seen on my travels that there was a tattoo salon up in Cabo Roig that we could walk to. So one Saturday we set off, he'd decided that he wanted a Sun medallion on his lower back. I had thought about it and decided on getting the word 'serendipity' done as a bracelet around my left wrist. According to the dictionary it means 'the occurrence and development of events by chance in a happy or beneficial way' or 'an aptitude for making desirable discoveries by accident; good fortune, luck' I felt that it was a positive idea that good things can just appear, that life can throw a curve ball. The first time that I walked in to Bagwa Tattoo with Keith I was immediately hit by how different the atmosphere was there compared to all the other tattoo places that I had been to before. It was so tranquil and happy. Meeting Toby and Sarah for the first time I was just in awe as to how cool they were, so approachable and chatty. I remember that day that there kept being short power cuts which meant that we spent a good 6 or 7 hours determinedly waiting around to get our tattoos done that day. It meant that we observed all the different people coming and going and how Toby and Sarah interacted with everybody. They were such cool characters and as a married couple I thought it was amazing the way that they worked together and talked to each other; instantly I thought that that was the kind of relationship I wanted to aspire to. Eventually Sarah did our tattoos and she asked me about the meaning of serendipity, as I explained it to her I couldn't help thinking that something serendipitous was happening right there and then. I could see Blue dancing through and flying around outside the window the whole time, she was really excited. Here were cool tattooed, interesting people who really inspired me; it was the best tattoo experience I'd had so far.

Come October I'd got my own apartment and because Keith still lived with his parents he spent most of the time crashing in my spare room until he'd basically moved in. He'd been working as a builder but during the summer the workers all took time off so I was buying him drinks and stuff because it was fun to have him around; it's a hard time of year to find work. The TV was only in Spanish so I gradually managed to pick up even more. It just so happened that my apartment was about 50 metres away from where Kerri lived with her family so we grew closer and became fast friends. In the autumn I met another girl called Nikki through work and the three of us ended up spending a lot of time together, they both loved singing so we'd do karaoke and go dancing. Mum and Barry had sold the post office that I worked in but on the agreement that Amanda and I stayed on to work for the new owners. They were nice enough but I was starting to want to try and find some sort of better job or career path. Mum and Barry were starting up a business importing traditional English food, mainly pasties and cakes. They planned to open another chain of cafes and Mum was pumping her divorce settlement into that new venture. The visions were still affecting me loads and I knew I was getting worse but everything else was going so well I just wanted to just wing it and ignore that anything was wrong. It was nice to have a circle of friends because Keith knew loads of people and so did Kerri I started to be accepted as a local and I didn't want to blow it. At the apartment we'd have parties before going out with friends, we met lots of tourists and also a great group of Spanish gays from the bar we'd go to. That Christmas we threw a party at the apartment the weekend before and invited my new bosses and parents and Amanda with her husband. We had great fun and drinks were flowing, even homemade jelly shots. But later on when we were heading out the visions just wouldn't let up and I was really struggling. When everyone had gone I hid in my room and just burst out crying, Keith came to check on me and couldn't understand what was wrong so I just blurted it all out about seeing things everywhere. I could tell he was weirded out but he just hugged me and cracked jokes to get me to go out and carry on partying. In one of the discos I was sat in the crowded bar and there was this female vision that I was seeing; it wasn't Blue but someone else. She was really nasty and kept saying things into my ear, that I was useless and a failure, that I should have topped myself years ago as things would never get better for me. She just kept telling me to get up and go kill myself, suggesting ways in which I could do it. It was really upsetting me and I was also freaked out. To the outside world it just looked like I was an emotional drunk but I was really fighting to stay sat on that stool and not follow the visions instructions like a zombie. One of the barmen who I knew, who used to go out with Kerri came over and gave me a shot and asked me if I was okay, Keith was off dancing around and although it was a nice gesture it embarrassed me even more that my distress was obvious to other people. When he was on his break the barman told me to get on the back of his motorbike and drove really fast round the block, I guess to knock some sense in to me. When we parked up back at the bar he kissed me saying "There does that make you feel better?" He was straight and I didn't know him that well at all but he'd clocked that something was wrong and had decided to try and help me. I just laughed and pretended that I was okay but just turned around and headed home by myself. I was determined to make it home safely to bed and sleep; I needed to ignore the vision telling me to kill myself. It was like fighting against the force of a magnet but I did manage it. The next morning Keith had a row with me saying that he couldn't deal with this kind of stuff, that he thought I was just a schizophrenic princess and I should man up and get over it all.

The visions got worse during the day and I was struggling at work. On Christmas Eve I knew I had to go and get gifts and when I was stood in the shops the visions kept telling me to buy random stuff, a recorder was one of them. It got so much trying to mentally fight it off that I fainted in the shop and the staff helped me to feel better. I got the gifts and struggled home and collapsed in a heap. I went to my Mum's for Christmas dinner then back home to my apartment. Kerri came over and spent the whole day trying to cheer me up and get me out of my shell but my brain was fried. She's such an amazing friend to me, a really beautiful soul. We decided that for New Year we would get matching tattoos to seal our friendship. We headed up to Bagwa and both had a letter K with a star attached to it because of our initials; mine was up on my shoulder and hers was on her wrist. We had it done in the afternoon on New Year's Eve so it was really special being down in the commercial centre at midnight watching the fireworks go off with our new inkings. That birthday I went out for a meal with Mum and Barry and went home by myself, the visions still haunting me.

<u>Being 26</u>

The visions got so bad that people started to notice that I was struggling. I would see figures dancing around everywhere and some of them would be telling me stuff to do; just things like where to walk or to go to the sea. At one point one was telling me I had to dreadlock my long hair so I got all the stuff and Kerri knotted my hair up. Once it was done the visions were telling me that I would gradually develop into one of them. I remember walking home from work and seeing this flock of angels high in the sky all swooping down around me. They male ones were all tattooed with long hair and some with dreadlocks. They kept saying to me that I would become one of them, that it was my destiny. I can still see them all clearly now years later. When I got in to my apartment I went straight to the bathroom and started trying to untangle the dreads and ended up cutting my hair off; convinced that if I had short hair I wouldn't be like thoe angels in the vision. I'd hit a brick wall and knew that I needed to get professional help once and for all. From past experience I really wanted to avoid just going to a GP and being put back on Prozac yet again. So with the help of a Spanish friend I went to try and see the mental health department in Torrevieja. To me it was an emergency I was at the end of my tether and needed to speak to someone as soon as possible. But in the Spanish system I had to see a GP then get referred to the psychiatric department, the earliest appointment to see anybody would be 12 weeks away. Knowing that I wouldn't survive that long I turned to my Mum and had to admit that I was going through stuff and I needed help. They took me to the private medical centre that they used where there was a psychologist that I could see. A few days later I was booked in for an appointment.

I knew that I had to be completely honest with the psychologist and just get a proper diagnosis whatever that may be. If they told me I was schizophrenic I would have to just deal with it and accept it. When I was sat in the waiting room a vision girl was dancing around and there were other angels flying around outside the window. The psychologist was a nice Spanish lady called Mercedes who spoke to me in English, when I sat at her desk I could see Blue sat in a chair at the edge of the room dressed in a powder Blue two piece and pill box hat like Jackie Onassis. I explained all the symptoms that I was experiencing and what my problem was. I told her about the situation with the national health appointment and she decided that she would see me once a week to build up a detailed picture of what was going on and then we'd keep that other appointment and relay a full case report. I was to keep a detailed journal of everything that was happening every day that we would go through in ore weekly sessions and discuss my history etc. I felt good that there was a plan and I was comfortable with writing it all down so my focus became about that. I'd document all the details of the visions and my dreams as well as how it affected my daily life. She asked me about my family and my sexuality, hunting for any glaring issues. She gave me exercises to work through to do with relaxation and controlling myself when I was in the midst of a vision. She advised me to find a new exercise regime or sports club and also that it'd be a great help if I got a dog. I started going running but couldn't have a pet in my apartment and with my work hours. She had contacted the national health and they sent me to get a brain scan at the hospital. They put a thing like a swimming cap on my head with all these wires coming out of it and did loads of tests. When the appointment came around Mercedes actually went with the hospital results and the case notes she'd made over the 3 months. When I saw her that week she relayed to me what had gone on, they had a diagnosis and a solution. I was to take Trileptal three times per day, every day for the rest of my life. They'd diagnosed me with a type of epilepsy. She explained to me that there were many kinds of epilepsy; it's just a type of brain damage. There are many pathways and connections in your brain and that somewhere they were broken. She said that the epilepsy was causing the visions and probably other things that I hadn't noticed which are called partial seizures. As there was a diagnosis she was confident that on the medication I would not need to see her anymore. So I just got my prescription and went home.

I obviously had an emotional connection with Blue and I felt that when I took that first pill I would somehow be killing her off. So I went down the beach and sat by the sea to take it; pretty soon after I felt the effects kicking in. My head was spinning and everything around me looked like a little model version of the world, it took everything I had to walk home and get in to bed. When I got up the next day I could tell the difference, I was kind of zombified; I was functional and fine but with no emotion. The panic of the visions that I was used to living with had gone but in its place was a sort of numbness. I had to tell all my friends about it because I wasn't allowed to drink alcohol whilst on the medication. I still went out with them and didn't mind not drinking mainly because I didn't mind anything; I was just numb.

I can't really say much about anything during that time because I was pretty disconnected with the world. I can tell you that I still had the visions but that they didn't emotionally affect me anymore, it was just part of the world that I saw. One young guy who I got to know called Luke was really in to spiritual stuff and said to me that he didn't think I was ill but that it was something spiritual. One night in my apartment he pointed the camera at where I could see Blue and every single time I did there were these things called orbs showing up on the photograph. He reckoned I should explore the spiritual side but I was alright just plodding along as I was, why rock the boat? Kerri went to live in the UK, that I went to work for Mum and Barry, that I had a tattoo that represented the diagnosis to me. I had a kind of optical illusion bunch of stars on my other shoulder. I spoke to Sarah about the diagnosis and about all the visions and stuff. I moved in to a shared house with two other gay guys. Because I didn't drink I became the designated driver and we'd go off to Murcia, Alicante or Benidorm on the gay scene. I started working on the van with Gary who worked for Mum and Barry. He's older than me and married but we get on really well and socialise together too. I did more porn work for a studio in Alicante and even got in to escorting. It wasn't the greatest career move and was mostly older guys but it doesn't bother me; I like having the money. Because of the medication I'm just a robot. I'd do house calls and massage, they call them Johns when they're clients. So I ended up with loads of friends called John, Juan, Ivan, and Giovanni and so on. Because they're all older and I do mainly massage it's all pretty tame; they're just lonely or want access to a young body. Gary knows about it and is cool about it. I did it for a while and then took a break to try dating. I met a guy who was half Spanish and half English called Pablo. We hit it off because my parents knew his parents and he was a good laugh. He didn't mind that I wasn't a drinker even though he was. After a few weeks he moved in with me and the guys because he lived with his parents out in the sticks. I could see he had issues like drinking a lot and taking drugs but he talked about wanting to settle down so we ended up looking for an apartment to buy rather than just renting. It took ages to organise the mortgage and find an apartment and in that time I could see he was a mess and we had blazing rows when he was really wasted. I just kept thinking that some stability and responsibility would help him out. He hated the fact that I was never anything other than blank emotionally. There'd be violent rows where he's be screaming and throwing stuff around and I'd just be numb. One of our friends had some puppies for sale so we got two dogs and moved in to our apartment. It hadn't been great for a while but the whole process was such an effort that it seemed difficult to halt the momentum. He kept having car accidents and changing jobs. So we both started training courses, his in being a personal trainer and mine in hairdressing. Mum and Barry's business was busy and work was okay because I spent most days on the van driving around Spain doing deliveries with Gary. He was having problems in his marriage too so we both just talked it out together.

Things between me and Pablo were totally dysfunctional but because we'd got the house and dogs in an attempt to settle down and have a normal life we were kind of stuck together. The biggest problem to me was his drinking and drug taking so after splitting up and getting back together a few times I decided to give him an ultimatum. I would commit to him properly and we could get married if he could lay off the drink and drugs for a year and prove it wasn't an addiction. We could find him rehab or counselling and we'd stay together. I got on really well with his family and they agreed that he needed help. He agreed to it and we commemorated the commitment by going to Bagwa and getting tattoos, he had some shooting stars on his hip and I put the letter P with a star and a heart on my wrist. Sarah and Toby were surprised to see me in a relationship and with the house and life and stuff but it was nice to catch up with them.

Well deal lasted for about two weeks before I found empty boxes of wine hidden under our bed and all over the apartment. I still gave him another chance as it was clue to Christmas and he'd started a new job. Christmas in our home was nice because we had his folks around and Gary with his new girlfriend. But on

New Year's we had a massive row because his drug mates were calling him up and he went off to meet them. I was left alone in the flat with the dogs, listening to all the fireworks go off at midnight. He turned up four days later and used my birthday as a way to try and make a mends but a couple of weeks after that I said that I couldn't stay in a relationship with him. I'd just turned 29 and my attempt at settling down and leading a normal life was a complete mess.

The Tattoo Year 2008

It was hell living in the flat with Pablo, I'd moved in to the spare room but the atmosphere was not surprisingly terrible. He was heartbroken and angry but I just knew that he wasn't going to change and I couldn't just keep going on the way we had been. As with everything you just have to persevere and let time do its job. He got a new job in a bar and a new boyfriend. I did more porn work and escorting, I figured I would just make the most of it whilst I was young. I built up a bunch of regular Johns, only a handful but it was kind of like dating them in a way. They wanted to go for meals or watch a movie and have the boyfriend experience. I was fine with that because I was done with relationships. The porn work was just occasional but it was kind of exciting because the other models were young and attractive. I kept up the hairdressing by cutting mates hair and I did enjoy it but what with a fulltime job with Mum I was keeping myself pretty busy.

I decided to change my image and bleached my long hair and put dread locks in again. I also decided to go to Bagwa and get a full sleeve tattoo done. I started researching ideas for it and was going for optical illusions, Escher style things and maybe a pin up to represent Blue. When I went to see Sarah she was really surprised that I wanted a sleeve and that I was looking for it to be bold and colourful as opposed to all the black ones that I had so far. But she said that she wanted to do a big sleeve of flowers, in Chinese culture all the flowers have meanings and she felt like I could carry it off. I just told her to go for it and design it herself, just use me as a canvas. The sleeve tattoo took a lot of hours over many weeks and I really got to know Sarah and Toby well. They were in to a lot of spiritual stuff and discussed it all with the clients who came in. It was kind of like therapy, just being able to talk about anything; Sarah had been told by a gay client who had come in that I was an escort, she asked me about it and I was honest with her. She said they didn't have any judgement at all and that became part of the conversation too. It was really liberating to be able to talk about anything and everything. I eventually talked about Blue with her and she was really intrigued, I couldn't believe that such a place like this existed. These two people had opened a business primarily to do tattoos and make a living but somehow with the talking therapy they were helping everybody who came in. As the time went on Sarah mentioned that during the summer they always have an assistant helping them out because it' so busy and asked me whether I was interested in doing it. She knew that I wanted to get another sleeve done on the other arm and the arrangement would be that I worked the summer in exchange for that. I was completely stoked, I could do my work on the van until the afternoon then go to the studio and work there in that great environment. I couldn't believe that I was being given the opportunity to be part of that place even just for the summer.

That summer was absolutely amazing I got to make drinks and chat to clients whilst they waited, make the transfers for the tattoos and even ended up designing some tattoos that people got done on them. It was such a buzz to see people walking out with stuff that I had just designed and now it was in their skin. I got to know Sarah and Toby better and also their Bagwa Tribe of clients who were like an extended family.

Adonai reached out to my arm and held it out so that he could inspect all the flowers. "So this is kind of that summer etched in to your skin."

"Yeah I'll never forget that summer, it completely changed my life. This how the story started out remember? That reading, the moment that changed me forever. I'd told Sarah about the visions and stuff and she'd sent me over the road from the tattoo studio to go and see a medium. I walked up the corridor to medium's apartment with some scepticism – expecting some colourful witch to theatrically spout a list of vague predictions to help me navigate my future. She'd say helpful things like beware of the man in the green jacket, look out for the number 7 it's very lucky for you or I can see you working with animals. Maybe she'd even give me some pointers on what to do next with my life – God knows I'm pretty desperate right now. I also had a certain amount of trepidation, what if she could somehow read my mind or see into my past and my secrets are all laid bare before her? What if there was bad news?

I knocked and was welcomed by a middle aged, normal – looking, northern woman who was wearing a distinctly confused expression.

"I have an appointment with Noelle at 2 o'clock"

"Crystal?"

"Um, no... Kristoff"

"Oh dear I thought you were a girl called Crystal! I must have misheard on the phone. So sorry do come in." If she had been expecting a girl named Crystal I can understand her surprise at opening the door to a young man with peroxide dreadlocks and a sleeve of tattoos. So far her powers of perception are not installing me with much confidence. She ushered me in and sat me down on a sofa and explained that she needed to inform her spirit guides of the mix up in client so that they could prepare for the right person. She proceeded to go out through a patio door onto a balcony where I observed her sit down bow her head and mutter under her breath for a few moments. I wasn't unfamiliar with the terms she was using as several of my friends are spiritualist but this was to be my first ever reading and I was beginning to feel nervous. The apartment was generic to the point of bland, no signs that anything magical happens here, no velvet, no wooden chest, and no book of shadows, magic wand or broomstick, just your typical apartment. Sarah and Toby had advised me to bring a pad and pen to make notes on the reading so I composed myself as Noelle sat in an armchair on the other side of a coffee table to me. Out of a pocket in her cardigan she retrieved a deck of tarot cards, handed them to me and asked me to shuffle them whilst thinking of a question I needed guidance with. All I could think as I shuffled the cards was that I wanted to know what to do next with my life, nothing particularly specific. She then directed me to pick cards and place them face down in a certain formation on the coffee table. Then she tilted her head as if someone was whispering in her ear and put up one hand as if to gesture to me to halt.

"Just give me a second, something's happening" She said. I presumed that the theatrics were commencing, a little dramatic performance that all of her clients must receive to prepare them for the magic that was about to happen with the cards. She was a good actress because she was really throwing herself into the role or maybe she was just well rehearsed.

"This has never happened before, you see normally I work with specific spirit guides but they've just told me to hang on because they need to go and find someone more qualified to deal with you. We won't be needing the tarot." This is when the question came.

"Do you know who you are?" She asks me. My brain presses pause. The room turns from white into Blue.

I must have glazed over at that point because she waved a hand over my face to catch my attention. It looked to me like she was a TV presenter communicating with a production team via an ear piece the way in which she was behaving, nodding and murmuring. She seemed genuinely flustered. Then she looked at me with a real sense of gravity and I felt a wave of awkwardness break over me, slightly embarrassed by her intensity.

"They've sent in the big boys, I've never spoken to these spirits before. It's a real privilege. It's very important that you develop." I didn't comprehend what she was saying but just made notes as she spoke.

"You are a loner who might not be meant to be with anyone, you'll have close friends and lovers but some people have to be alone because of the job you have to do. You have the spirit to know the right path and you are not interested in being rich or famous – just a pure soul who is very patient. The spectrum you are part of I can see moving around at the speed of light but very controlled. You need to start getting things into perspective and your life in order. Think in an orderly fashion. The repercussions of being laid back are immense. Start experimenting with feelings because in order to do the work you need to know how people feel, open up a bit. The job to be done concerns all mankind and when the time comes you'll need to guide people to help them understand. They've been waiting for you to come to be read so that they could communicate with you properly. You must now meditate, you must protect yourself put a bubble around you because you have such a strong spirit you'll attract a lot of spirits so you need to ask for protection. Once you start to develop people will arrive needing advice and guidance in their lives. Learn to empathise with them. The door is now open and that is permanent it cannot now be closed. Light attracts dark people who drain you but your light and path cannot be diminished. You are unemotional and take life as it comes, I can see angel wings on your back and you are a pure soul sent here to do a job bringing the light and spiritual word to others. There aren't many pure souls on earth – the only pure souls on earth are like angels walking amongst us. Because you volunteered for this job you will be kept safe and they'll make sure you have enough to get by on. You are one of the chosen ones who must have volunteered to come down and do this. When you meditate talk to them normally and ask them to teach you and take you on a journey. Ask the guide to slow things down for you so you can make sense of them. You have an extremely powerful guide. You'll be taken to amazing places and see things you will never have believed in the far reaches of the universe. You will join forces with five other psychics and together you will connect to be the light." She paused smiling at me in such a caring manner. My mind was already racing at all the information she had just given me. But what was about to come in the next sentence would blow my whole world and past apart.

She proceeded to tell me that she had someone there that she could see stood right next to her. In my eyes I could see that Blue was stood there. She said this is your partner in the spirit world, she's been with you in the life there and you've come here to be born and have this life and she's always been with you. She's showing me a scene to prove to you that this is real. Do you remember walking along the street on the way home from work and there was a flock of angels flying around you giving you a message? I was totally stunned; I'd never told anybody about that specific vision, there was no way that Noelle could be saying this unless it was actually happening. She went on to say that Blue is my lover and guardian and guide; she's been with me always. Now that she has made contact with me through somebody else she wants me to learn to contact her properly. Just as the message had said, they want me to meditate and reach the other side. She loves me and has confidence that I can do this. I should also ask my Mum about when I was tiny as there is a message for me there too. Blue smiled at me and winked, and then she just faded out in a cloud of blue glitter. Noelle said that she had gone and that was the end of the reading, everything had gone quiet. We sat there in stunned silence, she thanked me for coming for the reading and said it was like nothing he had experienced before; she was talking excitedly. She gave me advice about how to meditate and asked me if I was willing to do an experiment. We would both meditate separately and see if we could reach the place that I come from on the other side and then in a week we would meet up and compare notes. I just agreed because I was in shock.

When I left the apartment and made my way back over to the studio I really felt like I was living in the matrix. I kept going over the connotations of what had just happened. Blue was real. There was a spiritual world. Serendipity had lead me all my life to this moment right now, all the events and choices of my life had put me right here to experience this. I knew there was no way that Noelle would have known about the angel vision; Blue was the only one who could have told her or else she had some magical powers to read inside my memories. Either way magic exists and the spiritual world exists. When I got back in to the studio it was really busy so Sarah and Toby asked me how it had gone and they could tell by my face that something big had happened, I just said I'd talk to them alone later. Eventually I just handed them my notes of the reading, they were blown away too; but Sarah told me to go and get a second opinion too so that I wasn't basing stuff on what just one person had told me. I planned to go to the spiritualist church on the next Tuesday to sit in the crowd and see if anything came through. Apparently you just sit in the congregation and a medium stands at the front getting messages through for people.

When I got home that night I decided to lie on my bed and concentrating on trying to meditate and see what happens. It had been presented to me a couple of times in the past, doing A level psychology when I was 18 the teacher had taken me aside and described transcendental meditation to me and Mercedes had touched on it with the relaxation techniques to help with the epilepsy. So I just lay on my bed and put some music on in my headphones. Almost instantly my perspective changed and I was gradually looking down from the ceiling at my own body lying on the bed. My consciousness was outside of my body. In flash I moved upwards so fast that soon I was in the middle of space, zooming past stars until I was closing in on one. I slowed down until I was floating in front of a shining orb the size of a planet. Gradually I was pulled through the shining orb and into the atmosphere or sky of a world. It was like zooming down on Google maps; I landed down in a pure white room. There was a man sat crossed legged on the floor who looked like the stereotypical God figure with white robes and long hair and a beard. As I looked at him he hovered and morphed until he was looking like a professor in a lab coat sat on a chair; at the same time as he morphed so did the room. It transformed in to a science lab lined with book shelves and tables appeared laden with bubbling test tubes. He stood up off the chair and looked like the white suited Architect from The Matrix films and the room turned in to a giant game of chess. As he reached out to touch the white king piece he transformed into Mick Fleetwood from the 'Rumours' album cover holding a glass orb in his hand. He smiled at me and walked towards me holding the orb out for me to inspect; when I looked closer I could see that it was the planet earth. The clouds were moving and it looked alive. He took it in both hands and raised it up in front of me and then let it drop to the floor. As the orb hit the floor the whole room turned in to that street where I saw the flock of angels; he and I floated up above the street and we were in the perspective that the flying angels would have been. To look around it seemed as if we were actually there right now like I could land back down again and walk around and everything would be 'normal' He reached out for me to take his hand and as I did we zoomed back up through space again until we were back in the pure white room. He gestured for me to walk towards the wall and as I did a big wooden door appeared. I opened it and walked through. It was the hallway that I had seen in a dream with Blue years ago with a corridor leading off to the right or a stairway winding upwards.

I climbed the stairs until I came out in a room that was the one with the heart shaped bed from the vision with Blue years ago. I looked over the balcony down to the bed and there was Blue lay on the bed looking up, waiting for me to arrive. I slowly descended the stairs, the stone walls and bannister felt real to the touch, I could feel the cold floor beneath my feet. She reached out her hand and pulled me onto the bed with her, I'd never felt emotion like that before it was completely indescribable. She put her hand behind my head and pulled me in for a kiss. As our lips met I was suddenly back lying on my bed in the apartment, in Torrevieja, in Spain on planet Earth. As far as I could tell. I closed my eyes again and I was instantly back on the heart shaped bed and Blue was ascending the stairs beckoning me to follow her. She lead me to what I felt was our home, there was a 1950s looking kitchen like on the farm looking out onto a courtyard garden that was full of plants. She showed me the living room which just had big cushions piled around on the floor and what looked like musical instruments dotted around. I followed her out on to a balcony and the view was amazing. The apartment was part of a kind of castle that was carved out of a mountain, and at the foot of the mountain I could see a vast city spreading out in front of me. The mountain spread around both sides so that the city was nestled in its valley. There were water falls flowing down the mountain between the other balconies and holes where I could see other gardens. As I looked upwards I could see towers and turrets of a castle and bigger buildings jutting out and about. Blue was stood there looking at me taking the entire scene in; she smiled and tapped her wrist as if to say my time was up for this visit. She leant in and held my face in her hands and slowly kissed me on the lips and in a flash I was back in my bed again. I tried closing my eyes again but nothing happened, I was back here again. I didn't want to get up and about because I felt disappointed that I was back here rather than there so I just hugged into the duvet and rested my head on the pillow and drifted off to sleep.

At work that Monday I told my Mum that I'd had a reading and that they'd told me to ask her about when I was a baby. She looked a bit upset and told me that when I was born I was the second of the twins, once Peter had been born she was bleeding badly and she was suddenly looking down at herself from the ceiling watching everything happen. She could see the doctors and nurses doing stuff and me being born but she then passed out and woke up a while later. Then she told

me that I'd stayed in hospital for a long while to have
an operation on my stomach because I was really ill
and on the verge of death. When she'd taken me home
to the farm and put me and Pete in separate cots on
other sides of the room something weird happened.
She'd gone back downstairs to the lounge where
everybody else was, nobody left the room and a while
later she cam back up to check on us. I was in the cot
with Pete, she thought that someone had played a joke
on her and had a row with everybody else back
downstairs; she knew 100% that she'd put us in
different cots. I told her that the medium had said that
there was something spiritual going on with me and
Mum was a bit teary and just said she could well
believe that.

On the Tuesday I went to the Spiritualist church and
sat at the back not knowing what to expect. The lady
did a few messages to people and then she pointed
straight at me and said that the spirit was telling her
that I had lay in meditation and made contact with my
guide. She said there's a strong sense of love there and
that they are urging me to do it more and to develop
myself. The only other thing was that she was getting
the number 27 above my head. I did just that and went
home and meditated again. I rose up out of my body
again and zoomed off until I found myself lay on a
stone slab in a stone room like a mausoleum. As I
looked around me I had saw that I was wearing red
trousers and waistcoat and shirt with a big red cloak
spreading out around me. My blond dreadlocks were
longer and within each strand was flowing lights. I
stood up off the slab and went off to explore, I went

out into what seemed to me to be like a hospital and I had the sense that it was a vast building with loads more slab rooms just like the one I had just came out of. I walked past a big reception desk where there was a woman stood and as she saw me she looked really shocked so I just kept on moving up a flight of marble stairs. I came out on to a vast hallway I could feel the marble under my bare feet. There was a massive ornate doorway leading out on to a massive flight of stairs; I realised I was in that mountain again and the flight of stairs lead down into the city. The waterfalls were flowing down the mountain in amongst the balconies and gardens. At the bottom of the stairs was a wide and long onyx catwalk stretching out through the buildings. The buildings were all of different styles, some old some modern. There were people milling about all dressed in clothes from different eras and cultures, it was like I was in some big film set. Most of them looked at me with a shocked expression but one beautiful lady who looked like Michelle Pfeiffer smiled at me and gestured for me to follow her. She led me through the streets and out in to this vast park. There were trees of all different kinds and birds and animals all around. It occurred to me that for some reason nobody had actually said anything to me yet, perhaps I couldn't communicate here yet. The lady smiled at me and nodded. She span around and transformed into Marilyn Monroe, she giggled and blew me a kiss. With that I was back at home again. I tried going back again but couldn't do it.

Back at the studio I chatted to Sarah and Toby about the fact that I'd started meditating and experienced

OBEs, I didn't go into detail about where I'd gone. Toby was really interested and said that if I was getting into all the spiritual stuff then he had some good books for me to read. He gave me 'The Monk Who Sold His Ferrari' by Robin Sharma and 'The Road Less Travelled' by M Scott Peck. I soaked them all up, I was totally consumed by learning as much as I could about this other world and spiritual stuff. I was looking for clues as to whether anybody else had seen this place that I had gone to in meditation. The books were helpful and taught me stuff about life and spiritual evolution. M Scott Peck's definition of love is amazing that it's not a feeling but an activity; to love is to 'extend one's self for the purpose of nurturing one's own or another's spiritual growth' That really stuck with me and I definitely think that that is what Sarah and Toby were doing at Bagwa. Spiritual growth goes from zero all the way up a scale to oneness with the universe or source.

"Oh my god, way out man." Adonai purred while holding up the peace sign. "This whole thing is blowing my mind Kristoff. Keep going I wanna know the secret of life!"

"Ahaha, well I don't know about but I've definitely learned a lot along the way. When I was at the tattoo studio someone came in for a Marilyn Monroe piece and that reminded me of that lady in the meditation. I had also done my art GCSE with a portrait of Marilyn and read biographies about her; I didn't know whether it was some kind of clue they were trying to show me. I decided to look in to more of the OBE side of stuff and sure enough the first thing that came up was The Monroe Institute. I got straight in to reading Robert Monroe's last book because I figured it would all be summed up there. In 'Ultimate Journey' he writes about these levels of focus that you can progress your mind up through and at Level 27 is this Home level where there is a reception area and park and places that human spirits have created to help them progress in death and on-going evolution. I immediately recognised this place as the one that I had visited in my meditations/OBEs it really blew my mind. To me that was confirmation that all of this was real and that what he calls Level 27 is what I saw as home; also that's what the spiritualist medium had said to me was there was a number 27 above my head. I did an OBE that night and went straight home to Level 27. This time I saw myself in a mirror in the slab room and my body was different and alien. I had pointier ears and a tail, then it just became a light body then just sort of chemical symbols and stuff in the air. I lay back down on the slab and my dread locks connected through a halo into the wall. I had the idea that all of the slab rooms had were connected to each other in a big complex circuit. So all the souls are connected to each other, maybe that's where the collective unconscious comes from. He includes the idea of Belief System Territories people go to these places when they die according to what they believe about the afterlife and you can be hindered from reincarnating and having another life in order to carry on evolving. So it's really important to try and meditate into Level 27 and realise what the whole story is rather than just getting bogged down by religions that will end up restricting you.

When I went back to see Noelle and compared notes we realised that we had both visited the same place; she described the white room with the Godlike bloke sat in it and also the city. She had also drawn a picture that she'd seen me look like at Home and it was exactly what I'd seen in the mirror. I went on to have shared meditations with Melody and Victoria several times. Where we'd see the exact same things or they'd describe what they'd seen me do within the meditation when obviously there's no way of knowing that at all. I was starting on this amazing spiritual evolution that I'd kind of got thrown into. At home with Pablo things just got worse and worse and in October the financial crisis hit and Mum and Barry decided to close the business. It was a terrible time. I'd lost my main job and all over Spain it was happening to everyone, there were no jobs about and I couldn't claim benefits as I had been self-employed. Escorting was a sporadic and it wasn't feasible to rely just on hairdressing or even the porn work. I was surviving but barely; I couldn't contribute anything to the mortgage and bills because I was living hand to mouth. Through Bagwa I managed to start teaching Spanish lessons but it was just an hour here and there. Pablo just got more and more angry with me. The Johns were all really supportive and helped me survive with meals out. But at the start of 2009 it all came to a head and Pablo chucked me out of the flat. I managed to crash at a friend of my Mum's temporarily. It happened 4 days before my 30th birthday. On that day I was just really depressed, heartbroken that I'd lost my dogs, who were like children to me and my home. Pablo was calling me all the time and threatening me that he was going to get his drug mates to come and kill me because I'd left him with the bills. I was terrified because he had gone really crazy and smashed the flat up when he was chucking me out. I believed him that he would send me people after me. Luckily another mate I knew through Spanish lessons had an apartment that was empty that he was happy for me to use for as long as I needed. He felt sorry for me and wanted to give me a chance to get back on my feet. I moved my stuff in there in Punta Prima and just felt like I was at a dead end. I believed it had all happened for a reason but I just struggled to get through each hour. I had absolutely nothing and was just scrabbling to even get money to eat. Bagwa didn't need me up there because the winter is quiet and my Mum was selling up to return back to the UK. Barry had been ill for a while and things had broken down between them so she was moving back to the UK to start over again. She left a couple of weeks later and I was on my own.

Sarah and Toby spoke to me more and more about spiritual stuff and one day they were asking me at OBEs I was describing the way in which I had discovered that I could travel out of body in this world and see stuff that was going on. In real life I had never been to their new house but in an OBE I visited it. I never went in to any buildings as I thought that was quite weird because they're private. Outside their house I could see a man attached to the building just hovering around it and this thing he was holding on a lead that to me looked like a little fat puffer fish. I described the shape of the house and where the swimming pool was. When I relayed this to Sarah and Toby in one of our conversations they both gasped. They said that the old couple who they had bought the house from that sounded like the man and their dog was fat and round like a puffer fish. They'd viewed it last year but only were able to buy it because the man had died in the house and his wife wanted to return to the UK. Sarah said she had always felt like there was bad vibes or a presence in the house. They called Melody to go and do a kind of blessing on the house and told me to go along with her for the experience. She went around the house doing all the Reiki rituals and it weirded me out a bit. I just went in to a meditation/OBE I could see the old man hovering above the house so I went up and spoke to him. He was confused and didn't realise that he had died and that his wife had gone. I took his hand and helped him fly up until he zoomed up away from me. Blue came down in front of where I was actually sitting next to Melody dangling our legs in the swimming pool. She moved through the water and right up to me giving me a kiss. When we came out of the meditation Melody described seeing me darting about flying above the house and that she felt a massive force moving through the water to me at the end. That was another confirmation to me that this was all real, there was no way she could have guessed what was going on in my meditation. Melody invited me to sit in on some of her Reiki group meetings and the same thing kept happening, I could go in an OBE when they were doing distance healing and see the person that someone was concentrating on. When I spoke to Kerri on messenger I could describe the room that she was sitting in that I had never seen in real life, she was spooked but excited.

One day in March I was still living hand to mouth but surviving I popped in to Bagwa and Victoria was there getting an angel wings symbol tattooed on her shoulder. We got to chatting and decided to meet up and chat about spiritual stuff because we had similar beliefs. When we met up she told me that she thought I was psychic and that I should try and do a reading on her. I just concentrated and things started to play out like a film in my head. I could accurately describe loads of memories from her past, it just coming and coming; we carried on for hours that day. We started to spend a lot of time together and I showed her the reading I'd had and that I thought she could be one of the psychics I was supposed to connect up with. We spent all our time with each other talking about spiritual stuff and testing out how it works. In meditations I was being shown more and more about how the guides help us. It's a bit like in the film The Adjustment Bureau and The Matrix, they can't directly change things in the world but they can influence us with signs and dreams and inspiration. You can build your own signs that can help in that communication whether it's songs that mean stuff to you or words and numbers. I tested out with one of the Johns when we were talking about that stuff. I told him to think of a specific question and then switch the radio on and listen to three songs and there will be an answer to the question. He did exactly that and his mind was blown because it had worked.

"Wow Kristoff this is really cool, so looking at your other sleeve I can tell that it's full of all these symbols to do with that time right?"

"Definitely, Toby called me in to do the sleeve for me and I picked lots of symbolism from Chinese art that mean different stuff, he designed me a one off sugar skull and I got a brilliant handpicked butterfly done by their mentor Adam Starfish. Just as that arm was finished Victoria had to go back to the UK but we stayed in touch and I managed to get working as a chef in The Lansdown bar that used to be my local. For a few years it was all about just working and socialising and I did loads of research on the internet into everything I possibly could. I looked in to all the conspiracy theories, religions, psychology and everything. The Johns were still really supportive and I'd got a really good relationship with them now. We'd go on little holidays like to the Alhambra in Granada which blew me away because it totally reminded me of my spiritual home. I know that to them it's like a romantic relationship and I understand that, I'm eternally grateful for all of their support and I don't know what I would have done without them.

The Journey

So if I'm looking at the tattoos left that I've got to tell you about and in my story so far I guess it's my hands, neck and chest and the 3 dots by my eyes. I'll go with my neck one first, it's a symbol that kind of represents myself spiritually. Toby had been going to Reiki classes at Melody's with his an Sarah's son TJ. They were being taught all about the Reiki symbols that are used to focus different energies and do different things. When I had learnt about Reiki I came to the thinking that symbols and those things are just a way for us to more easily focus our intentions, it becomes part of that language with which we communicate with the guides at home. I knew what my symbol that represented me was and Toby asked me to see if I could find out what his and TJ's were. When I meditated on TJ's I was shown his energy and his potential. I've seen him grow up and his energy is so cool; he's going to be artistic and social and have this talent to really connect with people. It doesn't surprise me in the slightest that over time he has become a great photographer, into music, surrounded by good people and is involved in the outdoors and teaching. He's going to be an amazing human being; Sarah and Toby should be so proud of him and of themselves and the way that they have raised him. Toby's energy showed me more to do with the fact that he's in the right place with Sarah and with Bagwa. They're purpose is together and they are fulfilling it. People come to them not only for ink but also for guidance; they have helped so many people and affected so many peoples' lives. I know that for myself my life would be unrecognisable if I hadn't have gone for that first 'serendipity' tattoo. I was so privileged when they chose to give ma a bat symbol tattoo on my wrist that represents being part of the Bagwa Tattoo Tribe, at the same time I changed the P on my wrist to a B for Blue.

The two first tattoos I had on my hands were my ring fingers. The right hand side one was done in Las Vegas, I'd gone there with some friends who I'd met in Punta Prima when they went there to get married. We stayed in the Bellagio and went by helicopter and landed in the Grand Canyon where they got married. Las Vegas was an amazing place to explore and it really reminded me of Level 27 too, how there are all these different environments created for different experiences. I had to get a tattoo to commemorate it so I had a Blue heart to represent blue and a number 8 to represent Timothy Leary's 8 Circuits of Consciousness. It's about how we all evolve through different circuits of consciousness and how they affect our behaviour and help our spiritual evolution. The Blue heart to me also means that M Scott Peck's definition of love goes hand in hand with that. You have to actually do stuff to move towards spiritual evolution and that to me is the meaning of life in one finger! Home has taught me that the purpose of this world and universe and the meaning of life is evolution. The first one on the other hand was a lightning bolt because I got stuck by lightning; I didn't get any magic powers as far as I know. Victoria and I were walking along the road with umbrellas in a rain storm and suddenly a thunder storm kicked up. I suddenly saw a flash and in slow motion saw a tiny ball travel down my umbrella and across my body and Victoria jumped like she'd had an electric shock. I was really dazed and for a few days I had loads of static running through me; when we told Sarah and Toby about it they just pissed themselves and said that had to be a tattoo.

I discovered that the people I saw at Level 27 were able to show me different messages about the history of life; they came to me like dreams. If you start at the big bang there was a ball of energy with a force driving it to evolve, by trial and error with nothing other than the laws of physics holding it together it randomly evolved until there were planets and it had formed life and found a planet on which life could be sustained. Then the process of the evolution of life started on this planet. It's all still random and ruled by the laws of physics. Once sentient beings had evolved far enough up the eight circuits of consciousness to be conscious and form souls that reincarnated we started a journey as souls through all the different life forms that were available on this planet. As our souls got more advanced some broke through to the other dimension and started to create a place called level 27 to help souls evolve even more. I completely agree with Robert Monroe's idea that souls can get stuck in belief systems that trap souls into beliefs like Christianity or Islam etc. Those people who perpetuate those religions are only looking at one part of the elephant. They're the blind men touching the elephant and calling it a rope or a tree or a wall; not seeing the bigger picture. Here on earth they've set up systems and laws and norms that only divide us and hinder our spiritual evolution as individuals and as a human race in total. They became just a way in which those in power could control the masses; setting up laws that controlled their behaviour using the idea of eternal life as the end prize. Even now we see how much division and damage these religions are doing to humanity. It really surprised me that all the Abrahamic religions have a shared narrative, shared characters and are basically about the same things. Yet they have fought over the different ways that they have been interpreted. It's the human leaders of those religions that are perpetuating the divisions and destroying lives. Once we break down those ideas by trying to connect with Home and our souls then we will see that those religions were just signposts along the way and not the destination. Now that our souls have been cats and cows and dolphins and we are living human lives we are supposed to be experiencing everything we can and learning all the lessons we can being human. We then upload that information back up to our soul back at home. Our identities only exist for this particular life then we merge back in to our soul on death taking all our lessons back with us. By reincarnating and being born in to different situations, cultures, countries etc we try to experience and learn as much as we can. The aim is always to try and spiritually evolve our consciousness up through the 8 levels and with that up through the focus levels that Monroe talks about."

"I'm definitely going to hunt down these books and ideas – they sound fascinating. They're not connected to religion just to ideas about the mind and soul right?" Adonai asked.

"Yeah, they're really about your own mind; so through meditation, lucid dreaming, OBEs, dreams and all that you can just train your mind and to focus more like tuning through radio stations. Monroe uses this technology called hemisinc with binaural beats that by listening to them you can change the brainwaves. I think there are many different paths you can take to do that meditation; it's about what works for each individual. When I picked up a book about Buddhism I found that I already believed a lot of the ideas in it. To me it's about every person having the potential to be a Buddha, you just evolve yourself and aim for enlightenment. I think enlightenment is about stripping away the constructs of religions and the things that we have been told; there's a wall built up of what we're told about life and the world, as you break them down the light can get in. By evolving up the 8 circuits you will experience stuff that will enlighten you. It's about taking control of your thoughts every moment of the day and training your brain.

Another book that really helped me with this idea of training yourself was actually about Buddhism; 'How To Become A Buddha In 5 Weeks' by Giulio Cesare Giacobbe. It covers the ideas of Buddhism but breaks them down to practical activities that you can do. It's kind of like I've picked up these ideas and books that have really helped me to formulate ways of living every day and evolving my mind. I've read so many articles and books over the last few years and when they resonate with what I've experienced in meditations and at Level 27 I take them on board and add them to my arsenal of ways in which to evolve. Buddha was just a man who went through that process to and it's available to all of us, we can spiritually evolve to; we all have that potential. As M Scott

Peck's definition of love said it's just a decision we have to make to actively extend ourselves towards that spiritual growth. The great thing is that we are all in this together and we can help each other in that growth by the way in which we treat each other; it is a personal love but that also extends outwards to include everything else up to a universal love. That's the idea of being human and being here on earth. It's a bit like The Matrix where one self is unconscious on a slab at home and the other is here in this dimension walking around on earth uploading all the stuff we're experiencing here with the purpose of spiritually evolving. We're supposed to be learning how to do all the stuff that we think is paranormal. We're her within the confines of time and space and physics as a safe training ground for us to eventually graduate to a life in the other dimension. We're in a kind of training ground here to learn how to be an 'angel' and control all powers that an angel's body and mind can do. When I meditated on this the Michelle Pfeiffer lady showed me how the slab rooms work at home. There is a pure white room with no doors or windows. The walls, ceiling and floor are a milky shiny white. In the centre of this room is a body, it's on a slab, a solid block of the same material that forms the rest of the room. I walk over and look at the body. It is a human male. At first look I see his skin, and then as I focus more I can see blood vessels, then nerves, internal organs and right down to his skeleton. I can see the electricity moving through his brain and on out to the rest of his body. I can see that this electricity extends out of his body merges into the slab. Out of his body I can see his electromagnetic field and the energies that flow in it. In the core of his body the electricity weaves a circuit that shows an elaborate pattern of chakras all over the body and extending outwards into the magnetic field. It is a beautiful sight, actually seeing the biological body functioning along with the spirit body. The man's eyes open and as the lids unfold the room morphs into a hospital room and the slab turns into a bed and the man is covered in tubes coming out of his body and feeding down under the bed. He looks up at the ceiling and sees an identical hospital room, identical bed and himself, his eyes staring back up into his own. He closes his eyes and the room goes blank again. Then as he slowly opens them again the room becomes an ambulance and he's lying on the stretcher; he looks to his right and sees himself sat on seat in the ambulance in the hospital gown looking at himself. He recoils in fear, turns his head the other way and scrunches his eyes tight. He has rolled over in his own bed at home. He opens them again and he's in the middle of a beautiful blue ocean on a bright red lilo. He looks around and gets agitated, and then he jumps into the water. He comes up for air and wipes his face, and then he focuses. He's in a swimming pool, a real one he can remember; on holiday. He swims to the side of the pool, props himself up and watches his girlfriend walking up to him in a beautiful red swimming costume. She kneels down in front of him and kisses him, he closes his eyes. He can feel her lips leave his. He opens his eyes and he's stood against a wall at the foot of a sweeping flight of stairs; gleaming white marble. At the top of the stairway is a doorway filled with bright white light. He slowly climbs the stairs and as he stands in the doorway and looks through it he sees the original white slab room and he looks down at his body and realises he is lay on the slab. I can see the surge of energy inside of him flowering through his brain and fusing on down into his nervous system. It keeps surging as he begins to move his limbs. The strands of electricity move with him and still merge with block as if their energies are connected. He can see this and by the way he's staring at his hand I think he can see his body transparently like I can too. His electricity is now fizzling in multicolour and his chakras glisten and bloom. The field of energy is full with spiralling energies of every colour more chakras outside of his body start to illuminate. Just as he focuses on them the slab starts to change into a stone; as it fully morphs the floor turns into wooden floorboards. The ceiling turns into a painted heavenly scene and the walls are curtained completely in deep red velvet with intricate gold trimming. As he looks around and back above his head a tube of electricity leads down off the slab and along the floor; as it meets the curtain it starts to open. Its parting reveals a massive screen that is showing scenes from the man's life. He now reviews all the different events in his life; he can also hear the thoughts of the other people in the situation. Because all the slab room are linked to each other he can connect with the minds of the other people he has come in contact with in life. This is the purpose of Level 27; once you manage to believe that you can reincarnate you enter this process of reviewing the life you just had. Then you can wander around the city and park and meditate on those things. You upload them to your soul, you can talk to loved ones who are there and also get in contact with people still alive through dreams or via a medium or they may be able to see you as a spirit. All your identities are merged in to this one soul that is trying to evolve as much as it can; there can be any number of identities in your soul from the number of lives that you've had. In the future you can send another part of your soul down to have another life. All that you can plan is the genetics and location of your parents. Life is all about choices so everything else is down to the choices your parents make and then you; we all affect each other. Some of the course of your life will be down to biology and other things that are just random and mostly uncontrollable like natural disasters or global events. The guides at Home work with every single person and are there to try and help us all toward spiritual evolution; they communicate with us in so many different ways. Blue shows me ideas or signs in films and music; I will recognise something as a sign from her. It will be a sign about what I'm doing whether it's positive to show me I'm on the right path or negative to make me stop and examine what I'm doing. Sometimes I'll be shown a premonition and that tells me to concentrate when the scene comes up in real time. It may just be a symbol or picture that confirms and idea to me. Like when Avatar came out the aliens looked exactly like the one I saw years before in my first visits to Home; or Cloud Atlas that showed me ideas about reincarnation. I'll read something and formulate a belief, be shown as sign and to me then it becomes a known thing. Life always is changing every moment that passes and with every choice that everybody makes we are building the future. When I've done Medium readings and looked in to the future for someone I'm always aware that it is only one version of the future, all that can change by what a person chooses to do. The trick is to train your mind to make the best choices that you can in every moment, it's so fundamentally important. I read a book that really helped me with this idea, it's called 'The Four Agreements: A Practical Guide To Personal Freedom' by Don Miguel Ruiz. It taught me one way in which you can try and make the best choices in your everyday life. To boil it down it basically says to be impeccable with your word, don't take anything personally, don't make assumptions and always do your best. Obviously you're not going to do your absolute best in every situation but your best will be whatever it is in those conditions. Choices are so massively important, they are what life is all about, what build our future; so how to make good choices is the ultimate skill to learn. That's also why I have such a massive respect for what Sarah and Toby do at Bagwa because they actually get to talk to people about their lives and help them out with the choices that they are making. For some reason when somebody is sat in the tattoo chair they seem to open up about their situation and experiences. I suppose you have to make yourself physically vulnerable and have to totally trust the tattoo artist just on a physical level and somehow that makes you open up more emotionally too. It is a kind of secular therapy as well as an art form, but this art becomes part of you; it literally gets under your skin.

With this idea of love being so paramount in my evolution I remembered the quote that I got given back in secondary school. I had to hunt around on the internet to find out where it came from and eventually found that it was a section from the poem 'The Prophet' by Kahlil Gibran. Weirdly enough I had been given the quote that was just his words on love but I discovered that this beautiful book covered ideas on every aspect of life. Although his language come from a religious viewpoint I found that the ideas really resonated with me and it's one of my favourite things to read now; it reminds me of Home. I love the idea that some ideas that resonate with you, the ones that can be tested and researched and still stand the test of time and evolution cannot be broken. In the film 'V for Vendetta' I heard the line that says that ideas are bulletproof. That became one of my hand tattoos, the mask of Guy Fawkes with that quote around it. It's okay to have ideas or beliefs but you have to question them from every angle and if they survive they are the bulletproof ones and you can assimilate them to your soul; but never stop being open to testing them. When I'm at Level 27 it definitely looks like a scene from a Wachowski film but merged with the imagery of a Baz Luhrmann movie. Next to that tattoo on my hand I have to word 'protégé' tattooed to remind me that I'm the one who is learning from other people's teachings; whether it's art, films, music or writings I'm the student. On the other hand I have a tattoo of an eye with a lightning flash through it that represents the music of The Killers; they're music and lyric help me so much with meditation their energy takes me right Home. Around that is a blue feather to partly represent Blue as a guardian angel and also from a scene in the book 'Illusions: The Adventures of a Reluctant Messiah' by Richard Bach. That book was the seed that started me thinking about spiritual stuff in a different way and that magical things can happen. I think you can give yourself a kind of placebo with those kinds of ideas and the effect is the doors of your mind opening up to the magical spiritual world. All these rituals and symbols that people use are an elaborate placebo that they are giving themselves; building a context in which they believe that magic is going to happen. This is true to me in simple things like prayer, Reiki symbols, Voodoo, Wicca and loads of the religious ceremonies that people perform. They are all placebos that cultures have invented over the years, if you do x then the result will be y; would we perform these rituals if they hadn't been invented? How much of our religious ceremonies would we perform if we spent our entire lives on a deserted island? I really think about that analogy when people are fighting over religion, a lot of it has just been suggested by people hundreds and thousands of year ago. We only perform them because we're held hostage the idea of being a 'good' person; but that ideal has been formulated by religion. Even the laws on life that exist in the Old Testament don't bear much relevance to life in the 21st Century; those ideas weren't bullet proof. That's why around the eye on my hand I have the word 'revolutionary' because it symbolises the aim of this particular life. Evolution is a slow process which to me means things take a long time to change and develop; maybe over many lifetimes. But a revolution is a quick version of that, something that you can achieve in this lifetime. That is on a personal level and on a global level; we could have a spiritual revolution if the appropriate events happened. I think that's still to do with each individual connecting with Level 27 and realising for themselves how the afterlife works and the meaning of life. If enough people experienced that then our priorities here on earth would be completely different. That's what my hands and chest piece represent is that idea of the relationship between here and home. Metatron's Cube that I have on my chest is supposed to be the first human who graduated to be an angel; and the symbol holds all the shapes that there are that exist on earth all merged together as one. The three dots I have by me eye represent the Three Jewels of Buddhism that are the teacher, the teaching and community of believers, another meaning is the mind, body and soul. In tattoo tradition it mean 'Mi Vida Loca' my crazy life, I like my tattoos to represent several things because I think life is like that there are several layers to things. On my fingers I have a lots of little symbols, on the first pinkie I have pause and eject symbols reminding me to take a moment and think of the bigger picture or what my mind should be doing. The next has the lightning symbol and the word 'once' meaning that the time is now and make the most of the moment because you'll only live this moment once. The next is a cherry bomb and a blue star representing Blue and the fuse is lit and we're working against a clock. On the next finger I have a light bulb and the power button symbol, again meaning ideas and knowledge are the things that hold the power. On my thumb I have the contrast symbol that signifies me and Pete, my twin brother. The other thumb has a skull and crossbones on it to represent mortality, we're all going to die one day and this identity only occurs here and now. Next is an anchor and the alchemic symbol for gold, these are about being anchored down here to earth and this body and that we're trying to evolve ourselves into a purer soul. On my middle finger if have a Union Flag and a red star that's about where I was born and The Spice Girls and the red star signifies me at Home. Next is meaning of life finger and my other pinkie has a teardrop and a key, this signifies that we are each a teardrop in an ocean but an ocean is just a multitude of drops; we're all significant and without each drop the whole wouldn't exist and that is the key to knowing how important you are.

I've got so many plans for more tattoos that I want in the future and I'm sure that those will evolve as I do. Over the last few years my style has changed, I've been fat and thin, blonde, multi-coloured hair. I've stretched my ears in a nod to feeling part of a tribe at Home and Avatar. I've had multi-coloured dreadlocks for a long time too. I remember when I was working in the bar in Nottingham we used to get these monthly music videos of all the new releases; when I saw Pink's 'Don't let me get me' I was in love with her dreads. I'd always been inspired by the look of them and when I saw them at Home I tried to recreate that look here, I'd watched a documentary on Bob Marley and could really relate to the process and what was behind it. I didn't even realise that his father was white, people talk about cultural appropriation but dreadlocks have existed in many different cultures throughout history and with what I believe about your soul and being reincarnated it is quite random which culture you get born into. People should try not to make assumptions about cultural appropriation; they don't know what is going on in that other person's mind or their reasoning for having something like dreadlocks."

"Yes, for sure; like mine I've been growing for years now and I get a lot of prejudice about them. Personally it's an exercise in perseverance and a journey. When I'm knotting them up it's about self-care, about putting some love and attention to myself. They are a part of me and for me." Adonai said as he shook his dreads around. "In fact I think they could do with some more ocean time now that the sun is well on its way to setting. Let's get back in the water for a while we've been lay on the sand for an age now. I like your hair as it is now by the way." I get up and follow Adonai back in to the sea.

"Thanks man, last year I shaved my head and decided to just let my hair grow for a few years without doing anything to it, no colours or dreads just let it be natural. I'd love to have a fit body and I do yoga and work out with an app on my phone; it's a physical evolution I'd like to achieve too; just for myself. Even how I look now is a million miles away from how I looked when I was working as a chef in The Lansdown. Because of everything that had happened with the flat and turning 30 I had decided to come off the Trileptal so that I could have a drink. Then when I was working in that environment all the workers used to have a drink after work. Over time I piled on the pounds until I was quite fat. I just put myself on a low carb kick and thankfully managed to shift it off quite rapidly but my body image is always up and down; especially because of the bulimia in my past. To me I just want to feel comfortable in my own skin.

With Victoria being in the UK we were in contact on messenger but I became a psychonaut; a traveller using my mind. I would meditate and travel home, I would go on OBEs and travel this world, I did some Medium readings and lots more research in to the spiritual world. I also managed to write a lot of songs and met a guy who had a recording studio and got to experience recording some of my own songs, that was an amazing experience. When the restaurant I was working in closed down that guy gave me a job as a waiter in his Indian restaurant. I learnt so much about the Indian food and about the Muslim culture through getting to know the chefs. I was lucky enough to meet a girl called Lara who had the same beliefs as me and I could spend time with actually talking through some of the things I had learned. When her and her fiancé decided to go to Las Vegas and get married they invited me along with them. Victoria came back to pain to cover my shifts. When I got back we decided to share my job and she moved in with me. We spent all our time discussing spiritual stuff and conspiracy theories and all that stuff. 2012 was approaching and there was a massive belief that something significant was going to happen then. We both really bought in to it and at Home I couldn't see much past that date. All I could see was this image of a darkness taking over our souls at home like some black tar drowning us all. There was all this stuff about aliens and the Illuminati; I obviously believe in extra-terrestrials because I believe in other dimensions and beings. To me other religions do too with their beliefs in angels and gods, they are all extra-terrestrial beings. In terms of the Illuminati I believe that capitalism would always have created a ruling power group and it's part of human nature that people in power would be secretive and elite. They are trying to hold on to that power and make themselves out to be separate so they create these secret societies to protect that power. It's a product of capitalism rather than something magical. I think they're heavily in to transhumanism because that to them is the next logical step in human evolution and they have the funds to actually investigate it. I think that is the darkness that I could see around 2012. When nothing happened on that date that was catastrophic I re-examined those ideas and we may never know what happened on that day it may have been some kind of butterfly effect thing a choice or action was done that turns out to be significant but there was no sky falling in on that particular date. I t just reminded me that you should take a step back and question everything.

I feel very lucky to have been born in to Generation X

we were the last generation of people who experienced the world without so much technology but we were witness to the technological revolution. We've seen the world go from something simpler to this level of connection that we have now. Obviously there are advantages to how much information we have at our fingertips and I'm so grateful to have been able to reconnect with my family after a few years of not speaking because of the divorce and different things. Social media is good for that but there's also a dark side with the bullying and prejudice. Now we hear that the immediate future is going to be all about augmented reality, virtual reality transhumanism and artificial intelligence. They say that it is the biggest threat to humanity that there could soon be a technological singularity that artificial intelligence could reach a point where it is more intelligent and powerful than the humans that created it. I don't know what would happen to Home if humans start uploading their minds and merging with technology but it just makes me want to spiritually evolve as much as I can. I don't think artificial/technological evolution is the same as the organic or natural way of spiritually evolving. I don't believe that it is the next step in the evolution of the human race. Our human consciousness with all its emotions and hormones are the point of us being here learning to master our minds and bodies. If our minds are uploaded and just pure logic takes over I don't think the future will be bright for us. We need to concentrate on spiritual evolution even more right now because there's the real possibility that we could be the last generation of humanity as we know it. I was lucky enough to meet another guy who works nearby who is from the millennial generation called Donald; he's been such a great person to bounce ideas off and chat about all this stuff with. He's shown me that this generation are interested in all these things and he's shown me how society is evolving too. He's bisexual and shown me that nowadays there has been a real shift in the ideas of sexuality and gender. At Home on Level 27 our souls are androgynous because we've had lives as different genders in the past; we can see each other as a gender or something more fluid. So when Donald talks about being bisexual and I have experienced being gay and I see that transgender issues are being brought up it makes me see that society is getting closer to being like it is at Home. Being able to chat to him has been invaluable and especially when he lets me talk about my beliefs and questions them; there's something about having the freedom with someone to do that which is so great. The Johns have also allowed me to do that from another perspective because they are all from an older generation and experienced such vastly different lives to me. They sometimes humour me and other times test me and play devil's advocate; which is very healthy too.

This sense of urgency was also highlighted to me in a different way; when the Indian closed down I helped out part time in the bar next door for a year. Victoria had got a boyfriend and moved in with him. I concentrated on writing songs and trying to hone my beliefs and ideas for the future. Victoria eventually returned to the UK when the relationship didn't work and I also stopped working at the bar. I was struggling with migraines and when I went to the doctors they drummed in to me that I should still be on the Trileptal. She explained to me that the particular kind of partial seizures that I have can manifest as migraines, blank periods, déjà vu, jamais vu, sudden feelings of anger, sadness, happiness or nausea. It can vary from person to person but I have Temporal Lobe Epilepsy and it can cause hallucinations and all sorts of symptoms. She made sure I started back on the medication and I went away and properly looked in to the whole thing. I started to make a journal of my experiences and symptoms. The Johns really supported during this whole time because they could see that I had got gradually worse. I spent a lot of time with them so they were able to identify when I was having a seizure. They really care about me and I sort of evolved in to being a bit of a trophy boy to them allowing me to just do bits and pieces of translation and Spanish lessons with them cushioning me financially so that there was not so much pressure to get a full time job. I don't know what I would have done without them; I know that it is a mutually beneficial relationship but I'll be forever grateful that they were in my life at the time.

I believe the epilepsy has been around for a lot longer than I realised and that somehow it was the thing that opened the door to the spiritual world. I know that all the paranormal things that I've experienced are not just symptoms of a seizure because other people have shared those visions and corroborated Medium readings and things that have happened. I believe that my broken brain kind of allowed me access to another circuit, a crack in a wall that let me get through to another dimension. I have good days and bad days but I see epilepsy as a gift it's like the Japanese word 'Kintsukuroi' when a broken piece of ceramics is joined back together with gold; it is more beautiful because it was broken.

All through my spiritual journey I've been surrounded by some amazing people. I read somewhere that in order to evolve as a person you should make friends with a vast spectrum of people from different backgrounds. Some of the people who have really affected me are Kerri who is like my beautiful soul sister; we can go ages without seeing each other and just pick up where we left off. She's an inspiration to me and is a great mother to her daughter Brody; I love seeing her life evolve and I love her so much too. There's Victoria with whom I learnt so much about the spiritual world, my life would be so different if I had never met her; she was an education to me and a true angel. Also there's Bert my Belgian friend who is from a different culture and class than me and taught me so much about the differences between cultures. We spent a lot of time going walking along the coast and chilling on his terrace. He showed me how varied life is depending on where you got born. He's gay too and his relationship with his family is really nice to see. I was glad when I reconnected with my family I built a relationship with my Dad and I'm especially happy to have reconnected with my Mum. Both of her parents died in one year and they were such a massive part of my childhood on the farm. I have so much respect for their lives and the tribe that they raised. I'm really thankful to have that new connection with my Mum and to see Pete my twin brother and his tribe expanding and growing up. Kerri's aunty Chezzie has supported me for so long and was a bright and bubbly person who I loved spending time with. She's great company and we got to know each other when Kerri's Mum, who was Chezzie's twin, passed away. We used to go out once a week for a meal or coffee and spending time with her would be a really fun highlight of my week. The Johns have shown me so much care and love; they've given me stability and also shown me the world. I've been shown Valencia, Madrid, Rome and Las Vegas. They've given my life colour and given me the safety net during a time that I've been dealing with the epilepsy and trying to find my way. I physically wouldn't be here if it wasn't for their care and support. Of course Sarah and Toby goes without saying and obviously now there's you too Adonai. Taking an interest in my story and sitting here with me on the beach has really helped me. You've affected my life. I know now that I want to look in to doing what Sarah and Toby do; not only the tattooing that I'm passionate about but evolving enough to be able to share that with others. I want to express myself in art and writing and music. I've been sketching loads lately and I love it so much, it completely calms my mind down and I get in to a sense of flow. Art is the ultimate communication of your soul whether it's in writing or picture or sound. That's how we evolve by sharing."

"Thanks so much Kristoff that was an epic and mind

blowing story, thanks for sharing it. Can I ask you to share one more thing with me? Would you sing your best song to me?" He says splashing water ate me. "Look the sun has gone and now we can see stars, the ocean is twinkling with their light, from space. To think I might have not come down and spoke to you and not heard this story. You've given me a lot to think about, I'm going to go away and look for those books and maybe try to look for Home too. It's crazy that the story of your tattoos is so much more than I ever imagined when I asked about the story behind them. People probably walk past you and just see ink or they judge not knowing what the story is behind them. But I think our stories are what make the world go round and we should share them. That's how we grow and learn. Sing me your song and I'm going to head off dinner."

"Okay give me a sec I'll just psyche myself up." I look out across the water and see the reflection of the stars dancing across the waves. I look up into the sky at the vast universe stretching out above and I get a real sense of how small we are just two tiny people in a sea on a globe spinning through this space, I start to sing:

It's a big mirage in which we're swimming

All drowning in the illusion

Of the human race that no one's winning

We're lost in the confusion

If I am the single teardrop falling

Then I am the ocean too

But I can't stop those sirens calling

Seductively to you

We evolve today and the days to come

We've got to read the signs

Know when the human race is run

We were once upon a time

We can be the secret

I'll keep loving you

And it's magic this feeling falling for you

I will help you see it

Show this love is true

And this magic I'll keep it closer to you

Just feel my wavelengths breaking more

Cos I am the frequent sea

And you are the tide that makes me sure

I am that I am to be

My mind is a paper boat that's sinking

I've gotta get off of it

Got to stop myself from thinking

Or I'm going down with it

We evolve today and the days to come

We've got to read the signs

Know when the human race is run

We were once upon a time

We can be the secret

I'll keep loving you

And it's magic this feeling falling for you

I will help you see it

Show this love is true

And this magic I'll keep it closer to you"

Adonai had been swimming around me and as I fell silent he raised his finger to his lips so that I didn't say anything more. A beautiful broad smile lit up his face, he moved towards me opening his arms and scooping me up in a warm embrace. He kissed me on the cheek and for a moment stood back and stared into my eyes;

then he turned and swam towards shore. I didn't want to watch him go so I turned away and let myself float up in the water. As I looked up into the starry sky, the great expanse of the universe spread out in the heavens above me and I knew that I was just a teardrop in a vast ocean.

Printed in Great Britain
by Amazon